IT WILL ALL BE OVER BY CHRISTMAS

Memories of Portsmouth children of the Second World War

True stories collected and collated by
Margaret Foster

Edited by Donna Bish and Martin Chalk
Front cover illustration by Sue Standish-Murphy
Photograph of Donna Bish by
Stefan Venter -www.upixphotography.com

IT WILL ALL BE OVER BY CHRISTMAS
Memories of Portsmouth children of the Second World War
Margaret Foster

Text © Margaret Foster

Printed version ISBN: 978-1-909660-58-8
ePub ISBN: 978-1-909660-59-5
mobi ISBN: 978-1-909660-60-1

Published 2015 by Tricorn Books
131 High Street, Old Portsmouth
PO1 2HW
www.tricornbooks.co.uk

My special thanks go to all those who shared their stories with me:

Sidney Adlam, Florrie Allnut, Patricia Arnold, Percy Baigent, Pauline Brockwell, Barry Brett, Mary Chalk, Jenny Clark, Dean Clark, Margaret Cook, Les Cromeeke, Elspeth, Gillian Gemmell, Maureen Grady, Roy Herbert, Pat Istead, Nora Jagger, Les Jagger, Johnny Jarrett, Cyril Jones, Alan Kerry, Doris Leggett, Phyllis McGregor, Phyllis Maple, Phyllis Murphy, Peggy Jean O'Mara, Margaret Oram, Yvette Myriam Pearsey, Maureen Prett, Pauline Pritchard, Eddie Pritchard, Brian Smith, Coral Smith, Maisie Smith, Molly Smith, Kath Smith, Jennifer Trodd, Cyril Tutte, Pam Webb, Gwen Weeks.

Sadly, some of them have passed away since giving their interviews, and will be unable to see their stories finally in print.

This book also carries a remembrance to William Charles Todd. He was three years old when, whilst holding his sister Peggy's hand, an incendiary bomb was dropped and they were buried alive. Peggy was dug out but her little brother perished.

The photographs used in this book are reproduced by kind permission of their owners – the people who shared their stories.

I expect you are wondering why I myself felt the need to record more stories about World War Two.

When I was a young girl of about five or six I would sit by the open fire in our flat which was then Frazer House St Georges Square, Portsea, Portsmouth and listen to the tales of the times my dad, as a service man in the Army endured and the fun side of the War my mother and her sisters had while the men were serving in the armed forces.

We would sleep with dad's big Army coat on our bed, it served as an extra blanket in the very cold winters we had in them days and his belt, he would use to belt us with when we were naughty. How I recall with a flinch the pain that belt inflicted upon such smooth soft skin of my childhood.

The War was long since over when I was born but growing up in Portsea with bombed sites all around us showed how hard the area had taken a bashing from the bombers.

I heard stories from my uncles and stories from aunties and was always fascinated by them, and at times wished I was there.

The dance halls seemed so much fun to very young ears like mine and hearing about the different nationality soldiers would put me a dreamlike state. Just listening to mum and my aunts having a laugh about the dance hall at the bottom of Lake Road in Portsmouth that they would visit regular, it sounded so glamorous hearing how an American soldier would have my mum or aunt up dancing the night away or how they even managed to get to the dance hall fascinated me more because there was hardly any lights on the roads or it was pitch black, and then once a bomb had been dropped along the route how they managed to walk down with the great big craters in the road and gases hissing from the ground, and wires and debris everywhere, it must have been like an assault course getting down the road. But the girls, as they were then, needed that bit of fun as their outlet otherwise it was all doom and gloom because they just never knew what was going to happen next.

The interviews I have done for this book has been a good memory unlock for those that helped put this book together, we laughed and at times had tears in our eyes remembering the very harsh times they endured especially when they were children then came into adulthood as the War raged.

There is so much history in the stories in this book and places that have long since gone, but will always be remembered by those who read and remember the horrors of being a evacuee and a child of the War, or of the times doing national service in the War.

Margaret Foster

"The war years were very different"

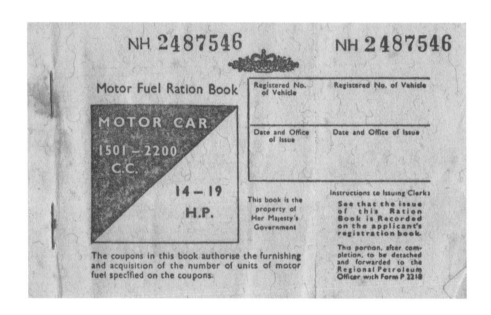

Patricia Arnold

I was born in Windsor in Berkshire on May 16 in 1930 and christened in the name of Jean Patricia Jones. I learned in later years that my parents had not been married when I was born, but I do recall that I did have a little brother who died in infancy. I remember the name Sonny being used but I have no other memories of him. It would have been good to have had a brother or a sister in my life, but that wasn't to be.

In 1933 when I was at the tender age of three my mother died at Windsor. This must have been a heart-breaking time for my father to have lost a son and now the mother of his children. Very soon though in 1935 my father must have decided he wanted a better life for me, I also realised later that he was ill. I was taken to a children's home in Harrow which was situated in North London. It was one of a group of homes under what I now think was an awful name - The Waifs and Strays Society, it sounded more like a refuge for lost cats and dogs. Since 1982 they have been known as The Children's Society. The home in Harrow was known as St Saviour's.

Then everything changed and it was never to be the same again because War had broken out. This was a new word which of course had no meaning for me but there did seem to be an air of urgency and the grown-ups looked more worried than usual. They seemed to speak quietly in small groups but to us there was an air of mystery and this of course is where my memories of being an evacuee begins.

We were taken several places of safety, usually deep in the countryside. The first of these, for a very short stay was St Agatha's in Prince's Risborough, Kent. Next came Upper Stowe, a village near Weedon in Northampton, then to Chislehurst in Kent where the schools could not cope with the influx of evacuees, and for a time we attended only morning classes and had a tutor at the home in the afternoons.

We had just about settled down here when it was decided by the powers that be to send ten of us girls, all under the age of ten, to yet another destination much further away this time in the Midlands. Usually children adapt well to change as long as the people they know and love are there to run to when hurt or afraid, and familiar toys are at hand when needed. The world of a child goes on much the same. The War years were very different.

Thousands of children were taken out of the big cities to places of safety in the countryside. This time their parents did not go with them and certainly for us, ten little girls from an orphanage in Harrow, being sent miles away to a remote village in Shropshire called Preston on the Weald Moors, was something of an ordeal. Also this was the fourth place of safety we had experienced. We didn't have parents that we had left behind, although my father was still alive and would sometimes write to me, but I remember how we missed the other girls that didn't come with us. I also missed certain toys I was not allowed to take with me, especially Rupert my lovely brown bear, a doll with a black velvet cape and a small beautifully illustrated book which I cannot now remember the author. The pictures in colour were of wild flowers and fairies sitting amongst them. The book when opened out and held to your face had a scent of pear drops about it. I wonder who had these things that I had left behind as I never saw them again.

We were marched in crocodile file each morning to the village school with our gas mask thrown over our shoulder just like millions of other children, but we were very lucky because apart from the air raid practices we were never involved in an actual air raid and for that I am truly thankful.

During the practices a loud bell would be rung which meant everyone lined up in the playground. We were then marched to the Reverend Thomas' Rectory and taken down into the cellars which were smelly and damp, so damp that we discovered frogs living down there.

I also remember the crisscross of tape that had been put on the school windows which made the room very dark and the blackout blinds which were used in the winter months so no light would show when the light was on. Pitch black when lights were turned off.

I had such fond memories of my time away in different places and sad ones too.

Phyllis McGregor

My name is Phyllis Miriam McGregor and I am the second daughter of daughter of Laura and James McGregor. I have an older sister and two brothers and we lived in the family home in Earnest Road in Portsmouth. Although when young money was very sparse we always enjoyed one and other's company especially around Christmas time.

As a child I went to the local elementary school which was an infant school, and the premises are still there today in New Road but the name of the school has changed and probably being used for other purposes.

At the age of five I was moved on then to the bigger girl's school and the entrance to that was at the back of the school in Balliol Road and I remained there till I was fourteen years of age. At the age of fourteen being a girl you had to think about a job or an occupation to help with the family income, because even though we did own our own home through our Grandparents quite a few things still had to be paid. But we were a united and happy family with a few luxury s in life.

I started a job with my friend in a factory which really was about the main employment in those days, and because of her appearance and because she was pretty clever in her own right she was sort of looking after us and the other jobs because she knew what she was doing, so they never had to tell her what to do. But I was a first starter and had to work roughly from about eight till six with an hour for lunch for six shillings and eight pence, and part of that went on your rent and you were not encouraged at that time to have any ambitions because father said the boys had to have some sort of occupation, because when they grew older they would have to support a family. So girls were not so important because as they grew older they would marry and be provided for.

I learned well and was good with figures so earned a bit more, then I was taken off that job and put into the factory doing hand lacing. I learned to stitch corsets with lace for eight pence an hour but I am afraid, when you were young like we were, it was impossible because we had to watch the jobs and it was hard.

The corset factory where I worked was situated in Cottage View and it was called Twilfit's Factory and I remember that you had to bend over on a small stool with a needle and thread and sit stitching the lace down on the corsets and also sewing little bows on them, and you had to stitch twelve pairs of these to get three pennies or three farthings for a dozen, and this was done because no one knew any other way to be going on for a very long time.

I stayed there for a very long time until my next job came along, and I remember every one rode a bicycle because that was the only means of getting anywhere at that time, and I can remember riding as far as Arundel and even Bognor, and taking a little pack of sandwiches and a bottle of lemonade and being out all day long and having a lovely time.

I remember a girl in our group by the name of Gladys Winkle who was a mouth organ player who was pretty good at it, and would play it on the way home from Arundel Park and we would all join in singing our heads off; don't know what people thought in Emsworth five girls riding through singing their heads off but it made the ride jolly good.

When we got home it was lovely because my mother would have tea ready for us, a real nice little tea party and that was how we got our pleasure in that way because we didn't go into places where you had to pay money like pictures and that, because we just couldn't afford that, but we were happy together.

We were told at the time about the wars that were going on in Europe but that seemed a long way away, but we were then encouraged to join something in the National Service so I joined The Red Cross Society because I wanted to be a nurse, but of course that was not to be.

In 1939 we were going to the old fire station for some training and rumours then were starting to get around, that I think was in the August. Then of course over the radio we were told hostilities were about to start, then we got word to report to the main Fire Station.

We were told to take a packet of sandwiches and a bottle of lemonade or something because we needed it to see us through the 24 hours. So we changed into uniform that we had to put together ourselves. Apart from the raincoat they issued we had to buy a skirt

9

from Marks Spencer which was four shillings eleven pennies, a gym blouse from Bull Pit which was also four pounds and eleven pennies and we were told because we were Auxiliaries we had to wear black stockings which were not to be nylon, and all this we had to pay for ourselves, and shoes we had to buy from Copnor Road which had to be lace ups and also, of all things, a pair of gauntlet gloves. What we were going to use them for I really didn't know.

But we all did as we were told and went without quite a lot of things to have sufficient money to pay for the uniform and the only thing we did get issued with was a red tin helmet and a gas mask, and when we got down to the centre station we were all booked in and was told we had to wait about, then we would be taken out to our Action Stations. So that was roughly just after six o clock 'til about midnight and they were taking girls here there and everywhere and then it was my turn to be sent out, and of all the places for me to be going to was the Gas Works at Rudmore and this was a place that I had never ever been to and had no idea what the place was like. And it was bad enough having to work with a load of men you didn't know and of course I had only ever worked with women, nevertheless you had to put up with it because you didn't know if it was good or bad because of the war in itself.

Well, I was taken by taxi to Rudmore where the Gas holders were and deposited me at the top of a small dark street that led out to the Rudmore water and was told to go down to the gates at the bottom and call out, and they would open the gates for me and of course off they went.

So I went down in the absolute pitch black road, and I could see the water and which looked like oil shimmering in the dark on top of the water with not another soul about. I shook the gates and rattled the chains on the gates but it seemed no one heard me, so I walked along this very dark passage way and saw three men sitting round this up-turned petrol drum which had a hurricane lamp on and they were playing cards.

I tried to get their attention but they just carried on playing so I said to myself "golly what should I do now?", so I started to walk and ended up walking back to Central Depot which was a very long walk indeed because I had to make my way back to the Guildhall, and as I walked along the old Commercial Road there was not one person, not a soul or anything about, But as I got to Charlotte Street by a shoe shop there which was called Dolcis I remember my shoes making a noise and all of a sudden two Policemen came out from the dark shadows of the door way of the shop. Once they see my Uniform they let me go on my way to Central then stepped back in the dark doorway.

By the time I got there every one had been sent out and there was no one there, so they decided I had to go back there so they must of rung this time to tell them that someone had to be at the gate and to let me go in once I arrived there .

With my kit bag on my back I was very worried, frightened and nervous because I just didn't know what was going on, but there I was back again at Rudmore and this time they were there to let me in and took me to a building what they called the Retort House. But I can't remember that but I do recall it was a great big chamber with like great big motor engines and the smell of Gas was everywhere, and there was a tiny blue light in the ceiling and they showed me over to a funny old telephone which I had never seen the like of it before and gladly would not have to use it. Then they showed me to an old wooden crate which had a hurricane lamp upon it and another crate was there to sit down on.

I sat there waiting and waiting and had never felt so isolated in my life during that period, because once they start to move you from point to point nobody even bothers to talk to you. They probably didn't realise how frightened you were and had never experienced anything else like it in your life, but of course there wasn't a great deal you could do about it.

After a while I don't know how long I had been there, I put my head down on my arms on this box because I was very tired, and it was six o'clock in the morning and there was a visit from the Controlling Officer from Young's Brewery who came in and saw me there and told me I could now get off home. They were making a visit to the area and visiting the Action Stations and seeing how everyone was getting on, and on seeing me must have felt very sorry for me because I was on my own. I hadn't even been told if there had been toilets and there was just me in this great big engine house. And then the Inspector had asked me how long I had been there and I told him that I had arrived at midnight and he then disturbed the men in their little cabin place and they came over and relieved me.

To think I had to lay my head onto my gas mask on this wooden box table to get some sleep had disturbed me because I had never had to do anything like this in my life before. One of the young workmen came over to me and was rather concerned for me to learn that I had not been relieved all night, and to be honest I do not know how I sat there like I did anyway wondering and waiting to see if you was going to see anybody. This young workman must have took pity because he showed me where the row of toilets were and when I went over to use them he stood guard, but there was no refreshments no cups of tea or water, so I just had to go back to the stall just sat there waiting and wonder what going to happen the next minute. Anyway because I had been there all night I was told to go home and be back there for six o clock that night and that in itself was an episode in its self because I didn't know how to get there, even though I had lived Portsmouth all my life I had never been there before for one, it was never considered a very clean area.

On my way back down to Commercial Road I stopped by another station and was told I could not go on down as a bomb had dropped at the top of Lake Road, but I had to go down there to let them know I had to go back to the Gas Works so I needed to get down there anyway, so I was told to go careful. But when I got to my station I was told I was not going back there because I being a woman on my own with all them men wasn't on.

In the end they had to contact the officer Mr Moor because they didn't know what to do with me once back on duty. So I was now told to go to Young's Brewery in Thomas Street where I would have a little office to sit in at the rear of the building because it was evening time and they had toilets which was a relief to hear. I think they even took pity on me when they learned my folks had gone away to a safe place and I had nowhere to go, but my friend's family house backed on to the Brewery and they took me in under their wing.

I also had a little office boy to keep me company which I was glad of because to use the toilet of a night time you had to run half way down the street with the rats and everything else coming into the building, and the little boy had to stand outside while I spent a penny. It was unbelievable when I think back now how on earth all that happened.

They built me a desk and a bed from hops that had come from the Brewery, but once again the toilets were not near the office I had, so the office boy had to come running down the street with me regardless of what time it was. Mind you, when the orders came through that I had to go back to the Gas Works at six that night and when the men came through got a coster cart from Charlotte Street it was lovely because it made you wonder what purpose it was to be there. Any way I had my little flask of tea and my pack of sandwiches that would see me through the night, but when I was ready to have a cuppa my flask had broken and had gone all through to my sandwiches. It must have happened when the men had made me my desk they must have dropped my pack which in turn had broken the flask so they had to be thrown away.

My friend's mother was very good with me, at least I had some where to go once I came off duty. God I can't get over the cabin thing in the old Cooper's building you had a light a bunk but the one thing you didn't have was washing facilities or a toilet so when we were allowed to use the office staff toilet we would be able to have a good wash up.

There was never any transport so you had to walk down to these places and I was the only woman, well girl with about eight to nine men and I just didn't know how to speak to them as they were typical Barrow Boys, you know, they just came off the stall in the evening and was billeted to an action station and of course they had to accept me.

When the Gas Works were bombed fortunately I was not there because during the day I would be in my little office in Cooper's old building and Gas Works the evening shift, but before the bombing had started I was told not to go but I was to stay at Young's Brewery where I had this telephone thing. Everything seemed so surreal but that's what was done.

Then it was decided I would have to go to St Mary's Hospital where they had an air raid shelter and I was put there where they had a proper little control room built there, and there were little tiny booths for burns at the side and better conditions for once, and once again I saw people and I don't know what it is about your body and the stresses it can take but you have to get on with it, but being there was a nice little happy feeling and you had to make the best of things at that time, and after the Gas Company and the Young's Brewery it seemed like a super hotel as far as I was concerned because it actually had a bath there.

In these like cubicles they had these like old fashioned lockers and they had a light bulb in but they were full of these wretched red ants, but still we could get them out and it was still like a hotel like a Paradise to me, how long was I there? Well I don't know but I remember another thing was a man came round on his cycle and knocked your door and would call out "Air Raid message Phil Yellow!" Then I would have to get out of my bed but I was already dressed, my trousers on the lot, then off I would go down to my action station and would have to stay there until I got the all clear. Then they decided that you didn't have to report until it was the Purple Call so that was another time you would be called and have to go to action stations until once again you got the all clear, then if there wasn't any action then they changed it again to enemy action, and the bombing was then in Buckland which was a long way away from where I was stationed.

I now recall when I got posted again near Smith's Garage which was situated in Old Commercial Road, this was opposite the old Savoy Cinema, and I was out shopping with my sister and the sirens had gone off and by this was a large bit of waste ground called the Rubber Park. This had an Anderson Shelter on it and I said to my sister "Here or the garage?" but the garage only had sand bags so we stayed in the shelter while lots of bombs were dropped on Lake Road, then one was dropped in Sultan Road and the ground beneath you just shuddered.

There used to be a furniture store on the corner of Buckingham Place it was called Spicknals and the milk place was there too but you get so used to seeing places and when they are gone it seems so surreal, but once again there was nothing we could do so went home.

Going back to the garage again we had to use the private accommodation so they built a little sort of cabin on the side of it so we had a wash room, and when we had the fires we had the sailors in and out and it was just like daylight, you could see all the houses on fire and then the water mains were hit so obviously they could not get the water to put the fires out, and we were over-run because we only had six or seven pumps across Portsmouth and that's what people were to use to try and put these fires out, and I remember being told that the horses were running around the streets because they had got out of their shuttered buildings. And in the middle of this people rallied around and just done what they could, they even moved people in to see what they could do and from the top of the Portsdown Hill looking down the city was ablaze but there just wasn't anything you could do about it, it was really just a hopeless job. But they ordered new pumps into the city to be stationed up on the hill but in Portsmouth the pumps were rounded and when the new pumps arrived we couldn't use them because they were threaded.

We not only had the Water Mains down but the Gas Mains took a hit too but we managed to get a bit of water down but Lake Road to Sultan Road was so badly hit there was nothing much one could do anyway.

Another thing that sticks in my mind was that when you was on duty you had no food no water. Then you would wonder "where were all our people, what about the air raid shelters that had been hit?" I think it made you become numb somehow.

You knew you had to get to work if you could and get about, but there was no food about so what the Army did was sent some old Corporation buses that was in store at North End and we were all gathered up and put on this bus and taken up to Hilsea Barracks to their mess rooms I think, because I think they all felt so sorry for us because they had never seen an over Guard or Fireman so dishevelled, and I remember having this aluminium bowl handed to me and me thinking it was very greasy but was I glad of it because it was so bitterly cold and it was January, and when you looked around you it made you feel that it was a welcomed break really, but it was just nice being there and carrying on in your own right in these premises, and the water and the food that was offered there and you knew you couldn't go anywhere because there was nowhere to go to .

When we came back down and on to work I would come down on my cycle from the Air Balloon and would have to get off and out the way because the men would be clearing and at their stations, but it was funny really because it was a nightmare but they did try to stop you in Sultan Road but you had to tell them that you had a duty to get on even though the planes were dropping bombs overhead. But it was not a case of being brave it was just a case of getting on with your duty, you just wasn't any good to Action Stations if you were the other side of the city. But this time I was pushed in to the air raid shelter for my own good while they were firing their guns above, and when it was safe I sort of come out the other end to the corset factory in Baker Street and see my red

helmet and sent a cheer up. It was sort of amazing and the comfort and how good you felt that someone had been watching.

Of course when I rode into the garage all you could see was these little smoke rings with these little cigarette ends on the floor and of

course another cheer would go up. It was very comforting because on your own it was really frightening but with people around you it made you feel good.

For one reason or other down in this garage they had installed long tables and had this gas stove so you could boil a kettle for a cuppa and cook, but I had never cooked in my life and of course I stuck this thing in the oven and of course it came out like solid concrete, and then they decided I best stick inside the office and let someone that knew how to cook get in there.

I do remember these poor souls being very hungry and of course you should not always go by the way people dress because I was only about 24 then, and the kindness they showed me was best to none because it was frightening at times and because I had never been anywhere in my life.

It wasn't always as hectic, there wasn't always the 24 hour bombing and sometimes it would quieten right down but then the men I worked alongside would get up to little bits of mischief, and I remember going outside one day and my cycle was strung up in the rafters and that was their idea of a joke, but I done a bit of protesting because I was one of those who like to get home to see how things were so down it came.

Well that was me I had served my apprenticeship.

We all had to go down to the Royal Naval Barracks then and of course when you got to your station and had to go out they would all give up a cheer as you arrived and it made you feel safe as anything and you would try and work your way through all of this in like an air raid shelter, it was very difficult because there was no way they could put in a reinforcing unit because there is no shelter and it probably would have been a target anyway.

Then when I got my second promotion I was sent back up to St. Mary's Hospital, it was a lovely place. All I had to do was give down the orders and we was allocated so much room and we also had a bathroom which was a blessing.

The fireman was stationed on the ground floor and they came up this day and sprayed us with water and me and the girls retaliated and started shaking talcum powder all over them so you can just imagine what they look like, wet through with talcum powder all over them. It's strange the things that made you laugh and it was nice to have such things to make you laugh because it was normal things like that.

We had two stations in Portsmouth that were manned by Canadian fireman, one area was Tressington Park by Canoe Lake and they were all volunteers from Canada. They all came in to man about three or four pumps. The area where the control room was they had a room, they thought it was a luxury and they was on their own and they weren't as bad as the others and they didn't seem to have the same attitude. And although they were sort of cleaners they kept themselves to themselves and I know they went to the pub on the corner of the road.

SAFE AND SOUND

Then the Americans came along and everything sort of held out and everyone sort of got separated but they was all wonderful people and the majority of them were really good and they were kind to us and gave us food parcels that we didn't have in our rations. The experience of being there in the air raids and the Doodlebugs was like listening to a motorbike cycle going along.

I remember being on duty and it must have been declared the end of the war because the things that were going on down at the Guildhall Square. I believe people were letting the celebration take the upper hand because people were burning everything, they went into pubs and started pulling the bars and the wood work down and sent everyone to the great big fire at the Guildhall stairs.

I think we all felt a little bit remote about it because it didn't seem to be frightening obviously apart from the odd one. I can remember riding down to the Guildhall on my bicycle and there was nothing to protect you from the shrapnel or any holes and we seemed to of lived like that. We must have been the first ones sent down evidently, and I think people started to talk about the things that had happened and what happened to it and of course you were still a member of the Fire Service at that time and as far as they were concerned, we were done. When we went back to the action station, the girls that were there remaining were all asked if they wanted to stay on.

Obviously, there is so much more to the war years than I have told and it must do something to your character, so many things that happened, what you heard, what you saw.

I carried on in the fire service for many, many years with promotion after promotion, up until I retired from the force.

Ode to the Mud-Larks.

Once upon a duty time,
So begins this little rythme,
When Firemen 4 made up the crew
Who manned the pump at Station.2.

From Police Headquarters came this plea,
"Will you rescue those in need,
In Baffins Pond mud firmly stuck
Are two Corporation ducks".

This, English hearts could not ignore,
Into action came the four,
Saving life the common bond,
Even ducks on Baffins Pond.

Their's is not to reason why,
Their's is but to do or die,
No one questioned why they ought-ter
Get the ducks out of the water.

Visualise the stirring sight,
Rescue operations at night,
Firemen working out ways and means
Of saving ducks and keeping clean.

From Jim the leader came this order,
"Run out the hose, turn on the water,
We will give our feathered friends,
The benefit of the watery end".

Forward strode the Fireman bold,
To rescue ducks went Nat "King" Gould,
Knee deep in mud our Nat took root,
And almost lost his rubber boots.

Harry had no time to dither
When on the bank he began to slither,
And joined the mud larks in their task
Of extricating mud bound ducks.

Holding down the branch was Trevor
Who in his Fireman's lift has never
Used the language when he slipped
On slimy mud and lost his grip.

Branch snaking wildly on the ground
Scattered the mud of Baffin round
Soaking all and did not spare,
Those who came to stand and stare.

Four little nigger boys, returning for a bath,
Gave the Control Room a mighty big laugh,
When black faced and mud drenched, but never subdued,
Reported, "Mission accomplished, ducks removed".

Alan Kerry

My name is Alan and I was born in 1933. I just don't know where to start so I will go back to my school days when I can remember sitting at my desk, writing at the top of my page 1939/40/41. Why these dates I do not know but they was firmly stuck in my mind. This was my school at Hither Green in South East London.

I recall a bomb site at one end of the school and each class had a piece of land or rubble to do what they wanted, I turned mine into a rockery garden and received a prize which was a green hardback gardening book which my elder brother tore up and I will never forget that.

I believe there was a fire station close by and also a railway station. I recall later years this station suffered a very bad crash. I can remember playing in the roads as there was not a lot of traffic in those days because of the War. I remember how we played football with no ball, we called it 'Tin Can Tommy' because it was a lidded tin with stones put in it.

I had a cycle wheel and a short stick, running with the wheel at my side down the road, or we played a game called 'Knock Down Ginger'. What we did was tie a long piece of string from on knocker to the other and knock the first door so when it opened it would knock the other door, but of course we were nowhere to be seen.

At one time I walked from Catford to Blackheath because it had a very large park with a large pond, I would go fishing there with other kids. No one had nets, we would use sacking. Sometimes you would be lucky and catch something but not always. Blackheath also held a very large fair once a year.

I can recall at the end of the common there was some very large iron gates that lead you through to a row of houses either side of the road and I recall an old chap that would be selling hot chestnuts, every year he would be there. Also at the end of that road was a very large tunnel with white tiles. It had a very large opening and all the kids would run right through under the Thames. I think it went right to the other end. We would come up the other side where the barges were in Greenwich. Us kids would spend all day mucking about by the river, then at the end of the day walk back home.

I recall everything was on ration and then we lived in Brookdale Road, Catford, London, SE6. There was only one shop on the main road and they would sell

Lyons Swiss Roll, mind you I had to queue a very long time to get one, but some things are worth the wait. I do remember as a treat my mother sent me to Woolworths to get some biscuits and I got chocolate ones knowing I had to get plain, so ate a couple on the way home before getting sent back to get them changed. They were more coupons than plain and I think the sale girl knew they were short but I still got away with it.

Some of the houses at the back of the shops had been bombed and was being cleared of the rubble, then the council had a brick wall built. It was as tall as me in a big square and they filled it with water ready for when the fire engines needed filing up again.

At the end of Brookdale Road, Catford we had a large park, Catford Dog Stadium was at the end of by the railway lines, and cars would draw up to the pavement to go to the races. I would then run up to a driver, open his car door or poke my head in the window and say, "Look after your car mister?" At the end of the evening, after the races I would be standing next to the car and if they had a win they would pay half a crown or two bob, or sometimes nothing if they lost.

I remember in the park in the corner were search lights and AK-AK guns and sometimes if you were out you could see the search lights shining up in the sky.

I remember every year the circus came and we would get free tickets to go because mum used to take in laundry and do all their laundry.

We had air raids day and night and at night you could hear them Doodlebugs go over and I would rush upstairs and watch them go on their way to London from my window. It made a droning noise and flames would be blowing at the back end of the, then it would go quiet as if it had run out of fuel. You would then know it was dropping to earth and minutes later you would hear a big bang and know some poor sod had got hit.

I remember one day me and my sisters were dressed in our best clothes and all had small suitcases and a tie-on label on our over coats with our names and date of birth. We also had a small box with a gas mask inside it and had to carry it at all times. I remember my sisters Marion and Joan and me boarding a train with lots of other kids on and some were crying, not me because it was on adventure and at last I was getting away from home.

It seemed to last all day on the train but we pulled in at a place called Abercwmoi, South Wales. It was a village and we were taken to the school where couples were waiting to house children and there wasn't many children left. Then a man and a woman came up, Mr and Mrs Savage, and took me. They lived in 16 Elm Street and would you believe my sisters were two doors along from me.

They had a son George who was in the Army. He was on leave when I arrived and sat me on his lap to make me feel welcome. He would then tell me stories about the War. I remember him going back and before we knew it he was home again but this time he was not the same man that we knew, I found out why and it was because he got gassed and boy did I feel sorry for him. I just can't think what his sister's name was but I do know she was a nurse.

The Savages were real church-goers, three times of a Sunday. I was at church with them and Wednesday evening I would then have to go Choir practice and dress the part as well.

It was great though to be out with the village kids as we played in the forest, free as birds we were. We would go up the side of the mountain and look down on the coal works, we had a clear view of the Co-op shop and I recall smoking my first fag which made me sick. Go fishing if allowed all night long.

In the village there was only one shop and us kids would play football and yes, of course I ducked down and the ball went through the shop window and we all had to pay for the repair. Later years people in the village still remembered that day.

Two years I stayed there as an evacuee. I have even been back in later years and watched the old men sitting on that pipe along the mountain side gasping for air with their bad chests because of working in the coal mines.

After the War when I went back to London we would go hop picking and fruit picking too as it was like a busman's holiday for a couple of years we did that, we were based by the Head Corn Rail Station in Kent.

The worst time I remember to pick hops was after a shower as you would pull a high vine from the ground and get wet through because the water would come tumbling down. It would also be sore on your hands but about five o'clock I would have to go back to the camp to get the fire started and peel the veg ready for dinner and get water on the boil for tea and the washing up. I would also help the farmer get the cows in for milking. I loved hop and fruit picking and working on the Farm, we earned money as well as being in the fresh air.

When the War did finish and we were back home I would go around all the houses to collect jars to make some money as I would get one penny for a pound jar and half penny for the smaller, but it still worked out it was worth collecting them, washing them and taking them back to Sainsbury's.

I would also go ragging and would sort them and keep some bits for me and make a couple rugs out of nice strips that I put on sack backing and they went down in our passage way. I would take the rest to the rag and bone man down the main road opposite the Hippodrome, there was a big clearing which had been a bombed site that the costermonger's sold their wares from, all sorts of bibs and bobs.

When trade got slow at the market the trader would load up the barrow with goods and go along the main road in Catford to sell and I would stand in the shop doorway as a lookout watching for the coppers, and as soon I see one he would quickly move on to the side street out of the way and hassle of being caught as the Main Road was out of bounds to Costermongers.

I also had a job clearing up after market, and went to Covent Garden with a stall holder to get his fruit vegetables, and after one Saturday when clearing up I found a dirty wet ten pound note, it was all crumpled up but I managed to straighten it and went straight round the ice cream shop and bought a very large one and saying sorry at the same time for the wet dirty note.

I also used to collect up the orange boxes that I would break up and sell for fire wood. It was all pocket money.

I remember always believing that I was the black sheep of the family because of how bad I was treated, poker across my back or hit with a copper stick, I always took the blame for everything that went wrong in the house and had the most jobs and chores to do. We had a three bedroomed house with lino floors that I had to wash through once a week, I also had to make sure I had chopped the wood ready for the fires or woe betide me if I let the wood run out. I had to do it for the Rayburn in the dining room that gave us hot water.

I remember a long like platform that was along the window that we sat upon for meal times. There would be a cane on the table and woe betide any of us kids if we spoke before being spoken to and if you had elbows on the table, you also had to eat all that was put in front of you or you would get if for supper or the next day until it was gone.

I remember in the small dining room of a Saturday night we would have the cottage tin bath on the floor in front of the fire and two at a time would fit in with knees up.

I had the job of cleaning the fireplaces as well as the boiler in the kitchen which I had to clean with red cardinal polish then go do the door step, I also had to collect clean newspapers and cut them into squares to loop a piece of string on the end and hang in the toilet. That was our toilet paper. I remember the toilet out in the back garden and it was painted white with distemper.

We also had our Anderson Shelter in the bottom of the garden where we spent many a-night with the air raids and hearing the bombs and AK-AK guns BLASTING.

Even today I have a bit of shrapnel from the War as a reminder. I recall I had to push a wheelchair for eight to ten miles from Catford to Sidham Gasworks to get two bags of coal and the weather would be bitter and foggy.

I remember my dad coming home for Christmas. He was in the Merchant Navy and it was our first time having an orange and box of crackers. By then my mother had a job delivering mail and I had no choice but to go with her, but this one time this lady called us in for a nice hot cup of tea. There I was in my welly boots and mittens drinking this lovely cup of tea when she produced a pair of shoes for me to try on, I had to have the cheek to ask to use her toilet so I could take my best socks off because if mum had seen them I would have been in for it. Then when we left, me with a nice pair of shoes but Wellington boots on with no socks in the cold and snow and with no complaint.

I remember the old lady that lived next door to us who had a son with a club foot who was a plumber or something, but also the vicar of the small church where we went Sunday School.

We had a sweet shop near us that two sisters ran, and once a month I would go to the Lewisham Hippodrome, Catford. I recall a man called Issy Bonn up on stage, he used to do tricks and we would run up on stage when he wanted someone. I think he must have been famous in his day.

I hated school meals but I would go across the road to the cafe and get two crusts with butter and jam that cost three pennies and go round to the park and eat it, much better than school dinner.

While I was at school for some reason I had it in my mind that I must have been in a children's home, in my mind it was a very large Victorian House with grounds at the back and front with stairs at one end, I also have a song in my head which goes like "We are Sidcup boys, we are the sons of the land", and this has always been with me and never goes away.

I had three sisters and three brothers, I have seen neither since the war. When I left school at fifteen and still to this day have my school reports. It stated that I should do well in my job but what one? I was a delivery boy delivering bread for the Co-op by horse and cart then on to a farm in Cambridgeshire to a place called Whistleford.

I left home on the 24th January which was a Monday, got a train back to Cambridge from Liverpool Street Station in London, sat in the carriage but when I got off the train with the man in my carriage he spoke to the guard who came to me and told me I had to pay more for travelling first class so I paid up out of the bit of pocket money I had and went on my way. Well I did not know the difference between the first class and second it was just a seat on a train to me.

I was also in the Army doing my National Service - two years deferred as I was working on a farm. Demob day came along after two years stationed in Germany. There was six of us lads at the time. My turn came in front of the adjutant. He wanted to know if I wanted to sign up for a longer stay in the Army and there was only me to worry about in life so I said yes.

I done another tour of duty but only if I was going away and not stationed here at home. He could not promise me that so I left because I was not getting a posting to Kenya or Malaya or Korea. He wanted my address so he could forward my paperwork on but I told him I didn't have one, I had been in lodgings before so the lad behind me said I could use his address and could also go home with him for a couple of weeks. So I spent two to three weeks in Liverpool in a place called Speke, there was an airport nearby which is now called The John Lennon airport. So it was time for me to leave and come on back to Cambridge before moving on to Portsmouth.

In 2009 I went to visit the War Museum which is on Southsea seafront as it was an open day all about the D Day Landings. I was so glad I went there because on display were photos, maps and mock ups and a few vehicles there as well, it was all about D Day Landings.

In one corner they had an Anderson air raid shelter which reminded me of the one we had in our back garden. One side of the shelter was cut away so that you could have a look in to get an idea of what it was like being inside it, it also had the slated forms on the ground where you would sleep and make your mattress out of anything you could stuff in it to lay on. We would also have a pail of water at hand and a couple bottles of lemonade as when there was an air raid you did not know how long you would be staying in them.

Where there was an opening to this shelter that would be the entrance and it was a dark entrance, but the lights would be flashing a red light as well, the effect was that a raid was on, with bangs going off at times but you needed to lie through it to be able to relate to it.

I stood staring at that entrance for ten minutes because it was so real, then a young couple came in with a young boy who was asking lots of questions but his dad was too young to know so I told him a story about it all from my own experience in my own shelter as a boy, it brought a tear to my eye, it is the one thing in my life I will never forget.

Part Two

My dad was in the Merchant Navy and the rest of the family by then was back home in Catford. Six months working on the farm soon went by and the farmer let me have the whole week end off so I could go visit the family. Off to London I went, only stayed a couple of days and off back to the farm I went in Cambridge.

I slept in a Sheppard's hut on the farm and I was very warm and cosy, I even had electric, very bare but it done me alright, I had my meals with the farmer and his wife. One night I woke with a shock - the air raid siren had gone off! I really thought the War had started again but it was a fire engine.

A few weeks went by and I received a letter from my uncle to tell me that my mum was very ill and in hospital in Lewisham, so the next day I went back up and was met by my uncle outside the hospital but had mum had passed away twenty minutes before I had got there, Dad was at sea all the time so did not see much of him. So I went back to the farm for another six months then thought I would go back to London to visit my family, it was a surprise visit but it was me who got the surprise because the house was empty and no one knew where my brothers or sisters had moved to.

Back to Cambridge I went and have lived my life since, not getting the blame for anything I didn't do and not a word from one of my family, but there again I suppose there were a few kids in the War had a worst time than me.

I think to myself a lot of people have different badges for different things, I reckon all those kids that were evacuated should get a badge because no one knew where they were going and only allowed to speak when spoken to not to mention the people that took us in. They were the ones that were forgotten.

I watched a film once on the television which summed up my life as well as all the other kids. Good Night Mr Tom acted by John Thaw.

I'm over seventy now and had a few jobs in my life, five all in and the last for eighteen year was working for a large cash and carry company in the print room where I was manager. That must have been the job that was mentioned in my school report all those years ago.

"You had to laugh or you would be forever crying"

Nora Jagger

My name is Nora Jagger nee Murphy and from a child I lived in Lake Road, Portsmouth with my mum, dad, brothers and sisters. I was seventeen when World War Two started and at that time I worked in Clarence Pier in a big posh restaurant just inside the Fairground, and it really was a lovely big restaurant and in the evening it became a dance hall and it was called the Clarence Pier. That was what I classed as my first job serving so that was counter assistant and waitress.

This particular morning I was going to work and the Prime Minister was heard on the news stating that he was waiting to hear if we were at War or not. He stated that if we didn't hear anything from him by eleven o'clock then we were at War. Everybody was waiting and watching and was very frightened, and then Mr Chamberlain came on the radio to announce that we were now at war with Germany. I went on to my job and being very young, I was very frightened and my bosses said to me "Are you alright?" and I said "No" and after my shift that night I decided I would go and live with my mum in Cowplain. The next day I went to work and told them that I was moving on to be with my family in Cowplain, and they were so kind in asking me if I had enough money and making sure I was OK.

My mum had moved from Portsmouth because of the War as everyone was so frightened, and the countryside was the best place to be. I came back to Portsmouth because I found the country was not for me and there was nothing for a seventeen year old girl to do and I was so lonely out there, so I said to my parents "I'm going back to Portsmouth and take my chances with the

bombs".

Nora's sister Jean and cousin Mick

I felt that after doing a few days' work I needed a bit of excitement in my life. So me and our Jean went to Broad Street in Old Portsmouth to make gas masks voluntarily for about two hours each day. I remember the first air raid I heard it was so awful, so frightening and even though we would go down to the Anderson Shelter every night, I will always remember the first night. And when the Germans started dropping their bombs, the first one came down on to the Blue Anchor Public House in North End, everyone thought they were looking for the Dockyard so that was the first pub that went, blasted to bits.

They started on other parts of Portsmouth the bombing was continuous. I just cannot describe what it was like then because we were all so hungry but all pulled together and shared what food they had. The people was so kind and that's how it went on right through to the end of the war.

We went to the dance halls every night, I stayed with my brother and his wife and we all went dancing at the City Hall and when I eventually got married that is where we went in the afternoon because there was nothing else to do, but that is another story.

I had a flat in Victoria Road and they built an air raid shelter right opposite which held fifty people, my sister was staying with me when the sirens started and I said to her, "Come on we better get down to the Anderson Shelter" and when we got there our Winn went go in but couldn't, I had a feeling about it and said "Let's go to the one further down the road". That was near the Plaza on Fratton Bridge, it was just me, our Winn and her three year old daughter Josephine who was wrapped in an eiderdown and we tried to get in the shelter by the Plaza but it was packed so we were told to go further along Fratton Bridge and you might get in one down there.

By this time we had got to the bottom and carried on walking, all the while they were dropping bombs all around us and we managed to get to the top of Lake Road and still could not get in to a shelter because they were so full up, so we carried on walking down Lake Road and all you could hear was this noise, it was a whizzing sound and it made you duck anywhere.

We did manage to get to the bottom of the road and the pub there was the Painter's Arms which still stands today. It was the Warden's place and we didn't know that until we knocked on the door and they said on opening the door, "Oh quick come on in!" and "Where are you going?" so we said, "Nowhere, can't we just get in anywhere" and they said back, "What you couldn't get in anywhere?" and I said, "No they are all completely full" so they said, "Alright we will sort you out" and gave us a little spring bed and let us stay the night. So we settled down and one of the wardens kept going over to the Painter's Arms with the chap that run it and filling up the buckets with beer and would sit and drink it all night, but because we were too young they kept making us cups of tea.

It was a horrendous night that I will never forget, the next morning we heard that the brick shelter had took a direct hit killing fifty people. Then we heard another got hit near St Mary's Road.

My sister-in-law Florence had a sister that lived opposite the corset factory which was in Arundel Street and they had a terrible bombing this particular night when she was getting her little boy ready for bed when the bomb came down on her neighbour's house and blew it to bits. They never found one bit of her and Flo's sister at the time of the explosion was washing her little boy and her son was gone so she was feeling around in the debris and dark but could not find him so the Air Raid Wardens came rushing over, where she had been digging about with her hands, they were all torn to pieces and when the wardens had seen what she pulled out they pushed it all back in.

They did eventually find the little boy but he was dead and in those days where there were so many dead they put them on stretchers and took them to different halls, and of course early morning people would have to go round all the churches to see if one of the dead belonged to you. Eventually they located the little boy that was only three years old and took him to my sister-in-law, he was so beautiful with blonde curly hair and these great big blue eyes, and he was laid out in the front room and they said to me, "Go and see him" but I said, "I can't bear to" but they kept on and on saying, "He is perfect, so go and see him."

So in the finish they convinced me to see the little boy and he just looked like he was asleep not a mark on him, but of course the blast had gone inwards, that's when the Air Raid Warden told us that the woman next door had gone and the baby had to be buried quick because of the blast going inwards.

At the same time the Princess Cinema had took a direct hit and blew the house opposite to bits at the bottom of Lake Road. I remember the film that was on that particular night, it was showing Margaret Lockwood in 'The Wicked Lady'.

Nora and Les

In between all this time I got married to my Les and he was stationed at Chattam, so I went to stay with him for a few weeks after my husband had told me about the cinema as I had arranged to meet him after his duty, and we would come down to Portsmouth together to what had happened because my mother's house by then was right opposite the cinema. She also came back to face the bombs because it was far too quiet in Cowplain.

I told my husband I could not wait till 4pm next day because I needed to know about my family so he agreed I could go on, so my sister came with me, there was nine of us in our family but as their houses got bombed moved in with one and other, it was an everyday thing then to do so.

I got the early train back but when I got to Commercial Road they would not let me through but I said I had to get down there to Lake Road but they said, "No you can't because of all the live wires" and told me to go to the top of Lake Road and go in that way but not to try and walk down because of the live wires and all, but I said, "I have to my people are all down there" and he then told me there were no houses left they had all been bombed. I kept on saying, "I have to go down there because of my family" so in the finish one of them said, "OK, but go so very careful and don't tread on any cables, even though it will take you twice as long to get down there."

But would you believe when I got to my house it was still standing but the roof had gone and my family were all sitting in the little room at the back. I was made a cup of tea and was so relieved to see them and I didn't worry about the top of the house and that night we lay in bed and was counting the stars.

Nora aged 15

Going back to my childhood days there was so much to do but so little time to do it. I went to Cottage Grove School as most of my family did and the school still stands today.

When I reached fourteen we moved to Aldershot because my dad was out of work and he was an engineer, it was nothing for people to move from one place to another because there houses was bombed so it was accepted as a natural thing. That was where I had my first job, I ended up in a little sweet shop.

After Aldershot we stayed in the house that got bombed until we got another one with a roof on. I then went on to work in Old Portsmouth working on naval shirts which was quite nice and I enjoyed doing that.

I remember a shop stating that if I bought a new coat they would give me a wedding cake. This is how things were, I got married as I said earlier and while he was away at sea I stayed with my family. We would go out for the day but never appreciated what we had before until it was gone and now it was either the pubs or the dance halls and we chose the dance halls and there wasn't many that we didn't visit in Portsmouth but the main one was the City Hall at the bottom of Lake Road.

My first boyfriend worked for Chapman's Laundry that was situated in Kingston Crescent, he was a driver and I thought that was great because sometimes we could have a little ride round, and of course through the War I got married and settled down like a lot of people, you heard people say enjoy today as it could be our last and that's how it was. We all made the best of what we had and it was real community spirit every one helped when they could and we felt very lucky to be alive.

I can remember one day as I was walking down the road this airplane came down very low and the next thing we heard was 'ti-ti-ti-ti-ti-ti' and it was machining the walls and if anyone was in line they would of got hit as well, it frightened the life out of us but we were very lucky because the bullets never touched us.

Then this particular night it had been very quiet then the sirens went but we had just put my niece Josephine to bed and got settled ourselves and got the cards out for a game of cards when I heard this terrible noise outside so ran along the long passage to the front room and thought "Oh my god it's on fire!" So I called my sister Winn quick, she put the duvet round Josephine and that's when we took her down Lake Road but couldn't get in anywhere as I said previous. We learned what had lit the place up was a Molotov

Nora's sister Winn with her children Freddie and Allan

Bomb, they had names for all the different bombs but was not sure but this is what we were told it was.

Before we left the flat our Winn went back to have a look and said, "No it's not our flat it's the one right opposite" but the way it lit our flat up you would of thought it was ours. We were very lucky that time.

There was a fish shop but couldn't get fish then, it was a pie shop really up the top of Lake Road on to Fratton Road and even though they were nice pies the pastry was yellow and people would line up after the Dance Hall closed and then sit on the steps and eat it. It was really laughable you know.

We had ration books then and it was awful, I would give mine to my little boy so when the grocery man came he used to have a Mars bar because he loved them. We used to have four eggs a month and I would boil mine so I could cut them in half to give to the children, and of course if you broke a chair leg or any furniture it could not be repaired or replaced.

Not many people had radios in those days but had what we called 'boxes', we had Radio Relay and they would come and put these boxes in and you would pay according to the number of boxes you had because as I said unless you were rich no one had a proper radio. The older people of course had them but the younger ones like me didn't.

The other thing we would do was to paint our legs to give us a nice tan or if we couldn't do that we would stand on a chair and get someone to draw the black line up the back of the leg to make it look as though we had stockings on.

The best times, the only real happy times were when the American ships came in because we went to their dances and had such gorgeous food although it was ordinary we thought it was wonderful, the whole family would turn up as well. We had three great big Battleships come in to Portsmouth and it caused more fights than enough because the woman didn't want to know our men. They wanted to know the Americans because they had the sweets, the stockings and they took the chances, and everyone you knew said you going to their dance as it brightened every one up, it was great.

We got so used to the air raids in the finish that when the bombs dropped we just didn't bother didn't rush to the Air raid shelters we just took a chance and enjoyed it but we were not alone, a lot of people were the same.

But I do remember when my son was born he was only three days old, it was terrible. The men got all the woman out and carried me out and my little Terry as the bombs rained down hard on the city into the Air raid shelter, what a night that was. In the morning there were all these cups and plates

and we didn't know who they belonged to, but people had started to make cakes and things and put them in for the evening as it was a natural thing in the end to go into the air raid shelter and you never bothered going in to the other roads and people also made their homes down in the gardens.

And I will always remember when my Les got promoted and had this lovely new suit on and slipped in the Air raid shelter where it had been raining and not only muddied it but torn it as well but my sister said, "Don't worry I can invisibly mend that for you" which of course she did and made a hash of it. They had to be so because he was an officer, I laugh now but didn't at the time.

All in all everyone enjoyed the War years and one of my sisters was working in the Dockyard making these torpedoes. My other sister Jane got a job in the munitions factory but only stayed the one day and gave her notice in like a lot of the jobs that came her way.

My sister Winn and our Jean all ended up living in Common Street and while I was there ready to take the kids out our Jane, Patsy and Jean came running in and said we got a proposition for you and asked me if I would be able to do them a snack at dinner time and they would pay me at the end of the week when they got paid, because they had got a job in the factory around the corner which made the bottles of bleach or substance the same as bleach. I said, "I tell you what, I will cook you a dinner, then we can all go so much" and they all said "Oh alright."

After the first day when our Jane came in I said, "What's up with your finger?" in which she replied "I don't know I must of hurt it and put a plaster on it." And then the next day when they came in for their dinner our Patsy had two fingers plastered up so I said, "What you doing, where you working?" and again they said, "With bottles of bleach" and I said, "At this rate you won't have any bloody fingers left, you can't stay there and do that" because their fingers were really sore. And I said to our Jane, laughing, "Well you only got a couple fingers left now so you better leave while the going is good" and so she left.

Needless to say I never got no bloody money for the cooked dinners every day I done at my expense. Next day our Winn came round and said "Lend me a pound and I'll give you it back next Thursday." It was a lot of money in those days but I lent her it, then she would pay me back, then borrow it again on the Friday, so in the end when she ask if she could lend a pound I said, "Oh you want to borrow my pound do you or is it your pound?" because it had gone on so long I had forgotten.

My Les was still away so I didn't see much of him and didn't even know where he was. When I wrote him a letter some would get blanked out because you couldn't just write anything in your letter as they were read in case you gave any secrets away about certain places or about the Dockyard, no contact at all, so Les never saw the babies till Terry was at least two and by then he screamed every time he saw his dad.

It was a weird thing when we heard about the invasion, most people thought it would happen but then they seemed to change their minds. It was a weird feeling inside of us which I just can't explain, it was as if people were saying, "You are not going to do it you're not going to beat us."

We would get Haw Haw on the radio telling us all sorts and it used to worry us but in the end people would just laugh and jeer at him and people never took no notice of it after a while, but he was a regular and every day it would be on and at first we would get upset but the men would say, "Ah, you don't want to take any notice of that" and then of course we learned to laugh it off. He got fed up in the end, this man called Haw Haw but I never put him on.

We were going to a dance one night and it was pitch black because you could not have any lights, and the previous night a bomb had gone off in Lake Road and the whole of the spiked fence had blown forward all over the pavement, and I said to the girls about the fence and told them to keep to the middle of the road. So you can imagine what it was like so we were all holding one another's hand and this sister-in-law of Vera said, "Oh I know where you mean, I have passed it several times" and as we were walking I said "You got it all wrong we got a bit further to go" and with that she walked straight into the fence and went head first and ended up with a big black eye as well as other injuries, but still went to the dance hall, and when she came out of City Hall at half time we would go down and have a drink rather than sit there and wait for it to start again.

This night though as we walked back in, a 'rip' one dropped, nothing like the ones in the garden - it was awful. The next night at home when I drew my curtains I looked and wondered how the hell we managed but of course you had to go about your daily chores as before, and winter nights were the worst when you had to get out of a warm bed to get to the Air raid shelter.

One night when me and our Winn was snuggled up warm in the bed she said, "If them Bastards drop a bomb tonight I am not getting out of this bed" and I said "Neither am I because I am past it now" and every time we got up as much debris as we could and swept and cleaned and made the most of what we had. The Germans could not break our spirits that's for sure, we all mucked in together. The War Years were very frightening but we all have many a happy memory to think back on and share as well as sad ones but hey, life is for living so don't dwell on what might have been.

Part Two

I did not tell you about the gas masks, that we would have to go down several times in the week to help make them and once done they would be supplied to everybody, the baby's ones that were made was special cradles and you just didn't go anywhere without them. If you tried to get in the Cinema with it, it was closed to you so you had to have your Gas Mask plus your identity card along with it so where ever you went those two things went with us.

The first one we got supplied with we had to go to a Gents' hat shop and they would be left there for each and every one that need a gas mask that did not have one. I remember the first time when we had to try the gas mask I said to our Jean "When we go into this shop do not look at me because you will start laughing and it will start me off" and she promised me faithfully she would not. Well anyway, we went in and it was an elderly gentleman who was dealing with us and he said, "Have a seat young ladies."

He then proceeded to put the gas mask on our Jean and I could see she was splitting her sides and when he finished I could she couldn't wait to get to the door to get out before she let rip with the loudest laugh. When I look back now over the years I can see why because when she put her mask on she looked straight at me and there was me ripped with laughter.

I know we had a lot of bleak moments but there was also happy ones like this when you could have a good chuckle about what we looked like in our gas mask. We had to keep these for a long time and in the meantime great big buildings were being made for the people, sturdy Anderson Shelters as I mentioned before.

Going back to the Air raid shelter I did not tell you I had to be carried out from one when my baby was only two days old and my other little fellow Terry was only two, it was a really bad night for us because Jerry was pounding us rotten and two men came in, pick me and baby up and carried me to the Air raid shelter and  gave us hot tea, and in the morning gave us more tea then carried me back to my rooms as in those days you were bed bound for a fortnight before you trod on ground. They were so kind so it really helped me and took the fear away from Terry.

I told you our house got hit and one night we slept in the bed looking up at the stars.

The furniture in them days was very big solid wood wardrobes and dressers and this night and one night one got wedged in the window so they had to come in and move it for everyone's safety.

It was such a shame to see the destruction all around you and children having to sleep in muddy shelters and places outside in the gardens, it made it hard times very hard indeed but we carried on.

My cousin Vera had her dark moments because she had been bombed several times and each time she lost a bit more of her furniture or it was spoilt, but her father had moved to Ringwood where it was not bombed so she decided that because she had been bombed so many times and lost so much, her furniture etc. that she too would move out and follow him and went down to the Guildhall to tell them that she was moving and asked them if they could pay for a bit of furniture. But they hummed and hahhed and said "No" and while in Ringwood her house here in Portsmouth took a direct hit and as a result she received a letter from the Guildhall then telling her that they would help her get her bits for her house, but she turned round and told them they need not bother because they had finished her house off the night before so don't worry about it.

She had quite a time of it and lost more than any of us but luckily enough we were all saved. We can't complain about that.

Part Three

Funny thing once you start to take your mind back so many years when things have been buried so deep then it's brought to mind.

I think I told you that I worked for Palmers the Brush Factory that was at Fratton, I worked there for two weeks and tried to leave three times because I hated it there. I tried smoking because it was banned because of the inflammables used in the factory, so I went into the toilets got a ciggie off one of the girls and started, but even though I got reported all I got was a habit I enjoyed not the sack. I became a smoker from that day.

Palmers was a very hard job and you only got paid after you did 144 brush heads then you earned a penny. After the smoking and not getting instant dismissal I went and gave my notice in but was told its War work so cannot leave. So I went and got married at eighteen and left and went to live up in Scotland, I might have already shared that bit with you.

I had so many short term jobs, I worked the Cinema as an usherette and ice cream seller, and when on that the men would say, "Have one for yourself" so I would say "Thank you I will have it in a bit" and pocket the money, and by the end of my shift I would go home with quite a bit. I forgot to mention earlier in my story that I worked in a tobacco factory inside the Barracks, we made cigarettes called Ticklers and tobacco would arrive in big blocks and we would have to tease it apart before feeding it in to the machine. My boss was really nice his name was Alex and we would together get the pipe tobacco ready for the officers. No pass to get into barracks meant you could not work so you had to remember your pass every day, I must of held that one down for four to six months, that was before I married, and pay day I would head for CA clothes shop in Commercial Road and spend best part of my wages. And one day had my eye on this dress I wanted and on pay day everyone but me got wages so before Alex left I shouted, "You forgot my wage packet!" so he shouted back, "Help yourself to petty cash in the tin!"

I just had to I had to have that dress. I would have to wait if not 'til Monday but wanted my dress for the dance hall that night so that's what I did.

There was one shop, I don't know if I mentioned before, but if you bought a coat or shoes you would be given a wedding cake free if you were getting married so I was given one after I purchased my coat and packed it on top on my wardrobe only to find the bloody mice had started eating it.

I lived at 259 Lake Road and there was a second-hand shop next door and a fruit and vegetable shop opposite on the other side of road next to the Swan Public House that still stands today.

I think I told you I worked Twilfit Corset Factory doing hook and eyes and buttons but didn't tell you about the little shake below that sold the best donuts and cream ones at that, but they cost an arm and leg and was best part of your wage, but you just had to have one now and again because they were the best. I think I mentioned earlier about me living at Nazareth House and being called Jacky because another girl there was called Nora Murphy but at the age of sixteen I told the family I wanted to be called Nora again.

I also had a job at the Black Cat Café in Commercial Road that only lasted a week thanks to our Jean, then we went to work together in bar work but our Jean once again got us the sack so I said "Bugger to this" and when our Dawsie's husband got killed I decided to try my luck with her at Brickwood's Brewery down in Portsea. We laughed seeing the girls in clogs until we got the job, funny thing is all the women there was hard as nails but took pity on our Dawsie and gave her a Guinness every single day to help build her up and get her over her bereavement.

Even though bombs were dropping everywhere you never thought for one minute it was going to be you next.

Brian Smith

I was born in St Marks Road in Stamshaw that was in 1934, but we had to move from there to a house in Chichester Road but I can't remember when that was, but I do remember my brother being born in 1938 and one day mother laying down on the bed with the baby laying in the middle and mother saying to me one day you are going to have to look after your brother.

Again in 1939 we moved house again to the old part of Paulsgrove at the back of a pub called the Old House at Home. There was also a race track and stables in them days and was run by a jockey by the name of Topper Brown and we go down there and help him out with his horses.

My gran lived in number four and we lived in number five. I can't remember who lived in the other four bungalows but I do remember there was a great big field at the back and there was pig sties in the field right through to Portsdown Hill, and at the back of the pig sties there was a Dairy Farm.

I was evacuated to a place called Black Water to a Mrs Onion and six of us had to top and tail in one bed, three up the top and three down the bottom and she fed us nothing but soup.

I remember one of the boys that were there with me could do sign language for the deaf and I will always remember that when parents came to visit us she was always there watching us so we knew what not to say, and this day this boy started to sign language to his dad what was going on and we were then all sent home.

Then in 1942 my mum died and we had to move in with my Granddad in Ranleigh Road in Stamshaw and we stayed on there for about a year also with my aunt, who lost her husband in the war so we couldn't stay there then, so we had to go back to our house in Paulsgrove and of course by this time my father had remarried so then we had a step mum who didn't really want us anyway.

I went to an infant school in Castle Street in Portchester and then when I became eleven I had to go to school in Cosham to Portsdown School and had to walk there from the Old House at Home right across the fields 'til I reached a public house called The Clacton and there was no houses there at that time, and where we lived only three of us attended that school. That was myself, a boy called Samuel Glide and Alex Marsh, but all my cousins all went to the Senior School at Portchester but they wouldn't have me. I just couldn't believe it 'cause my step mother would knock us around a lot, it would of helped being in the same school as family I think.

Then my brother was sent away to Naval School then we moved on to Eastney by then I was fifteen and a half and I walked out of my dad's house and never saw him again for years then he died in 1988.

Going back to the War years I remember the roads in Paulsgrove being built by Prisoners of War and if I caught a bus I could get off at Bert's Café then walk up the lane in Southampton Road and on one side of the lane you had Stables, then when you walked under the bridge you had Piggeries Slaughter House and behind that you had rhubarb fields so I would nick the rhubarb. Then if you walked along the Southampton Row you had Cooper's Slaughter House and the blood when they killed the cattle would run across the road into the sea. We would go up there and play as kids and watch, they also owned a very big house. Behind there was all fields that led right up to the hill.

In the War when the bombs were being dropped a car got hit and it blew it right across the fields from the dirt track road right outside our house, and we had a concrete water tank outside our house as well for when the bombs fell and caused fires, and I also remember when our one panes of glass window blew in we had to have an asbestos one put in to replace the glass one that had blown so we ended up with one of each.

We had our own garden with rabbits and chickens and it was my job to look after them because we had our own plots to look after.

During the War they made a film up Southampton Road and we had to skate up and down the promenade on scooters. It was a black and white film and I can't remember what it was called now but they shot film that came out after the War.

We would sit watch the prisoners of War walk up the main road to their Mess and we would go over there stand outside and they would give us corned beef and bread which was something we couldn't get and they would also make us little toys out of tin and we could flick them up in the air and they would fly.

Portsdown School while I was there had some prefab class rooms built at the back of it and some of us got transferred to them. I then left school in 1939.

The other thing I remember is when the Irish navvies' were working on the tunnel up on the hill and when they came down the hill we went up and stole one of their little trucks and pushed it down the field into a well, but it didn't go down and of course this idiot (ME) jumped on it to make it go down and lucky for me I grabbed hold of a tree branch and my cousins just managed to pull me out as it went down.

We could sit up the top of the hill and watched the dog fights going on with the German planes.

At the back of the Old House At Home Pub they had a water tank too.

I knew a family that lived in Hamilton Road by the name of Carter, then along by Vosper's was John Pounds who then had two Dalmatian Dogs which belonged to his wife.

We had tugs in the water at that time by Paulsgrove that had been recovered in the War, mostly German, and they would get dragged in there and we would jump off them into the water till they cut them up for scrap .

Going back to my evacuee days I went first to a Mrs Seymour who had a well at the bottom of the garden and I had to go fetch the water. I remember she also had a shepherd dog which was lovely and friendly like her and her husband, but Mr Seymour died then we were sent to Mrs Onion who was really horrible to us hence the reason we were sent home as told earlier. We never got starved but was fed this horrible watery soup and she did knock us around too and I will always remember that.

My dad was in the Navy in the War and stationed at HMS Nelson in Queen Street, Portsea and when we used to go and meet him we were never allowed to stand near the gates, always had to stand at the end of the road.

Then I got called up myself in 1954 for my National Service but I only served seven months because I was disabled out with lung and heart disease.

I then went as an apprenticeship brick layer which I packed up then moved on to London to manage a supermarket then retired and came home in 1999.

Jennifer Trodd

I was born August when it was glorious summer, mostly all day sunshine with the occasional light warm rain. My memory takes me back to when I was a baby

in my big coach-built pram, what age I do not recall but I can remember my grandparents always taking me out, and as I grew into a small child I recall the smell of summer with the blossom of our Buddleia tree and its beautiful big mauve blossoms hanging heavy down and the scent it gave out.

My father was a soldier in the Northumberland Fusiliers and was sent to Egypt because we were at War and it was the 1940s. My uncles were away also as father for a good few years so it was up to my dear Grandfather to look out for us. He had served his time in the First World War so lucky for us he was too old to be called back up.

He made me wonderful wooden toys by the plenty, a lovely doll's house followed by my wheelbarrow and of course a grand rabbit hutch for my beloved Snowdrop.

It was not always smiles and laughter because when the bombs dropped we along with my aunties had to go into the shelters, but Granddad being an Air Raid Warden for our town would always pop in to make sure all was OK and we had nice bales of hay to sit on. That was one benefit living in Bedhampton, I remember the songs everyone would sing and how well the family and all the neighbours laughed with Granddad when he popped his head in while on duty.

The bombs were so loud when they fell and it frightened me a lot, and I would cover my ears to try and get that horrid sound out of my mind. I remember as it was yesterday when one fell so near to the shelter just by Granddad's allotment, and I had my doll's pram in the shelter with me and the pram jumped high in the air to my utter dismay. The flames of the bombs would light up the sky red over Portsmouth and I sat in wonderment.

As the flames died down and it darkened once again you could see the glow worms shining along the garden path as we slowly walked back to the house having heard the cry of all clear. There in the yard the toilet door was ajar and a shivering little field mouse was backed in a corner, looked like he was shivering from fear too, so my loving Granddad put a little milk sop down just by the door for it and of course by the morning it had recovered and gone.

On the odd quiet night we would sit in the garden just watching the stars and the search lights with me sat in my granddad's big strong arms feeling very safe and content. We had flower pots and candles in the shelter which made us glow. I myself would put my gas mask on and run around pretending to be Mickey Mouse. To me as a child that is what they made you look like.

Havant was lots of fields in them days so on a summer's day it looked glorious everywhere you looked, of course where mum and dad lived in Bedhampton was very much the same. My brother Michael was a war baby, we had lots of animals; rabbits, mice, cats and of course my beloved Waggles a little fox terrier Granddad bought me for my sixth birthday. As my brother got older he was bought a collie bitch which he called Lassie. I remember there was never much room to sit if the cats were in because they would stretch themselves out like a big fur carpet on the settee and would not budge until you gave a small shove, then they would look at you as if to say "What do you think you are doing?"

Because we lived outside of the city we did not get evacuated neither did my friends. Over at Marie's house in her garden she had rabbits and a shed that housed ferrets that her father would use to catch wild rabbits. This put rabbit stew and pies on the table and very nice to eat they were. You could always smell the sweet smell of the hay bales at hers as well.

We would laze about watching the different colours and sizes of the butterflies that would land on her blossoms of the tree. Sometime throughout this hot sunny day we would climb the tree armed with our sketch pads to try and draw the nature that we were surrounded by, and also take in the breath-taking views looking out over Bedhampton. You hardly heard a car or a dog bark but you could watch wild rabbits running through the grass, or just sat watching us watching them so quiet and peaceful until the next bomb came. It was days like this you would not think a war was on until you looked at the ruins and devastation the bombs had left and the many homeless people that had lost their homes.

Of course to children you didn't concern yourself with such worries, we had a river by us as well and we played safe in the fields and in the wonderful woods, God how lucky we were not to have lived in the city.

As children we had happy war years. My friends all played with Christopher the farmer's son in a drive. The farm was called Berkley Farm and they were allowed to help with hay making and ride on the hay cart with the brown horse pulling it along. I recall the pony we were allowed to ride, on his name was Tiny and he was black and small that is why they named him Tiny I think, because of his size. The farmer would sometimes give us milk straight from the cows which was creamy and warm.

Tuesday was my favourite day because it was market day and my grandparents lived in Waterloo Road just across from it, so luck was on my side because at the market they sold livestock. You could buy goats and allsorts, but you could stand and watch the cattle get weighed and the sheep in the pens, but how I hated seeing the men with the pinchers that would make the pigs cry as they got the ear clipped.

One side of the market would have boxes with little yellow chicks and chickens but they were so crammed in some would end up with broken wings and they would get thrown out, so I picked up a few so Granddad could make them better. He would make little sticks and put on broken legs to help heal them, but of course they never survived but he kept me happy.

I begged to have a baby goat but of course it would have ate the flower and cabbages in the garden so I was refused. I remember meeting up with my friends and we would chase the little animals that had escaped, it was fun. I remember picking up a cockerel and running back to Grandma's and putting it in with the hens in the cage, but sadly the man that owned it had been around to ask if anyone had seen it. Granddad got a shock when he saw it with the hens walking so proud round their pen, but of course this put poor Granddad in somewhat an awkward position but of course he returned it to the man straight away. I was seen running in the back gate with it so I could not say it was mine.

I do recall gypsies in one of the fields, and I started to hang about fascinated by the great big well-kept horses and colourful wooden caravans that the horses pulled. The men was always brushing the horses down until they shone, the ladies would scrub the caravans like shiny pins. How lovely they were in side, not a thing out of place and beautiful coloured china on the walls and very big inside, not what you would imagine, so clean. But the people looked dirty even though they were not, it was the brown tanned skins that made them look so dirty - weather worn. I made friends with one of the girls but picked up such bad language, kept telling people to shut their gob much to Granddad's dismay. But he quickly got me out of that because I fell in love with a stuffed heron in a glass box that was promised if I stopped talking like the gypsy girl. I kept it until my teens and in the end sold it to a butcher.

When dad came back from the war I knew no more bombs were going to drop and no more in the shelter and of course I had four grown-ups to spoil me and my brother, it was lovely. Dad would wake me early and we would go pick mushrooms in the fields or winkling down by Bud's Farm and sometimes would take the little boat to Hayling Island, it was fun. We would watch the gypsies make pegs then go round the doors to sell them.

Dad eventually got a job working in the Dockyard for the MOD, he was a Military Policeman and stood very proud on the gate 'til eventually he had to retire. He cycled every day to work from Bedhampton and on a day off would bring me by tram down to see the mudlarkers in the mud at the Hard. I forgave my ice cream just so I could throw pennies down into the mud for the children below. Oh how I loved days like that.

The children below that bridge reminded me of the gypsy girl with the brown face ,the mud dried in giving the appearance of dark skin, that is how I will remember my friends who vanished as quick as they came and the mudlarks calling up for pennies. The War long forgotten.

Welcome Home

Underneath the beech tree waiting in the rain, dogs and me

Yellow leaves a-falling at our feet and little brown nuts for the squirrels to eat

The wind is blowing; leaves dancing everywhere soon this old tree will be bare.

Your train is coming, horn sounding at the station as it arrives

Little dog is dancing on two legs to welcome you home from the war zone.

Let's walk home in the rain with kit bag on shoulder, soon to be by the fireside with dog at your feet.

Hot milk and Whisky is granddad's little treat.

Hush of the rain drops on the window so pull the deep red curtains

Solider battle weary, kick off your well-worn boots

And dog will bring your slippers as she always would.

Hear the crackle of fire...it's not the guns resounding

Hear the cricket whistling on the warm hearth stone, some will say you're lucky to have one in your home.

But in your dreams you're hearing your mates whistling the old war songs.

I will say goodnight sleep safe my soldier son.

By Jennifer Trodd

HAVANT AND DISTRICT WAR WEAPONS WEEK

(Continued from Page 3)

HAVANT'S BUSY WEEK

Baby Show

Two of the chief events of Monday's programme were the Baby Show at the British Legion Club and the Fancy Dress Parade.

The judges at the Baby Show were Dr. Dewhurst senr., Mrs. Young (Southbourne), Mrs. Little (Harting) and Mrs. Jestico. The following were the awards:—

Up to 9 months—1, Leonard Cooper; 2, Christopher Leaver; 3, Pearl Arnett.

9 to 18 months—1, Patricia Viney; 2, Wendy Coleman; 3, Karina Spilman.

18 months to 2½ years—1, Wendy Duly; 2, Patricia Stallard; 3, Marie Waller; Masters Rees (twins), highly commended.

2½ to 3½ years—1, Maureen Yoxall; 2, Verity Mullins; 3, Betty Pearson.

Over 3½ years—1, Muriel Wiggins; 2, Ronald Pascoe; 3, Jean Wallis.

Fancy Dress Parade

A large crowd witnessed the Fancy Dress Parade held in the Park.

The judges were Lady Pink, Miss Pauline White, and Mrs. Courtney Mitchell, and the awards were as follows:—

Class 1 (up to 7 years)—1, Jennifer Abbott; 2, J. Fletcher; 3, L. Roberts.

Class 2—1, Alfred Allen; 2, Elizabeth North; special, Barbara Hedger.

Class 3—1, Mrs. Whiting (John Bull and dog); 2, Mrs. Burchell (gipsy woman); 3, Mr. Roberts (1870 soldier).

Decorated cycles—1, Brian Boxall; 2, Master Braithwaite.

Miss Edna Gibbs, in a dress composed entirely of patchwork, is running a competition all the week— "Guess the number of my patches."

Other events on Monday were a well executed Maypole dance by the scholars of the Council School; a tableau, "Nurseryland," by children of the Methodist Sunday School, under the leadership of Mrs. Niall; a whist drive in Bedhampton Hut; display by the First Aid Party and Drummond, Portchester, 7/6; N.

Havant Baby Show Winners

The programme for Monday in connexion with War Weapons Week was full of interest, and each event was well patronized. In the afternoon a baby show was held in the British Legion Hall, where Dr. J. H. Dewhurst, of Bedhampton), Mrs. Young (Southbourne), Mrs. Little (Harting), and Mrs. Jestie were the judges. Their awards were as follow: Up to 9 months: 1, Leonard Cooper; 2, Christopher Leaver; 3, Pearl Annett. 9-18 months: 1, Patricia Viney; 2, Wendy Coleman; 3, Karina Spilman. 18 months to 2½ years: 1, Wendy Derly; 2, Patricia Stallard; 3, Marie Walker. The Masters Rees (twins) were highly commended in this class. 2½ to 3½ years: 1, Maureen Voxall; 2, Verity Mullins; 3, Betty Pearson. 3½ to 5 years: 1, Muriel Wiggins; 2, Ronald Pascoe; 3, Jean Walls.

A competition for a portrait by Mrs. Marshall was won by Mrs. Hart, Market Lane, Havant.

In the evening Havant Park was the centre of attractions, and the proceedings were given a bright and cheerful send off by a pretty display of Maypole and country dances by pupils of the Council School. This was followed by a fancy dress parade. The judges were Lady Pink, Miss Pauline White and Mrs. Courtney Mitchell, and the results were as follow:— Up to 7 years: 1, Jennifer Abbott; 2, J. Fletcher; 3, L. Roberts. Up to 14 years: 1, Alfred Allen; 2, Elizabeth North; 3, Barbara and Edmund Hedger. Adults: 1, Mrs. Whiting (John Bull and Dog): 2, Mrs. Burchell (Ginsy); 3, Mr. Roberts (1870 soldier). Decorated cycles: 1, Brian Boxall; 2, A. Braithwaite.

The prizes were presented by Lady North.

The concluding item on the programme was a display by the First Aid and Casualty Services and thrilling episodes carried out by the Fire Brigade and A.F.S.

The Urban District Council of Havant and Waterloo.

If Undelivered Please Return to
The Chief Financial Officer,
Town Hall, Havant.

CLASS 6

11

FANCY DRESS COMPETITION.

Class 7.

1st Prize.

JULY 28th 1941

Jennifer winning the Fancy Dress Parade

Pauline Brockwell

My name is Pauline Brockwell and I am now eighty two years old. I am now going back seventy years to when I was evacuated as an evacuee at eleven years old.

I was evacuated with my two sisters and my brother and my youngest brother stayed with our mum. We were taken to Croydon Station, put on the train to Crowborough and stayed there for a couple of nights with people that took us in. We then went on to a place called Framfield and stayed with a middle-aged couple who never had any children and the man was not as he should have been, and there was other evacuees there same as us and they were two boys, two girls, one who was then fourteen, and unfortunately we found out that things were not as they should have been, and the fourteen year old girl was going to the mans bed. It did not interfere with us but we all knew what was going on.

I used to have to go out sometimes just to pick dandelion leaves to be put into sandwiches and this we would have to do and take it in turns. This is what we had for our tea and if we didn't have that then we would have nothing so of course we would eat it.

We got on quite well with the children in Framfield and people were quite kind to us but when mum found out what was going on she came and got us and took us into Blackboys, and I remember how we would walk for miles and miles to one place to another but of course we did it. Once when I went back there in August this year I couldn't believe the miles we had walked but I did like living in Blackboys and we were always together, my two sisters and me and my little brother.

At the age of fourteen I went into service as a kitchen maid and so did my sister and it was quite good, and my wage was about thirty shilling a month and I would have to get up six in the morning get the dog and get over the fields and try and get mushrooms for the lady's breakfast, but I never did get any mushrooms cause I took the dog round and round on my bike.

When the War first started I was out in the garden with my sister and my cousin and we were playing in the air raid shelter when I suddenly looked up and saw all these planes, then all these bombs being dropped and they landed on Croydon Air Port. I came from Croydon and it was terrifying and my poor mother was running around trying to find us all as we were all in different places. I just could not believe when I looked up and saw all these bombs dropping, my sister and self screamed and we all had to stay in the air raid shelter.

When I was evacuated we had this air raid shelter that was like a little house and we would have to go in there and of course the toilet was right up the top of the garden and you couldn't see what you were doing.

When as I said we went on to Blackboys we stayed with Mrs Barton, and a couple of years before the War ended my mum came to stay in a little cottage in Sir Reginald Bench's garden with my youngest brother who was quite ill, and she had this really old fashioned pram and walk right down this hill and put it in the bushes and pick him up and take him to school, then do the same again when she had to pick him up again. My mum would walk for miles and miles as we all did.

I started to work in Upfield in a little tiny café and it was really tiny as well, and my sister worked in Wirells in Upfield and we would have all the Canadian soldiers in for beans on toast, and they would sit out along the kerb. They were all very kind to us and because we only had one bus which was at half past eight in the morning, and if you didn't catch that then you didn't go to work. Well my sister always managed to get on the bus, but because I was always dragging along I missed it so one morning I arrived at work on a Tank, another in a Jeep, then on a Motor Bike, then when I was in the Tank I kept going up and down up and down and burned me-self.

It was a strange life when you think about it because now I am eighty two and I think we were very lucky because some people were treated very bad who they were billeted with, but some were alright and kind, and then there was one couple who wanted us but they only really wanted the money so all in all we were OK. And my sisters and I all had bikes and we would go for miles and miles in the evenings all around the country and it was lovely.

We never went to school but we had an old Nissan Hut in a field in Blackboys and we used to have our food in there, and the headmaster that came with us used to teach us and he stayed with us. Mr Alerver his name was and he was very kind and would take us for nature walks and anything else he could think of because we were not getting real schooling. In the end when I think I was about thirteen they managed to get us in to a real school but it was only for a year if that.

Blackboys is a lovely place and when I think back I know we were the lucky ones. We were fairly cared for and the fact that having our mother with us did help us.

It's a strange life and now when I think about it at my age, it was six years we were away from it and my mother away from my father the last two years of the War, so really and truthfully because we were all together it was a good thing even though we were billeted at different places we see each other every day.

When I was twelve and my sister eleven, and even to this day I don't know why, but we decided to be Baptised but of course we had to go on our own which we did of course, went to the little church in Framfield and I was Confirmed but my sister wasn't, but why we did that on our own I don't know but we did. When I went back for a visit everything all came back to me and the church has not changed a bit.

I remembered when I was in Framfield I would go potato picking anything in the fields that would earn us a bit, we were fortunate we didn't have a bad life but it could have been, but we looked after ourselves and nothing really happened to us.

I do remember one day when I was walking down the lanes and the planes was coming over and the bombs started to drop and the Doodlebug stopped, and down the bottom of the lane was a searchlight party in the ditch just across the road, and as the Doodlebug dropped a soldier jumped out of the trench and pulled me in just as it hit and I was saved. We did have them Doodlebugs come over and planes, and we lived in a little cottage then and my dad had made a ditch all around it so we could jump in the ditch when the bombs were dropping. It was so frightening because if they dropped a Doodlebug when it stopped you didn't know if you were going to get hit next.

We were very fortunate and when I think about it, it was frightening. I met my husband in Portsmouth age twenty three when he was in the Navy but unfortunately he died a very young age of forty five, but I am glad I did not live here in the War because I heard how badly bombed it got here, but I love living in Portsmouth and have always found the people very kind and I have always been very happy here with my lovely children.

Going back to when I lived with Mrs Barton there stood a very tiny cottage right in the field, it seems so strange now when you go back and I would like to say up 'til last year my brother went back every year to see Mrs Barton 'til his wife died last year because he had so many memories and they did not have children of their own and he was so happy with them.

I feel so happy now.

Maureen Prett

My name is Maureen Prett and in 1938 I was working in a factory and a young man came to the factory to work, and at the same time as he started at the factory the country were going to be calling young men up at twenty one to work six months in the militia, but they were not going to be wearing khaki they were going to be trained as soldiers but were going to wear navy blazers, grey trousers and navy beret. This young man I met in the factory was due to be called up because I had met him late 1938 and in 1939 he was called up for service.

The first time he came home on leave my father, who had been a Prisoner in the First World War, burst in to tears. This was because when he walked in to the house he was wearing the uniform of the 1914 - 18 soldiers wore. He never ever came home in the navy blazer and of course the six months for my husband that was stated went on for eight years.

As I was only fifteen and he was twenty and because he had asked me out for a date I said to him "You will have to ask my dad." But of course I was an only child and I could talk to my mum and dad about anything and everything, so my dad said "Yes that's OK, but tell that young man to come and see me." Tom did and my dad said "Yes that's alright" and told him what time I had to be home and that was that.

Then we was not at war so we spent that Christmas together then the next, but then he was called up and then stationed in Leeds, and luckily my father's family lived in Leeds so, far and in between I went to stay with them for the New Year. That was 1940 and so glad I did because a week after I came back from staying with them being able to see Tom in Leeds.

Tom then came home on his embarkation leave and that was it, he said "I don't know where we are going but we have been issued with these" which were his shorts and things like that. He then went over to the desert.

In them days you didn't hear things and on one occasion I went to the cinema and there was this terrible news of this terrible train crash, it was sabotaged of course and a lot of the soldiers had been killed on that train and they didn't say who or what, and of course Tom's letters were far and in between and if he had written anything he should not have done of course it was blacked out.

The War then started to turn for us at the Battle of Alamein in the Middle East. Tom then went through to fight in Tobruk and by that time it was 1943 and suddenly they were brought home and I can remember him saying to me;

"I don't know why we have been brought home, it must be something big because we are a crack Regiment and the Seventh Brigade had gone over to Italy and the eighth Bomber Brigade had been brought home."

He had fourteen days' leave with a forty eight hour and a twenty four hour Embarkation Leave and they was not allowed to write home but I now know that they were training up in Scotland up in the Highlands, and it was not 'til he missed his train after his forty eight hour leave had been cancelled that I now realise it could have been a disaster really, but one thing that did come out of that night was my daughter.

When I walked into the station and was told we had landed in Normandy. I thought "I wonder if he was involved in it?" as he had been through so much fighting and I was absolutely terrified, but can you believe he was not, only in the first landings on D Day. But he was also at Armin "The Bridge too Far" and was cut off there and was the first troops into Berlin, and he finished his war liberating Norway.

Years later when discussing the terrible train crash he told me that when he was in Norway and leave was given out, but only so many soldiers could have leave, they would put all the names into something and pick out names that way and his name was drew out, I believe they drew his name out on purpose because I had a daughter and his daughter was two month old before he even knew that he had got a baby.

Tom didn't want me to join the Armed Forces, don't know what he thought I would get up to, so I joined the Fire Service and the Firemen were no better, but I choose the Fire Service and it was such an experience and the girls then wouldn't do as they do now and go to the fires they were in the Control Room.

We lived in Leister and what the habit the Germans got into was to hold on to the last bomb after they went to bomb Coventry or where ever and the spare one they would drop on Leister on the way back, and no one then heard of bomb dropping and if you were in the air raid shelter it was really scary. We had four continuous raids on Leister and if you were home on leave sitting in the shelter you could hear this hiss, then you would hear a whistle and you can imagine what it felt like because you didn't know if it was going to fall on you or not, it was horrible absolutely horrible.

The men were great. We sent the Firemen here to Portsmouth when you had the raids, but anywhere Coventry, you know anywhere you went and the worst thing you could send them to was a plane crash and it didn't matter whether it was a German plane or British plane, they would come back and each one of them reacted differently. Some would sit and not talk and we would get used to how to deal with them because they would just sit. But the two comedians of the Station, which every station seemed to have, acted dafter than ever, that was the way they coped with it but it really and truly used to upset them. They didn't mind if the Pilot had got out but of course nine times out of ten they had not, but I will always remember that.

And I remember once that once the American's got involved in the War an American plane came down and I think they were just fighting machines because they just brought one parachute home and they had this parachute under the table and nobody could touch it, and you can imagine hardly any clothing coupons and this was pure silk, and we were all glad when the Americans came and collected it. It really was a bad time for the Fire Station.

What springs to mind now is the two Firemen that died recently how they died, we had two Firemen in Leister who died like that. We had sent them to the Blitz and my uncle was with this Fire Engine and the firemen went up to the top of the ladder and the Officer said to my uncle "We are leaving" and with that my uncle was shouting to him to come down but he didn't, so my uncle went up and he was dead in the same way those two men died. He brought all that back to me.

War actually started on my sixteenth birthday the 3rd September 1939 and I longed to be sixteen so of course. I will never forget it and of course this year I am reminding everybody what the day was because when you stop to think we had all those terrible, terrible years and yes we learned to laugh and went dancing because you would have gone mad otherwise, but you lost your defence because when you picked the paper up you just thought "Yes I know."

A man I was at school with, can you believe, on the very last day of the Japanese War was a sailor on board his ship when this Japanese pilot crashed his plane onto his ship and it killed him along with many others.

They didn't tell you what ships got hit and when sailors walked around they just had HMS on their hats, no name ,they couldn't give them a name because that would give information to the enemy.

Rations, yes we were rationed and for many years after the war but we didn't starve. Being in the Fire Service we had to give up our Rations books but I managed to give or get my mother her sweets because we lived at the Station not at home, and the clothing coupon was taken for our uniform. But we had enough to buy stockings and notice how I say "stockings" because tights were never invented then and your shoes you would get from the Fire Service, but you had shirts to buy so they gave us a few coupons. And this might sound mad but if you saw a long queue you would join it because evidently it would mean that biscuits were in or something, but you never see a cream one or even a banana for years after the War. I had had two children before I saw a banana back in this country.

Woolworth in Leister was where you would see a queue and someone would go around and say "Its sweets!", but sweets didn't bother me so, can you believe it we had a sweet ration too? It didn't bother me because I was not a sweet person but my mother loved all the sweets, so I would get in the queue and can you believe some of the Firemen would give me the coupons for sweets for my mother and the wives would go mad. So no matter if you saw a queue you would get in it and people would say they got so and so, but it was always biscuits or sweets.

Make up, no we didn't have make up. I used to work in a shop, a very posh shop called Snelgroves, no it was called Adimist in those days. It was a very posh shop in Leister and nearly every one that used it had an account there, but you could not buy the make-up but small chemists started to make their own, and there used to be a road where I lived called Cherwell Street and a lot of little shops on either side. And you would hear in the city that Cherwell Street had make-up and the next thing you would see was these great big queues down the road.

Sounds ridiculous now but we did manage to get it but it was through that sort of thing and we made-do as long as we could get face cream and powder you treasured it, and of course you didn't misplace sweet coupons because it was all such a luxury, but we didn't starve .

The one thing that upset my mother and upset her for years was that we had never had margarine in our house oh no, but of course there was no butter only two ounces, so to help you out you had to have the margarine. And my mother never forgave the War for that because she had to have margarine in the house.

Sugar was another thing you had to be very careful with because it was very low, and we were rationed for a very long time after the War because a lot of the food, as you know, had to be brought in on the Merchant ships and of course they concentrated on the merchant ships.

Before we were married my husband-to-be came home from the middle east and we stayed at my mum's and I had to go back on duty because I didn't know he was coming, and of course when they knew they immediately gave me leave, and I said "I don't know how long he is here for" and they said "Don't worry about that, you come back when he goes back." And when I got home I said to my mum, "How is Tom?" and she said "Well, you will never guess. I went to take him a cup of tea up this morning and I found him a sleep under the bed." So she said "Tom what are you doing sleeping under the bed?" and he replied "Mum, I have either slept under the lorry or dug a hole in the sand while in the desert and found the bed uncomfortable, so slept under the bed."

But I can tell you by the time we got married he was sleeping in a bed.

It's just silly things but you forget, as I said we did have cinemas and you could buy refreshments in the bigger shops and we all managed and nobody walked around looking miserable and nearly everyone was in uniform. Living in Lester we were not that far from Coventry were they bombed all the time, you could look up and see the red in the sky.

I was telling you before about this train with all the soldiers on. Tom came home on that leave, but was on that train and they must of known that them soldiers were on the train going over to the Middle East, and listen because this is what happened to my husband Tom all through the War. The soldier he was with said "Come on we will go in this carriage" and a voice said to my Tom, "No" so he said, "We will go further on down the train". And they did. All the others in the carriages he said no to was killed.

Another time he was in a convoy in the desert and he said to the soldier that was driving, "Pull out!" and he replied "Don't be daft Tom, I can't pull out" and the convoy said, "I don't care, pull out!" So he did and every one of those lorries were blown up and only Tom's survived because it had been pulled out on to the side.

I was a Catholic and this followed him through and I always thought it was Our Lady who was talking to him. I used to pray to St Teresa for there not to be a War, and of course there was a War and being sixteen I said to her, "You have had it, I am not going to pray for you anymore" as you would think at that time, and this year 2010 we had St Teresa Relics brought to the Cathedral and in a flash I said to Father David who agreed with me that it was not Our Lady talking to Tom, it was St Teresa. And Cannon David laughed at me and I said, "I did apologise to her Father" but it suddenly dawned on me that she could not stop the War for me but she could look after my soldier, but always a voice told him quite clearly, "Move" and he did and I said to Father, "Do you think I am daft?" and he said "No Maureen I think you are right."

These things happened through the War and years later in Burstall the veterans would meet once a month, and the Eighth Army Vets would meet, and a man that went to our church but was in the Navy came over to tell me that he had met a girl in the war, fell in love with her then went home on leave, a forty eight hour leave, and when he got back to Portsmouth it had had very bad raids and she had got killed in an air raid shelter, and he was told that some had been built in the middle of the roads and her shelter had taken a direct hit.

Going back again, when my husband left here it was for D Day and everyone knew in the forces that you could not write, and when I walked in and heard the words "Monty's Fiftieth" I thought "Oh my God" but I think I would of known if he had got killed, and when he did come home it was a very long time before he could even talk about it, and I would tell the sailors this and they would love me for it.

"I was six days on the ship because of the weather" and he said "we landed on the beach and if you had ever seen the film the longest day," he said "that blessed plane was killing us left right and centre, and I thought I had been all over the desert and lived and now I am going to die on this little beach and so near home."

In Tom's words a Royal British ship shot it down and I said "God bless the British Navy".

My husband being a soldier all those years thought swearing was a waste of breath, but would say how we taught our children "dash blow bother". I never forget when at five I heard my grandson swearing and said to him "Don't use those words" and he said "Well what do I say then?" and I said "Dash blow bother", and a few weeks later he was putting on an act as we had friends in our house and shouted out "Grandma, what is them words I have to use instead of bugger and bloody?"

Going back again when Tom came home, our daughter was two years old and when I used to say to her "Kiss Daddy goodnight" she would always go and pick his army photograph up and kiss that. It must of upset him terrible but he never said, but for all the fighting he done, and he fought with the Ghurkhas, but he never ever lost his temper and everyone loved him, and we were married for fifty five years and very happy with it. And one day we were in our garden and Tom said to me "I won't be a minute darling, I am just going to fetch another tray of pansies" and on the gate stood a little crowd of boys watching, and when Tom came back said "Why is he calling you a different name, does Tom know your name is Maureen?" in which I replied "Yes why do you ask?"

By then Tom had returned and we had a way of communicating with one another just by looking. Then the boy said "Tom you do know her name is Maureen?" and he replied "Of course I do, why?" and the boy said "But you always call her Darling why?" and Tom said "Because I love her and she is my darling." Then they said "But we love her" and he said "Well you know what to do." And believe it or not these young men who have children of their own now, when I went back to Burstall one walked past me and said "Hello Maureen Darling".

In the beginning I told you how Tom had come to work in my factory and the reason was because his factory had gone bankrupt and mine was a corset factory, and they were the only ones who would take them on because they knew he was going to be called up because it was 1939. And after the War, would you believe, we couldn't afford to buy a house and the first people, would you believe, that did get council houses was those that had stayed at home. We didn't get one 'til we had our second daughter, no one cared.

I am eighty seven years old now, the same age as Bebe Daniels, she was an American comedian for those of you too young to know who she was, who stayed in this country to keep us laughing in the war, and she was always thirty two.

With my uniform my hat was called a Glengarry which was posher than all the others with a little peak.

The War had been over for some time and Tom had come home on leave from Norway in which they had liberated because the Germans had occupied Norway, and when Tom went in the Germans offered no resistance and not a shot fired, and he walked into the King's Palace and open a door and sat there was three high rank German Officers, "who could have killed me, but come to that I could have killed them" he said, but they gave up and offered no resistance as I already stated. Tom was offered leave but all the men's names went in to hat but I think they picked Tom's name on purpose really because he had not had leave for a long time.

So he came home but only had seven weeks to do then be demobbed, but they decided not to send him back to Norway so instead sent him to Aldershot, and because they had been fighting a long time they didn't go around with their uniform buttoned right up. So Tom had his jacket open up the top and was sauntering across the Parade Ground, which of course was forbidden, and a Sergeant Major saw him and shouted out "Soldier!" in which Tom turned around and stood to attention, and the Major then saw his Eighth Army ribbon and said "What the hell soldier are you doing here? I can't teach you anything about soldiering, you could teach me more!" Then asked Tom what he was doing and Tom told him he only had seven weeks to serve and the Major said "Follow me son, let's get you home, let's get that seven week's leave" which of course the Major did.

Tom didn't write because it happened so quick and of course I was in bed, heard this whistle, run down the stairs, out and across the road, nothing on the feet and of course he picked me up, swung me round and as we always said "How long?" and he replied "All the time in the world."

We had three years of night mares and sometimes I would wake up with his hands around my throat, then he would wake up and cry, really cry, and this is how I learned a lot of what happened.

Another time we went to cinema and a film about the battle of Alamein came on and I went to put my arm around him and he wasn't there, he was on the floor under the seat and the youngsters at the back looked and I turned around and sharply said to them "He was at this battle" and I then had to take him out of the cinema.

Another time we were getting ready for D Day and a horse and cart went over the cobbles and dray and it made a noise and he was flat on the floor and dragged me down with him, and I said "Tom it's a horse" and he said "No Maureen, it's a German tank" and said it by name too, and that happened along time after the War. And if he heard other noises by a wall he would be over the wall in a flash thinking he was back in the War, and this went on for a long time. And when I watch TV now I think do people today realise what you will be going through when you come home.

Tom became a Catholic and one day said to the Priest "Father, how can I forgive myself for the things I had to do?" and he replied "Tom you had do those things, it was your duty."

On that note I say farewell.

Part Two

This now near the close of the War when the Russians took part of Berlin and my friend Heidi was still there hiding in an empty burned out house and she saw this bicycle, and had kept her eye on this bicycle for a long time ready for her escape and took her opportunity one night to get on the bike and cycle to the river, but she knew the British soldiers were the other side and that's where she wanted to get because the Russians were raping young and old and killing, it just did not matter what they were doing. So she escaped and got to the river, and as she swam across dead bodies were bumping into her. She was twenty years old at the time and she got to the other side, and the British soldiers took care of her and she was sent back to England, then on to Ireland because her father was a German Officer and he had said to her "If ever you live through this Heidi don't stay here, go to England or America."

My husband told me this which I would like to share with you, if you took an Italian Prisoner of War you didn't turn your back on him, but if you took a German Prisoner of War you could.

I told you I came from Leister and we had a Polish Squadron and us girls would say if a Polish Pilot asked you out you had to take your best friend with you because you would have never had handled him on your own.

I had a Polish lady friend who had been in Auschwitz Concentration Camp who had watched her parents being taken to the Gas Chamber, and the reason she didn't finish up in the Gas Chamber was because one of the German Guards hid her and helped her to escape. And years later she ended up marrying a British soldier and had three sons, and every one of her sons when old enough joined the British Army.

So a happy ending was made.

"We never had a banana"

Mary Chalk

My name is Mary Wheeler which is my maiden name, but my family all called me Marie because my mother's name was Mary as well. I always answered to Marie. I was four years old when war broke out, I was born September 6th in 1935.

Before the War my life was a very happy life because we lived with my grandparents because my father being in the Royal Navy was always away on long three year and more commitions, some up to five years. When my father came home on leave my mother took me to the train station at the Hard in Portsea and she said "Stand at this entrance and when you see your dad hold on to his hand and wait for me because I will stand at another entrance in case we miss him."

There was hundreds of sailors in uniform them days all disembarking from the trains, and then my mother approached me holding hands with a sailor and said "What are you crying for?" and I said "What do he look like?" and she said "This is your father" and off we went.

This man then came in to my life with me not remembering him because he had been away for years and it put me out a lot. I had been the only person in my mother's life for such a long time, sleeping with her and being with her constantly and the only other people in my life was my grandparents.

I was very happy at school and I used to go to Church Street School which was off of Lake Road and that was a very happy period in my life being at that school.

When War was declared we used to sleep in the Anderson Shelter every night because at that time the bombs would come over all night and sometimes was worse than others because they were aiming for the Dockyard, many German planes dropping bombs and incendiaries. So it was agreed that I would sleep in the shelter and in it was a flower pot with a candle over it for a bit of warmth and a bit of heat but of course it was very damp but I just got on with it, and when the raids come on very fast and furious then my parents, my mother and grandparents they would also come down to the Anderson shelter as well.

I can remember having chilblains very badly, they used to bite and I would have to go to school with slippers on and this was probably due to me sleeping down the air raid shelter.

On one particular night the raid was so bad, and of course we lived right next door to The Royal Portsmouth Hospital in my gran's house, and the plane s were aiming for the Dockyard but discharged these land mines which then demolished the Royal Hospital. They were getting all the patients out of the wards and taking them down to vehicles away to safety and my mother's cousin who was a Petty Officer in the Royal Navy who was home on leave who went round to help, who was found with a couple of patients with his arms around both of them dead, they had been caught in the blast and all died. So he came home on leave just to die. I don't know if he was the only son of my grandmother's sister but it was a tragedy.

That night was a very bad night and it blew a lot of the roof off of the house, and it was decided we would not be able to stay there because it was too dangerous for anyone to live in them circumstances when you didn't have to. So I can remember being taken, and it must have been by train but I cannot remember the journey, and a long journey it must have been, to North Wales and we went to Llanfair PG [Llanfairpwllgwyngyllgogerychwyrndrobwllllantysiliogogogoch], the smallest village with the longest name.

I do remember being happy there in that little village and I can remember granny going to the well to get the water so I can only imagine it must have been a tiny little house. My grandfather was also with us and I think it must have been one of his family who owned the cottage, his name was William Wynne and my granny was called Catharine Wynne and I have enclosed a photograph of him taking me along the beach, it was the promenade at Rhyll. He must have been to visit the family he had.

He was a very tall gentleman and a lovely man. I had really lovely grandparents, they were really lovely, but my grandmother brought me back from this idyllic world back to these bombs and everything else because I had been taken ill with measles or mumps or one of the children's illnesses and was brought back to Portsmouth unfortunately, and I can remember my mother visiting with my father once to North Wales to visit us, and the woman in the village came out and as my parents walked down the road the woman wanted to touch his collar, they called it a 'dickey collar' for luck, and I remember them walking arm in arm. Then they must of caught the train back again and he went off again.

So the next thing I can remember is being in Portsmouth and going to school at Church Street, and through a family argument my mum left the family home and I was taken away from my grandparents and she moved to Gosport to stay with her eldest sister and I was still only a young little girl. And every morning I would have to get up catch the bus from Albemarle Ave which was in Elson to the ferry, then over to the Hard. And on the boat they would put me down the hatch and close it down because it must have been winter or something and it was very rough. Then when I got off at the Hard I would walk from there to Church Street School and continue my day, and because of the family argument I was not allowed to go to visit my grandparents so had to have dinner in the British Restaurant, again all on my own because my mother was doing War work in the Dockyard.

That was a big upheaval, a big thing in my life, and another thing I can remember another time was when we lived with my grandparents in the War and there was deprivation of food that my gran used to give me sugar, a bag of sugar, and I would take it to Charlotte Street to a shop which was called 'Old Jacks' which was a sweet shop and they would give me the equivalent of sweets for the bag of sugar. I didn't have to pay, just the bag of sugar and I would choose the fishes and any boiled sweets they sold, from humbugs to any boiled sweets, and it was a very well-known shop. And on the corner of my grandmother's street there was an Italian family had an ice cream shop which was called 'Tony Colletta's' and he still made the ice cream but couldn't get the wafers or biscuits because of the War, but we would take a cup and he would then fill it up for sixpence, and this ice cream was more water I expect but it was a real treat. And across the road in Thomas Street was another corner shop, and when you think of it all these tiny little shops and every one making a living from it and because they had no sweets because sweets was on ration I would spend my penny pocket money on a couple of Oxo cubes and suck those because there was nothing else to buy.

In my grandmother's road Fredrick Street in Landport right opposite our house was a fruit and veg shop, well it was a shop to me but really all it was was someone's house by the name of Farr, and they had turned their front room in to a shop as people did in them days, and I used to play with the boy of the family. And one summer day still in the War we went into the Hospital grounds to play and must have fallen asleep there in the heat in the long grass, and when we went home my mother gave me a good hiding and in her relief because she didn't know what had happened to me and his mother did not know what happened to him, and my mother had been round to the Cinema, the Savoy in Commercial Road, and asked them to put a notice up on the screen in case I had got in there somehow and if I was in there to go home immediately. She must have been out of her mind with worry because for hours we had just fallen asleep in the Hospital grounds because we had properly been up half the night due to the bombings.

I can remember this vividly that when we came back from school one day there was a Post Office on the corner of Thomas Street in Commercial Road next to a big water reservoir which they stored gallons and gallons of water to put out all the fires or help put out the fires in this big shopping centre, and next door to the Post Office was Reynolds who sold wallpaper paint etc. and it had sample books and it had been bombed and my friend Farr, who I cannot remember his first name, took a book each which we took home to my mother and said, "Look I brought this book for you, you can now paper the room" me thinking all these bits of paper child-like could be alright. But there was a knock at the door and of course I had been followed home by a Policeman and of course got in an awful lot of trouble with my mother for that and told off by the Policeman because it was stealing, stealing from a bombed-out premises and it was the sample book of the wallpapers.

Another memory walking to school after a big night of bombing down Lake Road and passing the shops that had been bombed, the smell which I can still smell today of plaster dust all mixed together, this smell where they had all come tumbling down.

In the bay window of one little shop which was a pretty little shop, there was all these blue bags which they used to pour sugar in to and wrap them up the sugar bags. I can remember them bringing out, they had a cordon around the shop and they brought these people out very blue - they had all been gassed and there was me still on my way to school just a little girl on my own and seeing the people that had been gassed.

Later on when we moved to Copnor, Vernon Road near the old Monckton Pub, it was just me and my mum then and she would send me across the road to Copnor Bakery but I cannot think of the name of it, I would have to buy half of a loaf because that was all the coupon would allow us because it was just my mother and me a little girl so I was a half, I remember coming home from school getting in the window and scraping this round oblong, I think it was margarine I think it was called Stork, because I was always hungry because we got less coupons and I was a growing child and a small little family like ours didn't have that much extra food.

Mum wouldn't buy any food or coupons on the Black Market it was against her beliefs. I remember eating just sugar because I was hungry however this because she was at work.

When we lived in Copnor Road the War ended and in the middle of Monkton Road and where it joined with Vernon Road they had a huge bonfire - that was for the celebration of the ending of the war. And it was through Vernon Road, if I remember rightly, the trestle tables came out and everybody brought out their odd chairs etc. and jelly and the usual to celebrate.

I am going to go back a bit because my father must have come home and found where we were living because he had been away for many years then in the war, and I expect we were cold because I clearly remember mum taking me to the cinema and you had to queue up in the cold and rain. Everyone used to attend the cinema in those days because they changed the films in the middle of the week to two films so you had two choices and it was somewhere to go of an evening to keep warm and company. And when we came home she would light the gas oven and I would sit with my feet in there to get warm and would sit with them underneath me in the cinema to try and get them warm, as I said before I did have chilblains and my circulation of my feet must have been terrible. Any way my father came home and I remember this - he went to the Gas Works which was at the back of well over the lines at Copnor Road, because the Gas Works was there with a Gasometer and he bought coke, his kit bag was full and he brought it home on a bicycle on the peddle to balance it and we had fires again, because before that as I said we had to make the fuel last so we didn't have much heat.

We lived better when dad came home we had more provisions and I can really remember this one, he brought some bananas - a hand of bananas home and no one knew what a banana was at my age and he put them in the window to ripen off and every child that could down the road had a banana but none of us knew how to eat it. We didn't know you had to peel them or anything so that was a bit of exotic fruit brought home from on his travels so things definitely picked up for us once my dad came home. There was more to eat, more to fun, he used to buy all sorts of games - a small billiard table and I think he used to treat me like the son he never had and I always played the games with him, and life picked up for me again then and so did the food effort.

On that note I say bye bye.

Les Cromeeke

My call up papers, well I wasn't very keen on where they were going to send me or what they were going to send me in so I walked down the road and saw this chap standing outside the Royal Marine Auditions [Recruitments] in his lovely new suit so I said to him "Can I have your suit?" and he said,

"Yea if you want to come in you can have it." So in I went thinking he was having me on and inside he said, "Sign here, sign here, you have now joined the Royal Marines" and I said "That's good" and he then said "Can you swim?" I said "Only if I can get both me feet off the bottom of the pool but normally they stay on the bottom firmly in the water." "Oh right" he said "You will be ok, they will teach you how to swim."

Then I was going down to Lympstone and this was in October 1943 and my father decided he was going to have a few words with me and asked me what I thought I would be like on my own because I had never been away before from mother or father and he decided he was going to tell me the facts of life, and I listened and listened and thought, "You silly old fool" and "Not done like that these days" but said "Yes Dad I know what you are talking about" and he said "You do then I won't tell you any more then so you be a good lad and off you go, where are you going?" and I said "Well I have been called up to Exeter and that was a fortnight after I signed the paper going down to a place called Lympstone." "Oh" he said, then I said "How far is that away?" "Oh" he said "about two, three hundred miles I think." Then I said "Oh no I've never been away on my own that far before have I?"

Anyhow, we got away and caught the train down to London then the Express Lympstone in Devon and was met there. We then got chased around for three months running and marching around Lympstone until we were all fit then we were moved on to what we were going to be doing, and I learned we were going on the landing craft and was going to Hayling Isle.

When we got to Hayling Island we decided "Oh this is a nice place" and we all had boats to tear around on the river and we thoroughly enjoyed ourselves, and they decided we could go ashore and we were allowed to go off the Island to Havant, but I got fed up trying to rush the ticket inspector as I was trying to get through on a platform ticket so we ended up coming across by one of our boats just from the strip of water there where the Hayling Ferry is today, and decided instead that we would go and have a look around Portsmouth because it sounded like a great place to be .

We were walking along but not too much could be seen of Portsmouth in those days until we got up on to the Seafront, then we saw a bit more scenery of the beach and all the houses that were along there, so we had a nice walk along the seafront and got as far as the Royal Marine Barracks and all of a sudden someone shouts out "Do that ruddy collar up!" and we looked over and there was a Sergeant Major or a Colour Sergeant or whatever he was standing on a mound of earth telling us to do our collar up, so we gave him the Marine salute and walked the other way back to the boat and back to Hayling Island. And that was the only time then that I saw Portsmouth until I arrived here again in 1990 I think it was.

When we came to Portsmouth in the War we were moved about then ended up in Scotland, but first of all went down to Westcliffe and was stationed along the Seafront there in the houses and I was sneaking home one Sunday afternoon to see mother and father for the first time and a Sergeant Major came running along the platform shouting "Where you going to?" and I replied "We are going to Pitsea to get some cockles." "Oh" he replied "that's alright, 'cause I thought you were going to London" and I said "No of course not I'm not going to London." But he then said "You just come with me because yes, you are going to London because you are on foreign draft in twenty minutes' time."

So we were rushed back into camp to pack our bags and given our marching orders and told to catch such and such a train and to go to London then go to Glasgow and join up with the rest of our crowd who had already gone, and once in Scotland in Glasgow we were met by Officer Meadows who took us down to the fortiller hut by jeep and said "Oh course lads you are going to be alright and be away again in the morning on foreign draft." We thought well, how do he know? They not meant to talk about things like that during the war.

Anyhow, we get to the camp and was told tea would be ready in about ten minutes' time and have your tea then get changed into number one uniform, your blue uniforms, and you're all going to a party tonight down at the Co-op Hall because the girls has invited you all to a party . Off we all go to the party and learn how to do all the jigging about and dancing and folk and Scottish dancing and thoroughly enjoying ourselves.

After that, back at the camp, we were all issued with duffle coats which made us think we were going north or somewhere like that and we all had guesses on to where we might be going and the girls was saying, "You are going to Bombay" and I replied, "Do what? Going to Bombay? Where is that?" and was told that's out in India and I went, "Oh don't know about that, that's a hot country we can't be going there because we all got duffle coats and all that."

And of course they were not meant to know anything but here they were telling us we were going and of course by this time we were ready to get down to the docks in the morning to board ship and the boxes coming aboard was all marked Bombay.

We all had to get up at five in the morning and run down to the boat. By then we knew we were going but didn't know why we all had duffle coats none of us had a clue. We ended up sailing about ten o'clock in the morning and seemed to go north but could not make out why, and of course it took us a month to get to Bombay and we found out why we needed the ruddy duffle coats because we ended up sailing through the Atlantic and sailing through Canada and turning off again and coming back through the Mediterranean. And we didn't do too bad because we had a bit of shore leave in Gibraltar and after that we carried on to India and after that I spent the rest of my time in India and Singapore looking around for Japanese and had quite a fair time in the Services.

When we came home it was on the old Indomitable and we done a lot of troop carrying on that, they gave me a nice job serving the Sergeant Major and them with wine the whole trip home which I thoroughly enjoyed.

Midnight the lads would be sitting up in their hammocks and say "What you got to drink tonight?" Of course I used to collect all the glasses and put all the left-over drinks in bottles and take it to the lads and they would be all sitting up drinking up merrily, good job the officers didn't know what happened to their drinks if they left any.

Of course I wasn't allowed to have any rum or anything on board because I was under eighteen that made it worse than ever, but of course we still got our rum and of course I made up for it when I was serving Officers again out in Singapore so we didn't do too bad.

I was demobbed three years and one week later in 1946 and I had quite a nice short service had a good service life so can't complain and glad I didn't go to

Europe like a lot of people did.   Considering I had never been to these places before in my life, not even Portsmouth or Devon I really enjoyed it.

Going back to my earlier lives, I lived in South Harrow in Middlesex which of course is now part of the London Borough and going back to before 1939 and everyone will remember when the War broke out. It was a Sunday morning and within an hour of War being declared the air raid sirens went off and everybody ran for shelter and me, well I was going out on a bicycle ride and that was not going to stop me because I was going out to Eton on my bike to have a punch up with the Eton boys, and there was a gang of us meeting up and we were all going on this Sunday to knock their straw hats off. But of course it did stop us and later on that day we got another air raid warning go off and by that time I was safely indoors and not allowed outside the door, and there's me wanting to go out into the garden to look up at the sky but was told, "No you must not do that in case you get a bomb on your head" and I reply, "Well I don't want a big lump on my head so I will stay in."

Going on from then I used to do a job in the local Cinema I was a doorman a foreman and boiler man all in one and night watchman, you name it I done it, and would sleep night and day in the theatre and was lucky to have a few hours in the day time.

When I went out one morning on my way home there was four policemen standing over a hole in the pavement and I walked up and said, "What you looking for then?" and they turned to me and said, "What you doing here?" and I said, "I've come to see what you are looking at" and one of 'em said, "You can't stay here, there is an unexploded bomb there" and I said, "Oh will that affect us if it's gone down there" and he said, "Come on laddy, where do you live? You should not be in the area everyone has been evacuated and where have you been all night?" And I said I been asleep in the cinema and told them I was the night watchman.

That was that.

Johnny Jarrett

I was born the first day of August in 1937 and that was at home in Station Road in Copnor Portsmouth, lots of my family lived in the same road so it was really good my Grandparents, uncles, aunties and cousins . Number three Station Road was a very small house which had a Larbert Range for cooking and this was made by Treadgolds in Portsea.

We shared a tin bath which hung up outside the toilet in the garden on the wall, we had the railway line running at the bottom of our garden and was sometimes lucky to find knobs of coal in the garden. Mum always had a moan because she could never hang the washing out on the line because the signal box was at the bottom of the garden and trains would sometimes have to stop. Lovely steam engines they were but of course if washing was out it would suffer and get all black marks on it from the engine.

I have so many memories of my childhood, my Granddad using the pub on the corner and often seen sitting in the old bus shelter having a natter, having a good smoke on his pipe, the shelter was opposite the cemetery and also you could see the ladies bringing back glasses of ale with a cloth over the top of the glass or faggots and peas from the bottom of New Road.

Being so young it seemed like we had a lot of visitors, the fish man then the vegetable man on his horse and cart, even a brush salesman that had a case full of everything apart from the kitchen sink.

Just before the ending of the War I was evacuated because so many bombs were dropping all over Portsmouth so I was packed off to a place with relatives in Alderbury near Salisbury, but only for a short time that was.

When I was eight mum and dad decided to buy another house the other side of Copnor Bridge and mum's parents moved in with us and it was a little bit crowed then. We were very lucky because we had an Anderson shelter already in the garden so it meant we didn't have to use the public ones.

I remember one day we were all in the shelter after a raid and when the all clear came. My grandparents were the first out, he would then say "It's OK, only a few window panes" and bits would be seen falling still from the aftershock of the bombings all around.

I can still to this day remember St Cuthbert's Church in Hayling Avenue being hit with an incendiary bomb and the flames from it lighting up the sky and seeing the big crater holes that were left.

We heard that the Gas Works up by Hilsea took a hit and two bombs were dropped by Baffins Pond, and then the next we heard was the Town Hall Guildhall had been bombed and burned to the ground.

Children were told to keep away from the craters, firstly because of how deep they were and secondly because how dangerous they could be.

After the War school was back to normal but my schooling was awful. I went Alderbury Kinder Garden followed by Copnor Junior then Modern. I did take my eleven plus and was promised a bike from dad if I passed. I was so hopeless I failed so it meant no Grammar School and no cycle for me and on to St Luke's for me which was all huts apart from the Assembly Hall and Church.

So dad not buying my bike meant I had to save up myself and buy one which I did and it was an old sit up and beg type and dad had to put blocks on the peddles because my feet would not reach.

At St Luke's I was in the gardening club and wasn't much use apart from laying grass but it was handy because I got out of a lot of other classes.

I would ride my bike to school from Copnor and would go Via New Road so I could pass the girls' school because by this time I was girl mad.

I loved fishing as well and spent many a day fishing at Baffins Pond, some days till very late into the evening. It was great fun and our rods were made from old Tank aerials, two sections screwed together and sewn on eyes etc., but hook, line and reels came from a small shop in Arundel Street which was run by the Cox Sisters.

The end of my school days came with no joy because I was stuck in hospital with a bad leg injury. My parents then had the worry of trying to find a job for me and would look in the papers in hope as I had little education and no qualifications so this was difficult.

Then one day they saw an advert in the paper for a young lad for Signal Man at Portsmouth and Southsea Station so I went with my dad to make some enquires and found out it was logging dates and times in the signal box of trains. Before starting I had to take a small exam and it was four sums which I got all wrong but was still sent for the medical, the M.O. was situated in Brighton Works.

Then I had to report back to Fred England who is sadly no longer with us, and he said "Right lad you start tomorrow morning" which was Wednesday 20th August 1952.

At the age of 18 I was called up to do my National Service which took me away from my job two years, I served in the Army and my father said it would make a man of me and it certainly did. My two years in the Army was not what I had expected, I had to do my training in Malvern in Worcestershire in the Royal Engineers I was a real squaddie sapper, I was one of the chaps from all different parts of the country with different accents.

The training at first was awful, we were up at dawn and marched everywhere, then we had lots of drills and rifle shooting - all the things to make a good soldier and it lasted six weeks.

When we got our postings I was a grade A2 so could only go to a home posting and for me that was Hamelin West Germany [Pied Piper Town] to nearest big city to Hanover and this is where I remained for all my service.

I was put in to a Bridge Building Squadron, erecting bridges over the River Weser and it was very hard work. Then for a short time I went in to the Regimental Police, which was situated at the top of the Town, set under the edge of a forest looking back towards the town and I had to cross a railway line to get to it. I was there to look after Sappers who were in cells for different misdemeanours.

They had to do odd jobs including cleaning the kit of the Sergeant Major ready for the next day's Parade. When I finished there I was told to report to the Transport M.O. Section was the change to the rest of my service.

The officer there asked me if I would like to join his section on Transport and asked if I could ride a motorbike and although I could not I was very willing to learn. Off I went to the quarters and met up with Roy Jones the Barracks dispatch rider boy and what he didn't know about bikes? All we had was 1937 BSA but he could certainly soup them up as he had his own bikes at home.

I pleased to say that after riding around and around the perimeter fence then took my test outside on the roads, passed with flying colours but told off for riding on the wrong side of the road but the instructor just said "Go easy."

That was it, two despatch riders now and that was me and Roy and the next morning got my first despatch to take to Hanover, then I was delivering all over West Germany. What an experience for someone like me that had never been away from home before.

I was not very big built and one would say skinny, even so it was an art to first get the hang of holding up my bike to stop it falling. Fifty miles an hour was good for these bikes and great on hills and grass talk about Steve McQueen in the Great Escape, it was like riding a horse, suspension forks, big saddle and no comfort. Much later we were given a 1956 Matchless with hydraulic suspension, it was sheer heaven.

During my dispatch rider days I did a spell with the German Service Organisation escorting convoys along the Autobahn. One day I got lost so rode into an American Unit called Cashe. I was so tired and hungry and the Americans was so shocked, but after a good night sleep and feed they put me and my bike on the back of a lorry and took me back to Barracks. I enjoyed my time in Germany and in time learned the lingo and was soon shopping and travelling on local trains and I also spent two Christmases there and it snowed both times.

As I could speak German it was my job to invite the girls from town to our dance nights which we held on several nights, and at one of these dances I fell in love with one particular girl that came regular to the dances. Her name was Lora and for eight months it was round to her parents' house whenever I was out on the bike, they lived near the river Weser.

Neither Lora or her parents spoke any English but we somehow managed to get by. Her brother was a big lad in the German Army and I was very jealous of his very smart uniform, mine was a mess compared to his but we all got on very well and would all pop to the local ale houses.

I was now coming to the end of my service and in a way was very sad, it was ending simply because it was great fun and I enjoyed it and properly because I had learned German and was used to being there and using the town like home.

I had to return to Andover for my demob then back to my parents in Copnor. I then made arrangements for my German girl friend to come over and stay until we got married and moved to our own house. Unfortunately because of me working long hours and her not knowing any one the marriage failed and she went to Wales to be with her sister.

I then returned to the railway to my old job as they kept it open while I did my National Service but my ambition then was to get back to signalling as soon as possible, but not many vacancies occurred locally so I had to apply for positions in outer suburbs of London.

While waiting for that I was offered the post of Porter Guard, I really enjoyed that job and met many train crew. I spent many years with the railways and worked my way up and have so many fond and sad memories, I remember the sugar beet trains that left from the village of Lavant it was a very busy line but something else that no longer exist.

My childhood memories I still go over in my mind like when I had to run for faggots and peas and also pick up the horse muck for granddad's allotment and the old Knife Grinder that came round with his barrow.

My uncle drove the coaches for the White Heather for years and most weekends we went on short trips, my aunties and uncles were all chefs and after the War that's what dad became he was a working manager he worked many pubs and bars in the city.

I told you about my fishing in Baffins Pond but didn't tell you I got ten bob a year. I said about the Cox Sisters who ran the little shop didn't I? Well I should have said we also got our worms there.

Did I mention the gangs I was in as a kid? The Portsea Boys and the Buckland Boys lots of gangs about then, we had the Lido, the Kiddies Corner with the train going all around it then the little boating lake near on all gone now but memories will live on, we will never forget the bomb damage and the friends we lost and the city near on destroyed, but nice memories we will keep was of our times Mudlarking, Cinema, the Dockies coming out of the Yard on the bikes, the Pubs and churches long since gone, but one thing that never leaves us is our roots where we lived, grew up where we are now, our past because it's our Life.

Roy Herbert

My earliest memories was of Rochester in Kent in 1934 but I now live in Portsmouth and am now seventy seven years old, but can remember back to before World War Two broke out when I went to school in Rochester and my mother being taken into hospital.

It was the summer before the War started and because I was left handed and Miss Honey said I had to write right handed and this led to my piece of paper I had covered in tears so she gave up in the end and let me carry on and it was never ever mentioned again, the School was situated in Strood High Street.

My father had joined the Navy in 1939 and at that time was away and he was a seaman by trade anyway so knew what he was going in to. My mother as I said previous was taken to hospital but me and two younger brothers didn't know much about that but we learned later that it was a miscarriage and unfortunately she died from it.

We were then taken in by my Aunt and Uncle who lived on the outskirts of Strood and then in 1942 my father was invalided out of the Navy and we then went to live with my Grandmother in the Fish and Chip shop in Chatham High Street, and I can remember the shop being packed at the weekend by sailors in uniform, it was a very good business because they sold cold wet fish during the day and fish and chips cooked fresh at night.

My father then remarried to a very young lady who was only 16 or 17 who didn't know what she was doing and by then my old man was very fond of the booze and we had moved on again back to Strood.

I remember going with my Grandmother to visit some cousins who had been evacuated to Surrey or Sussex I am not too sure what the county was but it was close to Hartsfield and Colborough Tunbridge Wells, so it was on the edge of Kent it was by coach and it would leave on the Sunday from Chatham and we would have to get out and walk up Bluebell Hill because the Coach wasn't up to much and would not have been able to make it.

My cousins was in a boarding school there which I thought was nice. I really was impressed with it and badgered my step mother until she agreed to me going there but you were not allowed to go there until you were nine and that was in the March we went, and then I was nine in the January and I can remember her walking me to Star Hill in Rochester where you picked up the coach and her telling me it was too late for me to change my mind but the thought had never occurred, I suppose it was just a bit unimaginable to me. And when we got to the Farm we were taken to what was the assembly room and the Matron showed us how to make our bed and then we were taken down to the Dormitory and shown to our beds which were double bunks which were iron and open fronted lockers to keep our belongings in, and after that we were unhappy for a few days but soon made friends but then got over it, and we spent nearly two and a half years happy years there and was very sad when the War was nearly over, went home and it was very sad waving to the boys and girls that stayed behind. It was three blocks each for boys and girls and an ablution block made of cedar wood which was situated in the middle of the woods about two and a half miles from Hartfield with a stream running up ways, so it was ideal playing arrangements, and schools on-site ran them like a boarding school and we were very very lucky and we all moaned about food and said it was a dump but most of us enjoyed it very much, and as I said had to come home in 1945 and go back to an ordinary school .

We wasn't greatly effected up there when the War was on in that part of the country but we did have a few bombs drop nearby so we would be hustled down to the shelters, but we thought the bombers was just getting rid of his bombs because I couldn't imagine anything there for them to bomb they just dropped them up on the heath. But there was a lot of soldiers around there because it was heath country, the Army would do manoeuvres and would also do mock battles and all the boys would go out after and hunt for ammunition and one boy got burned very badly by using a thing called a Bolder basher because it had not gone off and he put it into the fire and lit the end of it with cardboard because the fuse had gone, he thought he could throw it around and it would explode to simulate being in a battle and of course he held it too long and it went off in his hand.

I did believe that before I got there that some boys had been killed but that was just a rumour so I didn't know if it was a true story or not.

Even though the boy got burned the rest along with my cousins went scrumping for apples and would roast them over the fire and of course it led to a fire and we all had to turn out to put out the Heath Fire. When the Fire Brigade turned up it was too late and we were very proud of ourselves for doing that, but my cousins and his mates got taken off to juvenile court for it.

We had Canadians, British and Americans that had all stayed around there and just before D Day what we called Five Hundred Acre Wood which was between us and Colborough were huge dumps of ammunitions. It was piles and piles, stacks of boxes amongst the trees and one morning when we woke up, the Americans that had been in Five Hundred Acre Wood had gone, just up and went and we had never heard a thing.

Then of course we had an armada of Aeroplanes going over above us, and gliders which was a marvellous display which was unbelievable, and of course aeroplanes in them days did not fly so high.

During the Doodlebug period we actually had them flying overhead and one landed on the Army Camp only a few miles away from us which was more pure fluke, which killed quite a few soldiers I am afraid. I cannot remember how many now but it was a major which went in to double figures, and I recall Typhoons shooting down the Doodlebugs and if my memory serves me right I remember seeing a Typhoon actually flipping a Doodlebug over and on another occasion the pilot got too close to one and caught his wing and had to bail out and some of the older boys would be seen carrying his parachute off and of course would also pick up the empty cartridges and blanks because sometimes the soldiers would dig these little slip trenches and put these clips of cartridges in ready, and of course would leave them there at night and we would go get them when they moved out.

Some of the live ones would be hammered into a tree with a very long nail so we could set the detonator off it was marvellous what you got up to really we got up to a lot of things then with a great deal of secrecy but being kids you didn't care did you.

My step mother, as I said before, was very young and had no imagination but did her best what she knew I am sure and I often think back to when we were at school and she used to clean our shoes. We must have been sniffy little buggers because I used to sleep in my shirt and never even took my tie off and I decided one day that it was a bit dangerous so I would start taking it off and of course we didn't wear under pants until I was working and I could buy my own, we just didn't wear them when I was young, I don't know why not maybe because my old man was one of those that took the money out for his beer money, I just don't know and housekeeping came after so my stepmother had a struggle, and in the end my father ended up with seven children while they were together and none of them followed his path.

He was a clever man but unfortunately he wanted to spend his time down in the pub but we all grew none the worst for it I suppose.

"We got not water!"

Pat Istead

 My first memories of World War Two was when my sister was born in July 1937 and at that time we lived in a block of flats in Queen Street Portsea Portsmouth. My Aunt had come to see the new born baby and I was the only one who would let people up to see her and that was my first memory going back.

We then moved from that block of flats in 1939 because my dad knew that Portsea would be the first place to be bombed because of it being nearest to the Dockyard so we then moved out of area to Chesterfield Road in Copnor, I must have been four.

A friend of my parents worked in the Corset Factory and managed to get materiel out for mum to have dresses made for my sister and myself.

Copnor Bridge the lady lived and I recall one day when we were having our dress fitting and Air Raid siren went off the house was as I said on the bridge just behind St Joseph's Church, we all went to her basement and I remember sitting on the stairs and her front room door had been left open and I do remember seeing the Bomb dropped. The front room window blew inwards before going outwards with the shattered glass blown to smithereens, it was like a balloon in the front room before going out. Then when we came up and started our way home, we see a bus all scorched up in the front coming over Copnor Bridge and when we got home which was tea time mum wanted me to go upstairs to get her an apron from the drawer, I was a very nervous child and thought the Germans might be up there.

Then in 1941 we got bombed out of Chesterfield Road and at that time didn't have an air raid shelter ourselves so would sit under the stairs when there was an Air Raid, but later on the Council did build us a brick one. We must have been out when the house got hit.

I do remember January the 10th when there was another big Air Raid during the evening and night that we went into the brick Air raid shelter for the first time, but the lady next door shouted over "There is a load of us over here so come over" and because she had an Anderson shelter we did, and it was a good job we did because the blast of the bomb pulled the door clean off, and if we had been in there we would have been severely cut through the blast. I also recall when the all clear went someone went into one of the houses and shouted out the window "We got no water!"

We went from there to stay with my Aunt in Pitcroft Road which was in North End, we just took what we could in the pram and walked to Pitcroft Road and my great aunt Annie Brackley took us in and put us up like she did anybody there, she put a double bed in the front room for my parents and she put two cots in there for my sister and I, but my dad would always go around if there was any windows rattling and secure them because I thought the Germans was trying to get in.

From my aunt's we moved to St Pirans Avenue then on June 22nd in 1941 my mother committed suicide. My mum had always had very bad nerves from about when she was fourteen years old, it started when she came home from school one day and there was an ambulance stood outside her house and they were just taking her father away who also had just committed suicide so she always had bad nerves from then and having had children it made her very bad which resulted in me having to go into St James with her just after I was born.

They said that the nurses clumping up and down the wards made her worst and in fact she was worst when she came out than when she went in. When my sister was born she then suffered from post-natal depression so a neighbour looked after her and I was shipped out to Coventry for a little while, I was fostered out and my mother then went into Knowle Hospital for her nerves.

She was getting better before this but because of the War it did make her bad again and when dad used to go off to work she would say "I may not be here when you get back cause I might do myself in, kill myself" and he always tried not to do any over time and get back as soon as he could, but this particular day it was a beautiful sunny day and she sent Gill and I out into the garden to dig the garden with tea spoons and Gill's ribbon had came off and mum had been doing her ironing when we went out to play so we both went in to get it put on but we couldn't find her anywhere, so I went upstairs to look for her and one of the bedrooms door was locked, at this time I never went to school because it was too much for mum but I learned a lot and remember getting out a writing pad and a pen and was going to write a letter to my dad to say that I couldn't find mum, but he walked in the back gate soon after that and we told him we could not find mum and he then went up the stairs and broke the door open and in the bedroom was a big wardrobe that had big draws at the bottom and big coat hangers at the back of the wardrobe and mum had tied herself to the hanger while stood on the draws and then hung herself. She knew dad would be home soon and us girls would not be left on our own for too long. It was also the evening when Anne Blackley would come down from North End to bring meat for us for Sunday meal and she would take us back so dad could sort everything out and I remember the doctor coming in and going up to the bedroom and my dad was to carry her through to the bedroom.

After this myself and my sister was evacuated to my mother's sister who had been in service with an elderly lady and cousin, and she had a brother in Northampton in a little village called Hemmington which was near to Peterborough and she found someone there that would look after Gill and myself.

We spent the rest of the War there but we used to come home again Christmas to Annie Brackley and Annie was a marvellous old lady.

My own grandmother died in childbirth so Annie brought the two boys up, my uncle Jim at that time was three and they were brought up as her own then she had a baby so the three was brought up as brothers. As I said before when the War came on and any one needed a room she would give them a bed, she also had my dad's two brothers who were in the Army and when they came home from leave they too would be there, her own son was born in 1926 so did not go into the Army and was eighteen a couple years before the end of the War, she also had a lodger a Mr Randle who lived there who I didn't know where he came from, but would go home in the holidays but came back and even after the War still lived there. Then there was her husband Arthur Brackley and another cousin by the name of Fred who also lived there as well.

My uncle Jim then got married in 1941, he and Peggy went on to have a daughter and at Christmas when Jim and I were at home they turned up but naturally they lived at her mother's because Uncle Jim was still in the army. Her mother lived in Gosport and this day when she turned up she had a row with her parents hence the reason she turned up so they then stayed there until the end of the War.

So there was all these people living there plus the lady next door Mrs Gale who was a widow who was too scared to sleep in her own house at night would come in and also sleep, so there was a couple people that slept on the floor and we would all share beds, but those are my most vivid memories at the moment about the War but it will come in a minute or so.

Annie Brackley who I was talking about before was, as I said, my great aunt and she and her sister were members of the John Pounds Memorial Church but in them days it was the High Street Unitarian Church that was in High Street Old Portsmouth, and I believe they had gone to the Church from a very early age, my great great grandmother Ann Amelia Richmond and her sister Georgina were pupils of the John Pounds when he actually died.

In the stories about John Pounds who you read about had his Ragged School in St Mary's Street and Amelia and her family also lived in St Mary's Street and lived there right up until she died in 1906, later on they changed it to Highbury Street and that was 31 Highbury Street where she died and can be verified because we have just obtained a copy of her Will with that address on. Aunt Annie and her granddaughters would all come to the Unitarian Church in the High Street every Sunday and my dad would go with them and the week before my dad died he told us that the Chapel then had a balcony and it had an organ on the balcony and it was his job to pump the organ for the hymn singing, and once a month a Boys Brigade that came from the Garrison Church would parade along the High Street and he would be pumping the organ for the hymns but would be looking out of the window watching them go by and forget to pump the organ so it would stop in the middle of the hymn, that was one of his great stories.

Edie I believe died in child birth in 1916, but still Annie and Mabel went to the Chapel that was demolished on January 10th 1941, and at that time I was in the Royal Hospital up town with scarlet fever and it was the Blitz and the nurses came and put us with our bedding underneath the beds, and I remember when the Doctor came around with his tin helmet on and looking underneath and making sure we were all alright, and in that ward which was J6 ward I believe was one side scarlet fever and the other side was diphtheria and when I was up and allowed to walk around I was told not to go to the other side of the ward. But I do recall an elderly lady who called me across and I remember touching the bottom of her bed and then looking at my hands to see if I had caught diphtheria, and parents wasn't allowed in and the ward had glass doors into the ward at the far end and they could come as far as them so when they came they could only wave to you from behind this glass door and when I was allowed to walk around I was allowed to the end bed so I was a bit nearer to see my mum, and if they had brought anything in like sweets, eggs it had to be handed in to the sister to be shared amongst everybody, but as I said when I was allowed to walk to the end of the last bed mum was able to throw me a sweet which she had given me for myself.

Getting back to Annie and Mable, they were absolutely devastated when the old Chapel was bombed because the only surviving bits left were the end two walls and the Memorial to John Pounds which was buried in the garden but now in the Chapel that was rebuilt but his bones still remain in the garden today. So when it was demolished they then had to decide whether to carry on or not and I have the copies of the AGM reports to show Mabel was the Secretary of the Chapel committee and a Mrs Wetton was chairman and she said they could use a room in her house to have the meeting, so a couple of days later the meeting took place and Mr Cole who was the Minister said if they raised their subscriptions from sixpence a week to a shilling they could keep going.

So they eventually found rooms in Kinston Crescent in a house where they went on to have their services so eventually Jim Sturgess, who had been a committee member at that time who then became a Minister because Rev Cole as he was then had gone back to New Zealand ,their dream was to rebuild the Chapel or a Church and in time they eventually got the permission to build and had monies from the War Funds so just had to raise lots of other for bits of extras and things for fixtures and fittings and would get a bit fed up with the fund raising, so Aunt Annie said "I will make some coconut ice and chocolate sponges" and Aunty Mable made some cream donuts and at Aunty Annie's funeral in 1965 John Sturgess said the foundation of this John Pounds' Memorial Church was built on coconut ice and chocolate sponges and cream donuts, and the church was actually opened in 1956 I think.

My father went on to marry my mother's youngest sister in December 1944 and because he kept the St Pirans Avenue house during the War myself and Gill had some where to move back to. There was no Church built then so they got married in St Marks Church, and even though there was no John Pounds Church they would still hold garden parties and coach trips and also Christmas parties.

There would be a lot of Aunt Mabel's family because she had quite a lot of family and Auntie Annie with her family, and of course my dad and us and lots of other people would turn up and we would say "But who are all these other people at our parties?" and it wasn't till years later we realised it was their party and we were the visitors. By this time they were too old to be involved with anything but still stayed on the committee.

Mable Hepplewhite's daughter Eddie was the very last bride to have got married in the old church before it was demolished in December 1940 and in 1964 Myra, that was Mabel's granddaughter, also got married that same year and the little one that came with her mum in the Christmas holidays. Uncle Jim's daughter also got married there and Annie Brackley's granddaughter Linda and Mary was the very first to be named in this church here at the John Pounds' Memorial Church and at home I have a photograph of Annie Blackley and Arthur Blackley sitting on the bench and Cecil their son with my two brothers, because they were brought up as brothers, standing at the back of them and the two young girls and all of us in it, Ann was sixteen along with Peter and it was a lovely family photograph sat in the John Pounds garden.

Another story about the three boys, as my brothers got older was that during the War they could only afford one suit so had to take turns in who was going to go out because it was "our suit" and would only go out one at a time because it was who is going to wear "our suit" today.

That was another story.

Florrie Allnut

It was 1939 I think the War started and we were all very concerned and very scared about the Bombings we were to expect.

Leethem /Twilfit Ltd Corset Factory had four or five factory s all over Portsmouth in which I worked in the Buckland one and I must say we all enjoyed our work there. Mind you if you were not at your desk or machine by seven thirty in the morning you didn't get a start, you had to go back home so of course you lost the money for that.

They were very strict but a very good firm to work for and in 1941 the Sultan Road Factory was bombed while I was working there and of course we all stood there in morning looking at the ruins all very up upset. The other factory was in Eastney off of the Highland Road so some of us had to go to a meeting there next day and being as I was a supervisor I had to say which girls I wanted in my department and I must say it was not easy neither was it for the rest of the super visors that was also there. The girls that you didn't choose either went into munitions or into services and I myself would of liked to have gone into one of those, I did have four calling up papers but the Boss just would not let me go so I had to stay with the firm.

That firm then went on 'til 1950 and the firm had a big building built at Farlington near to the railway so those that knew the work was sent there, the firm had sent machinery out to the country before the War started so they had enough to start another service there and it was a lovely building and we all enjoyed working there.

Going back to the 'When we were at War', when the siren went off we all had to evacuate our desks and go into the Air raid shelter and a lot of the girls took knitting to do while they were sitting there and of course it was not an easy time because the girls that were sitting there just wasn't earning any money at that time and of course a lot of us lost a lot of money.

One day I got a bit fed up and I said to the Boss I am going home I have been sitting in that Air raid shelter for hours and I knew my mother would be at home on her own, so I went and got my bike out and off I went but riding along the Kingston Road a German Plane dive-bombed me and machine gunned me and I was just near a shelter and the shelter man shouted "Get off that bike quickly and get in here!" so I did for a time.

The War went on and on and we were spending more time in the Air raid shelters than at our machines so it was decided that there would be a Red Alert. This meant that we would ignore the sirens, put someone on watch then dash to the shelter when they called us.

On odd occasions at lunch times we had a concert party to entertain us, it was one of them days that I just mentioned when the German plane machined gunned me and I was very lucky that day not to have been injured or even killed. Lucky I fell off my bike into the nearest Air raid shelter or I wouldn't be telling my story today at the age of 97.

When you left work at the end of the day you always wondered if you would see each other again and also if you had a house to return to. Two of my friends were killed in an Air raid shelter by the Dockyard as this was a prime target.

One of my Friends who lived in Beecham Road told me her house had been bombed and could not find her dog. Lucky for my friend the house was not completely destroyed but of course the Police would not let us near to try and find her dog as it was not safe. Two days later a policeman on patrol passing the house heard a dog barking and went to investigate and found the dog safe and sound hiding under the table.

One day I was visiting a friend in Purbrook when the sirens went off and as time went on and on it was agreed that I would spend the night there, later I found out that on the same night a friend had gone to visit me and had to spend the night in my house and someone had also gone to visit her and had to do the same. In those days there were very few telephones about so other members of the family just had to worry 'til you arrived home again.

On one occasion on my way home I saw my neighbour walking up the road and asked why she were not in the shelter and she replied, "I am a bit scared" so I said "Come on then come in there with me." So I took her in to my shelter and we sat there and waited for the all clear signal.

It was a very bad time for every one and when I see pictures nowadays of how it was it brings back memories of all those houses that had burned down and was destroyed, and I realise how fortunate we were because we only had a few windows blown out in our house and a lot of people lost everything they had, and a lot of the girls didn't come back because they were killed in Air raid shelters.

As I said before when we all went home at night we always said goodnight because you never knew if you would see one and other next day, it was a very sad time and I would never want to go through that again.

Bedford Street I lived which was off the Kingston Road and that was the first bombing we had in Portsmouth, the Pub and the Library was scattered there when the bomb dropped on them there. My father worked in the Dockyard and it was just the three of us at home with mother, he worked all day and mother would have to have a dinner on the table at quarter past twelve for him to cycle from the Dockyard home every day so that we all sat down together for dinner.

I was born in 1913 and have lived here all my life, I did have a brother and a sister and my brother was at Dunkirk and we were very worried about that, and I remember one day mother coming up to the factory with a telegram in her hand and she said, "I have had this telegram from the authorities" and she said "Arthur is alright but he wants us to send money where he is now he is living on the pavement but wants us to send money to the post office there" and because I had passed my test in 1938 and was able to drive mother wanted me to drive there and take her to see him, but I said no because the roads would be crowded and you would not get to see him so she said, "Oh all right then." So when the boss came in I asked if I could take mother home because we wanted to see what we needed to do about this money, so on the way home I popped into the post office and was allowed to send ten pounds and I was lucky to have a ten pond note on me in my bag so we sent that ten pounds and Arthur was very pleased with that and thanks us after because he was able to treat his chums as well. That was one episode I would not forget.

My sister was married at the end of 1940 and went abroad to live, I told you we had an Anderson Shelter in the garden and when people came in we would make tea and that.

Did I tell you that I was five when mother took me over to the Church on the corner of Queens Road to the Sunday School and I enjoyed the company there and still keep in touch with them.

I remember it was D Day in Portsmouth on the 6th June 1944 and it was 7 o'clock in the morning and I was cycling along Fratton Road to work when lorry after lorry passed me and each one was full of soldiers in their uniforms going off to war. I was crying with tears streaming down my face to think that they were only young men and were having to go off to fight. One man shouted out "Don't cry Ma we will be back soon!" This I will never know, did any of those young men come back?

Another thing that comes to my mind is that there was never much to eat but mother always put a good meal on the table, sometimes we would have to queue and queue for food like bread and milk and some went without, rations were awful and we were all glad when things got back to normal after the war.

I recall another sad time when two of my friends who were twin girls were killed in the Air raid shelter near the Dockyard that I mentioned before, there was a lot of casualties that day and around Portsmouth.

When we came into decimalisation in 1971 we had a work study man come to the factory to see what the girls were doing and how much they were being paid, well the seamers who were seaming the corsets were paid a penny three farthings per corset so you had to work all that out, so I had a friend who was very good with arithmetic and so I asked her to help me so I could get it right down to change that. So after about a couple of months Mr Jones said take one list off so that then left 1.3 list so he took one list off but that was cutting the price down, and by the time you added it all up it had shrunk quite a bit, so I thought, "I am not doing that anymore" and about six months after he said, "I don't think we will need that other list, we will take that off" and I said "We will not" and he said "I think we will" but I said "No we will not" and he said "I will take you into Mr Holaroid" and my stomach went over but I said "Alright I don't care I will come with you."

Then he thought about it saw that I was adamant. But we went into Mr Holaroid and he said "Well what do you want Mr Jones?" and he said what he wanted and Mr Holaroid said, "Well give Miss Allnutt what she wants" and I think he would of killed me but I was very very pleased what I did for those girls, so when I retired the boss said the girls did well by you and he did tell them. "She did fight for you girls you know" and I replied, "Yes and I enjoyed doing it." And of course they didn't want me to leave but after forty years I had had enough and being I still had mother at home it was time.

The War years were very sad and we will never forget what we all went through, some worse than others.

Elspeth

My name is Elspeth and I was born in 1930 in Landport, which over the years has changed so much - and so have the people. When I was a child, it was mostly houses and we lived in a three bedroomed house, with a parlour and back sitting room, just off Lake Road.

Like everyone else when the War began, we didn't have much. My father worked at the Docks unloading coal and coke and we always had a warm cosy house because of his job. He would bring a few small bags every day, what had fallen by the Quayside, so come winter we always had enough.

As long as I live, which I don't think will be many more years, I will never forget the War and being torn away from mother and father because of the horrendous amount of bombs dropped on Portsmouth.

We had a lovely house, and a pretty garden to go with it, because father liked to potter and plant whenever he had time to do so. The house always smelt of honeysuckle or lily of the valley, when it was the season for it. We had a lovely lilac tree at the back of the garden that gave a lovely scent, which mum somehow preserved in a jar with a little of olive oil that kept the scent smell for a long time after it died off. Mum could have been famous, had she had known years later they made air fresheners, just like she used to do with her beloved flowers.

Father worked, but Mother did not and the War for her and me was horrid, left at home all day until Father finished work and these bombs being dropped and Mother grabbing my hand and us running for dear life to the tin shack known as an air raid shelter. Once there mind, there was a lot of merriment, people would hum or sing softly and play dominos or cards, depending if they thought they were going to be there for a long time.

"God," I recall people saying "that was a near miss" and Mother holding my hand so tight I would want to weep and sometimes did. She would embrace me and say "Sorry, darling", but sometimes it never made up for the pain I felt. Though that was trivial to what I went through later on in the War when I was evacuated. I went from a very happy child to a frightened little mouse, who thought Mother would die or be killed if my secret was ever told, but at that time there was no one to tell.

I was placed with a family a short train ride away because my parents thought it best for me to go to the country. I remember the day even though it was raining very heavy. I was ten, I think at the beginning of the war and we went to the train station in Commercial Road which still stands proud today. First though, mum had to go to the Post Office the one opposite the train station. She put some money into my little beaded purse for when I needed it, but from that day I never saw my purse again or the cash.

I was put with a man, his wife, and a boy Edward age thirteen who I recall had ginger hair and freckles and was rotten to the core. I cannot mention where I was or their names, in case they have surviving family. I do know they are no longer with us, because their shelter took a hit and they were in it. Luckily for me, Edward was bullying me that day and I had been left tied to a hay stack, because I cried because of what he made me do.

I expect you have heard some very sad stories, but some people will not tell if they were sexually interfered with, like I was at that time, and had kept it a secret locked away for nearly a lifetime. I was beaten on a daily basis by this young bully, and my scraps of food I was given by 'Mother 2' - that's all I remember her by and hated calling her it, because I had my own Mother. He took my food when they were not looking, unless I scoffed it in my mouth first, and if got caught, I went without. Anyway, I lived or existed by very little food, but I did eat seasonal fruit which kept me healthy, gooseberries, when ripe, were plenty and my favourite, as well as blackberries.

We had to work on the farm from very early in the morning, and even as a child my back felt like it would split in half because of the long hours and how heavy the work was. I had to tie young shoots to start with, to trellises in very long rows, and it was row after row and then water them to give them a good start. So that would take up to dinner time each day, because it took weeks to get the job done before going onto the next thing.

I had to clean the chicken coups and collect the eggs. We always had bread and dripping for dinner and nothing else till supper. But give her due she did cook good food, just a shame the brute got to get most of it off my plate. I swear they turned a blind eye and knew what he was up to.

My getaway was the barn, because it had steps up to the hay loft and it was very warm in there for some reason on cold days. Sometimes the chickens somehow got up there and I would climb the ladder and get them back down. One day, he,

105

the boy, came in the barn when I was coming down with the chicken, and said: "Let me help you down". On doing so, somehow he lost his hand in my drawers, but as soon as I stiffened, he laughed and said it was an accident. He slowly pulled his hand away, but not before having a grope.

I was mystified by this and could not understand what had happened, but knew it was wrong. My heart was beating so fast with fear, I thought it would stop. Of course, he said: "Don't go saying nothing to nobody or else you will get it." Those words went on for the whole time I was away from my dear Mother. Every time the brute could corner me, he would again do horrid things to me. Then, he started talking dirty things that I had not heard of before until I was much older.

There were lots of little streams all over the fields, so you could paddle and wash the hot sun from your face and body. I used to do this to keep clean, because 'Mother 2' hardly washed the clothes we wore or hardly kept the farmhouse clean, not like my own loving mother who brushed and cleaned every single day. Him, the man of the house, was hardly ever seen but at meal times would stare at me as though I was not welcome. I think, because he didn't really want me there, he turned a blind eye to the bully son. I remember once, he came into the barn when the boy assaulted me and instead of doing something or saying something, he just rubbed himself below and let the brute carry on and stood watching until he had seen enough, then just left me to the brute's mercy.

Even 'Mother 2', when I cried of being so sore below, just told me to change my underwear and wash more, because, she said, it was where I wet myself and that made me sore. I will never forget what I went through because of that family.

My mother came to visit a couple of times, but I was so scared to say anything, because he said he would kill my mother. I just pretended all was ok and I was being looked after, but she did notice the bruises I had and inquired how I happened to have them on my upper arms and legs. This was put down to being helped out of a bog, hence the bruises on the arms. 'Mother 2' would bake a lovely cake for my mother's visit and would be really lovely on that day, as well as the day before. After then, back to normal with hardly saying a word and just looking at me. Now I am an adult, I think they were not 'the full shilling' so to speak. The boy nor myself never went to school while I stayed there. Once at home, I did.

I remember, some nights you could look up to the sky and it would look red, orange and black, where fires and bombs were ravishing the earth. The noise sometimes made me think we are next, when a bomb was dropped near. We must have been near the water, because you could clearly see the searchlights. I would hear them talking, funny thing, it was so cosy, not having a television. I would sit by the grate and read, and occasionally the brute would slyly kick my ankle. I did laugh on one occasion when 'Mother 2' caught him red-handed. She had no alternative but to punish him, because he kicked me so hard, I fell off the seat onto the earth. He got a good slap around his ear that time, but of course I suffered later on.

As I said, I had a miserable time of it living away from my family and even worse when they got hit in the shelter, because I was alone for quite a while before anyone came to my rescue.

When I did go home, I was a different girl altogether. My skin was very bronzed and a bit rougher, as I worked out in all weathers. Plus, my hair was dull and very long. The worst thing for me was to realise the love I had missed and the attention. But, of course, I was a changed child, abused and used and never said a word to anyone. Now though it's too late. I think a lot of the children that were evacuated had a raw deal, one way or another. Maybe not what I went through, but worked and underfed and felt unwanted by the families they were placed with, because some families had no choice - they had to take a child.

I was so glad when the War ended and things started to get back to as near normal as possible. No bombing or raging fires or sirens going off. It took people a long time to get used to that, mother said. She often would sit me beneath her feet and brush my hair and ask me if I enjoyed my time in the country. What else but "Yes, mother" could I say? It was so good to eat normally again and have no grease on bread. I was allowed the occasional sugar bread, but my best treat was mother baking rhubarb tart, which was so nice it melted in your mouth. And scones with a little preserve in them. I can visualise nice warm sunny days when we moved back to our old house in Landport after the War. Mother had had to move while I was away, because our street was severely bombed. Along with most the streets, our house had the roof almost blown off. But the street behind ours had to all be demolished because it took so many direct hits.

We had a different lifestyle than today, and appreciated all that we were given and had. It's not like today, although I have lived very comfortably. No children, just myself and a dear husband who passed over a long time ago. I have buried a lot of memories but must say, now, this interview I have given has lifted a little dark cloud buried for a long time and I thank you for that.

I hope the book is published while I am still alive, but if I have gone to pastures new, I know someone will be reading my story and thinking: "Oh, what a shame." But there's no shame any more.

Part Two

I do remember I think before the War when there were live Elephants kept in the city ready for when they were performing in the Circus, and I remember the horses and other animals being paraded through the streets and the funny looking people that worked for the circus. The Elephants I recall lived in a stable and people used to live on top of the stables.

My aunt lived in a flat in Portsea and her husband who was a rag and bone man kept a horse in the yard. I remember hating going to visit because sometimes we would walk pass the slaughter house and the smell was horrid, and if you were very unlucky they might have bled the animals and hosed down which would drain outside. Mum always bought me a sweet to help me get over the sickness I would feel.

Queen Street as I remember it had lots of Pubs and shops, you could purchase more or less anything from shoes to a coffin down there. Very vibrant in its heyday when it was a proper naval city, not like today very modern with less pubs and hardly any shops. I have ventured lots of time to the harbour and sat in my later years and felt not much if anything has really changed there, apart from the bus depot that was never there years ago.

Did I tell you that when I first got evacuated it was to Petersfield, which was all countryside and farms, lots of lanes and you had to walk for miles before you came to anything normal like a garage or village store?

I only stayed there for a couple of weeks because the lady that had the farm only had one son and he was sent to War and was killed so she didn't want me there after that, but while I was with her my time was full of "what next?" because she let me explore and milk the cows with her and feed pigs and chase her goats, but the best thing was she let me help her in her kitchen. On her stove you had to put the kettle and pots, her oven was like a kiln, she made bread and her friends would come and give her home made jam in place of the loaf. I can taste that bread now as we speak I have never tasted any like it throughout my life. The smell would waft off down the lanes and it could be smelt for hours after it had been baked in that magic oven of her, she pulled the tray of bread out with a big flat spade and I would look on in awe.

After she got the news about her son the light in her eyes went out and she wanted no part of me and gone as quick as. It was such a shame because I didn't want to stay with her in the beginning and in the end after just a couple of weeks didn't want to leave, but there you are it was time to move on and mother came and collected me and after one night at home with mother and father I was taken to the mission hall and sent off again to the other farm which was not so nice and no happy memories.

I remember though as a child Victoria Park also had small animals in and a bandstand and Sundays everyone would put Sunday best clothes on, and after church if they went would go and relax in the park.

It is funny how things can jog your memory, I have remembered so much just sitting letting my mind go back since I last spoke to you.

Reg Tungatt

My name is Reg Tungatt and I was born 1948, and I remember the War years or rather the after math of the War. I lived in Bishop Street in Portsea as a child. I was one of eight children and on the corner of our road stood the Salvation Army which we could go and have a farthing breakfast or for five days get one for a penny, but of course you had to take your own sugar or butter or you just had toast on its own or you could have porridge with no sugar.

I spent many a day around the aftermath bomb sites round the old Brickwoods site which was where what is now known The Admiralty Quarter in Cross Street on the North side of Portsea. We would find big lumps of shrapnel and take it off to the scrap yard and that would help a few ends to meet.

We used to knock our own carts up to do bag carrying to and from the ferry and trains for the people that came over, and in between we used to go Mud larking down on the foreshore there, and we had a regular Policeman that would come down and shout at us but could not get us because we were knee deep in mud, and we would just laugh at him and carry on what we were doing.

I went to Beneficial School which is now Groundling's Theatre in Kent Street, Portsea and Miss Powell was then the Headmistress which was quite a nice school and a very nice lady head who always kept a budgie in her office. She was very strict but very fair to all the children.

There was quite a few bomb sites around the area around that time and it was great for us kids to play on and better when we found the old lamp stands on these old houses, that was until they started to come along with a big crane with a big metal bomb on the end of it that would just go and knock the houses down, demolition ball it was. And I have a secret that I should not say at this time which was an incident with the demolition crane which at the time was quite hilarious at that time for us kids, but not for the person who owned that house at that time.

I was one of eight children and we did struggle like most families did after the War, and the one thing you don't see today like you did in them days was if you was ill or anything like that people gathered around and brought food to the door and if mum was ill the other ladies would come in and look after her, and at that time it was getting to the tail end of having to get the Doctor in the evenings and having to give him a shilling or he just did not come in. And of course there was only ever one telephone box and that was at the end of the street and you could understand that if it was an emergency that was the only way you could contact the outside world. And if you had an injury you had to try and put them on a cart and get them down to the Hospital yourself, which we had to do on one occasion because my brother Douglas was playing with old bits of the Air raid shelter in our back garden, drop the corrugated metal and it went straight down his leg, from his knee down to his ankle was wide open but somehow it did not bleed at all and we had to put him on our little cart that we had and took him up to the Royal Hospital. And nothing at all happened and the bone was all exposed until they put the first injection in it and we had to get out quick while they stitch him up.

There was mum at home terrified sitting on her own crying her eyes out but it was left to us children to deal with it on her behalf while our father was still out working hard.

I heard recently about the Air raid shelter that was bombed which I have known for many a year because it was known as the School Meal Hut because that is where all the school meals across the city were cooked and then delivered to the different schools on a daily basis. This was situated on the Besant Road and Arundel Street itself with very large buildings that were very large inside that they would prepare and cook all the meals, then they went out soon on the road for delivery.

It was that shelter that took the direct hit and it was only this year that somebody has made the effort to recognise it, over the last thirty odd years I have always said a memorial should have been placed there a long time ago, then everyone could have had their condolences added to this site. But this site has changed on so many occasions so we hope this plaque will still stay there because that was put in place long after the War and when the hospital was demolished years later.

The same thing will happen in Commercial Road if Sainsbury goes because we have a plaque in memory of The Royal Hospital there and if the new Northern Quarter goes ahead like The News has stated then I wonder what will happen to that plaque. I sincerely hope that will stay where it is with so many of our people that were in there before and after the War that died, it would be a great shame to lose such a memoir that belongs to this great City we have.

Life living in Portsea those early years was very hard for everybody but you made ends meet and you went down like we did often to Charlotte Street and would find a wooden crate that would be given to us by the Green Grocer there, and we would be sitting there cutting them up and putting the sticks into bundles and would sell them around the doors to the people for just pennies which was a lot cheaper than the Iron Mongers so would buy ours and sometimes it wasn't so much as the making of the money it was the little smiles on their faces when we knocked their doors with our little hand cart delivering to them. Even when the weather was bad we still went out delivering and in them days was on the tail end of sweets.

We was on the tail end of the rations by then and at this point the sugar and sweetie stuff was still on ration till 1953 so you still had to queue up to the Butcher shop tore out a coupon and paid in cash if it was over, and out you came and especially at Christmas time it was really hard, but powdered egg was still in use and it was a luxury to even see a cake let alone even eat one and this is why we all looked forward to Christmas.

People laugh today over their silly Play Stations and all that, but to us the greatest thing to us was to wake up to an apple or an orange and we always had a little sock hanging on the end of the bed, and that was a luxury that kids wouldn't appreciate today. They go on and on about lap tops and all that, they ought to get back to reality and bring it back.

In Bishop Street there was a place called Treadgolds where I used to spend some Saturdays there for sixpence and work the bellows all day, and was amazed when that shut down because I only lived a few doors away. They done the old fashioned nails and if you had a latch for the toilet doors in the back garden and it broke you could go up there and the man on the forge would work his magic and redo it because some of them were not as they are later where they all came as a set design. Those in them days came as individuals and these gentlemen up there could make literally anything, and the amazing thing about it I can remember at a young age was that he could go to any drawer and know where every nut, bolt or screw was, even washer, which even at today's standard was amazing, and I just hope that Treadgolds will reopen again properly as a museum one day in memory of the people that were there, especially as somebody as humble as me who actually worked the bellows.

When I left school I worked for a building firm Boldring's and when I found out things wasn't right I wasn't happy so decided to spread out myself.

That secret I was talking about in the beginning I can now tell you about because I have taken legal advice.

A man who lived in Queen Street who was very obnoxious to children and as we were at that young impressionable age to read and write we found that they were writing "SB OUT" on the side of houses with white paint on the wall just before the house got demolished and we thought we would have a good laugh to do it to this gentleman's house, not realising the repercussions which we found out a few hours later that when the man came home from work he had no house. It was gone with the big metal ball that had knocked his house down completely with the contents. I laugh today but it wasn't such a laugh then after we saw he had no house. We never knew what happened after that because we didn't see him no more.

So there you go that's just another chapter of someone else's life after the terrible bombing we took in Portsmouth.

Les Jagger

I was a child of four when the aftermath of the World War Two to children was a dream come true and the stories my family talked about will stay with me forever, because as you will read some was very funny and some very sad, but to children it was one big adventure.

This story was told to me by my uncle Reg and he called it "The Scream in the Blackout."

My aunt Florence (Flo) told me this story about a wartime walk through the black out. She and uncle Reg, her husband, and other members of the family had been having a drink in one of the many public houses that lined Lake Road. By the time they had left the pub it was pitch black, and that craved very wary walking, because their route home was littered with bomb damage debris. In addition to this it was very overcast which made it even darker in the strictly enforced blackout, it was like walking through an ink bottle.

People frequently fell over or walked straight into all sorts of unseen objects hurting themselves very badly.

On such a night, then my resilient relations, primed with drink, made their best efforts for a safe landfall at their garden gate. But as with many other Pompey people in those fatal darkened nights, their progress would not be like a day on the beach. In the blackness of night suddenly went up a fearful racket of a stricken man's scream. Aunt Florence recognising instantly that it was her husband who made this outburst that had shocked them all to a shivering standstill gamely made her way tottering to where it came from.

Whereupon she quickly besought Reg, the reason for such a horrendous scream, it was such a blood curdling scream she wondered what he had done to himself, it was such a chilling scream she thought he had hurt himself very badly but his anguished reply was that he had been searching around in his coat pocket and realised he had lost Two Bob, would you believe!

This is another story told to me. My cousin Dennis Murphy was born in Portsmouth in 1933, which meant he was well acquainted with the intense bombing that afflicted the city during World War Two.

This will show how The German Luftwaffe changed my cousin Dennis' religion.

His father, my uncle Reg, was born into a Catholic family and consequently Dennis found himself a young pupil in one of Portsmouth Catholic schools. His route to and from school happened to take him under one of the German Luftwaffe's bombing lanes, and this understandable consternation for his Protestant mother, my aunt Florence who I have mentioned previously.

So concerned was she that she petitioned uncle Reg to consider moving Dennis from his ill-placed Catholic school to the comparative safety of a Protestant school that roosted well away from the offending bomb lane.

Uncle Reg was what can be described as a Catholic who treated his beliefs with a dash of levity, who had a poor Sunday attendance record and who immediately saw the good sense in the relocation of Dennis to the Protestant school, accepting the fact that Dennis, if he wanted to, could still cling to his Catholic beliefs.

I think Dennis would have been more particular in his religious predilections than his loose-leafed dad, but he must have also considered the reduced possibility of his copping the odd bomb here and there. So he acceded to his parent's suggestion and far from clinging to his Catholic beliefs, he took to Protestantism like a duck to water and not just for the duration of the War but for the rest of his life.

Thus Dennis was converted from the old to the new religion.

During the War the Germans did their level best to destroy Portsmouth and our Dockyard and shipping, and largely failed in this endeavour. Their bombing was none too accurate at times as was verified with the first bomb dropped and resulted in the destruction of the old Blue Anchor public house which was situated in Kingston Crescent, they were well off the beam of the Dockyard.

This was just the beginning, and the people and the City were to suffer further massive damage in both the Commercial Road and residential areas.

Yet this too proved ultimately to be a defeat for the enemy, as the courageous people, civil and military, battled on heroically to clear the collateral damage, rebuilt their shattered streets and buildings where required and prayed for their loved ones lost.

At the end of that long War, the German Luftwaffe plans for the people of Portsmouth, their city and their Dockyard came to nought.

In fact I would surmise herein that the only event they did achieve which endured not only after the War but well into the Millennium was something that they would never have included in their logbooks as they knew nothing about it -they had unknowingly paved the way for the conversion of my cheerful cousin Dennis Murphy to Protestantism.

A WW2 story of my cousin Mike Murphy: Part 1
by Les Jagger

This story was told to me by my Aunt Flo (Florence) in the late sixties.

My cousin Mike, born and brought up in Portsmouth, was not old enough for military call-up at the beginning of the WW2 hostilities. This provided him with the opportunity to see the aerial dog-fights that raged over the city whenever the German Luftwaffe made their unwelcome bombing raids, and the population damned them for their destructive capabilities: but not cousin Mike. Whenever he was at home and the air-raid warnings sounded he would scramble up onto a convenient support on the roof of his parent's house, where, with a handy pair of binoculars, he was able to stare up in utter fascination as the fearful battles between the invaders and the Royal Air Force destroyed both in the air and massively at ground level throughout the city.

Such was his fascination with aircraft that he decided he would join the RAF as soon as his call-up papers arrived, due midway through the war. Upon the arrival of those documents he immediately volunteered for the RAF and was accepted as a rear gunner, a career move the news of which he cheerfully passed on to his unknowing parents. Flushed with triumph, he broke the news to them with the words "You know I wanted to join the RAF - well I've been accepted into bomber command, and I'm going to be a rear-gunner". This brief delivery activated strikingly different elicitations from both parents. His dad, my uncle Reg, knowing that the service life-span of rear-gunners was notoriously short, raged at him for not having selected something more ground-based, such as a cook etc. Aunt Florence, by contrast, not being up to snuff with the precise disciplines of rear-gunnery, and surmising that it meant Mike would be part of a firmly grounded anti-aircraft gun crew, tried to assuage her husband's ire with the soothing words of a relieved mother; "Now, now, Reg - if the boy wants a career as a rear-gunner, why not let him have his choice - I'm sure he will do very well in his chosen career, and we will both be proud of him", or words to that effect. Only after Uncle Reg had thundered out the nature of what rear-gunners' responsibilities were was my Aunt won over, and Mike now came under fire from both irate parents as they delivered blistering condemnations about his foolishness. Despite their anger, driven after all by an intense concern for their son's safety, Mike's determination won the day: he became a rear gunner, and in so doing paved the way for PART 2 of his wartime story, detailed below.

Part 2

This story was told to me by Cousin Mike at different times in his later years after he was demobbed from the RAF, and had concluded a career as a sergeant with the security police in Heathrow airport and graduated with a degree in social science from Brunel University.

After Mike had won his first wartime skirmish with his parents to achieve his wish to be a rear gunner, he signed on with the RAF, who promptly whisked him away to India. Here he quickly found himself on long-hour bomber flights where they flew across the border into Burma, and then southwards to attack Japanese installations, and having deposited their bombs upon the aroused and riled enemy, swung around and made their weary way back to their base camp. These long flights sometimes lasted as long as nine hours. The return flights were often in pitch blackness due to cloud cover, which did nothing for flight navigation. The flights were uncomfortably noisy, and because they had to fly high to minimise the prospect of being shot down by enemy anti-aircraft fire, it was always bitterly cold. Mike said that the only part of the flight that made them forget these discomforts was when they went into attack mode.

The prospect of being shot down once the planes crossed the border into Japanese occupied Burma was always there. However, Mike and his comrades continued with their bombing raids for some time without the enemy being able to get a bead on their lucky bomber. Inevitably though, their luck eventually ran out. They had completed one particular mission, and were tired as they made their way northwards in pitch-black darkness, a massive blankness that provided them with at least some protection from the waiting enemy anti-aircraft batteries. They had almost cleared Japanese occupied territory near the Burmese border and were anticipating the relief that safety would bring as they flew on over friendly India.

But this was to be their ill-met night, and suddenly Mike and his fellow crewmen found themselves in a bomber ablaze. The brave Australian pilot, who tried to fly as far as he could from enemy held ground, was unable to maintain a correct course, and with the flames beginning to spread throughout the fuselage, he ordered all the crew to exit from the plane. This was going to be Mike's first parachute jump, and diving into utter darkness over jungle territory populated with snakes and tigers, etc., he wasn't keen to make the jump. But as he said, spreading flames in a confined space can be very persuasive, and he took his place in the queue as each man made his dive into the abyss. He said the only thing he can remember before he made his own jump was the bottom of the boots of the man in front, by chance a fellow Pompey man also. He recalled that the image of the soles on his mate's boots gleaming in the flaming plane always remained in his mind years afterwards, but he was damned if he could actually remember leaping into that dreadful night.

Mike said his parachute was his only comfort as he dropped towards whatever lay beneath him. Understandably, his mind was fixed on what he would land on. It turned out to be a malarial swamp. He couldn't see clearly and consequently broke a leg on landing. There was no choice but to lie where he was and await the light that dawn would bring. He did not call out to check if any other of his fellow crewmen were in the vicinity because enemy patrols may have been in the area. When the dawn broke he decided he had to get out of the swamp which may have had snakes on-site, and he started to crawl, in agony with the broken leg. Once clear of the water he laid still and waited, hoping that the plane's approach had been picked up on British radar.

Waiting was the only option, and he tried to make the most of it. And then suddenly, after all the bad luck he had already suffered during the luckless night, he now saw what at first he envisaged was to be the end of his short life. Coming towards him at a steady pace were some fierce-looking tribesmen, festooned with an array of malignant looking weapons. As this wasn't working out to be the luckiest day of his life, his immediate, fleeting, dismal thought was that his visitors might be cannibals. He knew that both the British and Japanese gave cash to locals who handed over any stray servicemen to them, but the appearance of the approaching band of ne'er- do-wells gave him no hope of salvation. But he couldn't have been more wrong, for his wild-looking arrivals were local Naga tribesmen, fiercely opposed to the Japanese invaders, and happily in the pay of the British.

So; a most relieving ending after Mike's earlier unhappy adventures. The leg was swiftly attended to by the RAF and young as he was, it quickly healed, and he never again had any problems with it. But he was quickly diagnosed as having malaria - a result of his unfortunate landing in the swamp, and he suffered for many years after with the disease, which did not fully fade until late in his life. After the war, like many other airmen who had parachuted to safety, he applied for, and was accepted into, the Silkworm Society for his life-saving parachute jump.

Thus ends my story of Cousin Mike whilst he proudly wore the uniform of the Royal Air Force in the Second World War. After demob, this quiet, modest man tried various jobs, including a spell in the merchant navy, during which time he was on a ship that was sunk in Danish waters in 1947 after it had struck a stray German war-time mine that had broken its restraining chains due to a rough sea storm. As the ship swiftly sank, he and all the crew, with much gratitude, were rescued by the gallant crew of a German fishing ship, but that is another story. He married, and joined the Heathrow security police force. When he asked for promotion after some years of service he was advised that only officers with certain GCE college certifications could apply. So he went to night-school, got his certificates, and obtained his promotion. Later in life, he retired from the police force, studied hard, and obtained a Social Services degree from the University of London. Not an inconsiderable achievement for a Pompey boy whose childhood schooling was fairly basic.

He died in 1996, and his loss was grieved by his family and friends then, and he will still be missed until all of us who knew him are ourselves long gone.

"I would not have missed it for a moment"

Phyllis Murphy, known as Betty

My name is Phyllis Murphy (nee Summers) but I am known to all as Betty. I am now 88 years of age and was born and raised on the Isle of Wight.

When I left school and the War was on I worked here on the Island in a factory as a Riveter, the factory was called Ranelagh and we built Pontoon Bridges. The work was very hard and I only stood 4 foot eleven inches in stocking feet so I was up to my arm pits in rivets. I loved the camaraderie of being with other teenagers because I had grown up being the only child.

My father died at a very young age so it was just mother and me so she became very over protective and insular, so working in the factory for me was like breaking free and leading a normal life, just being myself despite the fact that the War was on.

Of course we knew the War was coming but it really hit home to me the day was when the Air Raid siren went off and me and my mate Jessie was having a real good gossip in the rest room, and by the time we got outside the factory the Aeroplanes were almost upon us so rather than risk being exposed and vulnerable we dove down the bank next to us into the thicket, which was a godsend because it gave us plenty of cover, even though it was prickly and uncomfortable.

As we look up to the sky we could see that it was a Spitfire and a German Plane having a one to one, or as we called it in them days a "Dog fight". It was awesome to watch and so terrifying at the same time but thrilling to see the Spitfire getting the better of Gerry. They were darting round the sky like a Tom and Jerry Cartoon 'til suddenly the German plane burst into flames and we were laughing and both crying at the same time, then cheering and laughing again with nerves as it came spiralling down into the Solent.

Its only when you get older and marry and have sons of your own that you look back and think of the German pilot and crew that died that day, someone's son or grandson and was properly equally loved as much, so it was heartache all around no matter what side you were on.

I was about sixteen when I went to work for Ranelagh and because we lived close to the Ryde Pier in Castle Street. Our top floor was rented out to Naval personnel, mostly of course officers on official business at HMS Medina which nowadays has become a great big holiday attraction known as Puckpool Park which is situated along the far end of the seafront wall near the small village of Seaview. We were so lucky because we also got extra rations and perks which of course we did share. I have never not even today tasted better scrambled eggs that mother made from powered egg out of a tin, it was the best.

 I hadn't met him yet but the love of my life was stationed at that naval base. His name was Percy (Patrick Michael William Standish Murphy) known to all as Zoe. He was also the favourite uncle of the author of this book, his niece Margaret Foster the daughter of his beloved sister Patricia, also known as Jane my dear sister-in-law that lived on the main land but would come over when we married often.

Moving on to the second rude awakening of the War and the dangers that were ahead was when mother made her weekly pilgrimage to the Ryde Cemetery to tend to my father's grave like she did most weeks as I said. It was a glorious warm sunny day and she was walking slowly along the wide straight path leading up to the cemetery to the big archway and gates and admiring the wild flowers that smelt and looked delicious, when all of a sudden she had a weird feeling come over her and was aware that three quarters near to the gate she was aware that an aeroplane was approaching her but of course the Air raid siren had not gone off so she didn't think nothing of it. So carried on to dad, did his grave and as she was leaving had this feeling of uneasiness and could of swore to this day she heard my dad's voice calling her as the plane looked like it was coming into land and she was still not near the gate, she had 30 yards to go in fact and started to try and locate a way out of its path.

It was at this point she looked up and see the German marking on the plane and at the same time it dawned on her it was aiming right at her, mum broke into a flat run and ran for her life to what she thought was the shelter but was in fact a crypt and right near the arch as he opened fire and shot at her. As she dove into the crypt she was being peppered by debris from the bullets thudded into the ground, not to mention the big chunks of masonry from statues one of which remains today in its place fifteen yards to the left as you walk in through the gates. There stands a beautiful statue of an angel complete still with a couple of bullet holes and the old crypt even though sunken by time is now closed but still there.

Fortunately for mum she made it to the gate as he circled then passed overhead. Mum then sat for a moment on the side of the road to gather her thoughts and composure, after a few minutes she got up and heading over the road to report the incident to the stone mason that was across the road, what mum didn't know was that the plane had circled one more and was coming in for another go. By this time mum was in the middle of the road and too far to run back to the arch of the cemetery and too far for the stone mason's yard or doorway. Nothing could afford her shelter as she see it so ran literally for her life as the bullets thudded into the wall beside her.

God must have been with her that day as she stumbled into the door way of Ellis the stonemason's and was dragged in by one of the workers who had witnessed the whole scene. As incredible as it sounds, he missed her just by inches and who knows what that German pilot gained from chasing a lone woman in a cemetery and wasting all that ammunition. Only God knows and he was with my dear mum that day for sure.

I married my love on the 25th February 1944 at the Trinity Church in Ryde it was a lovely white wedding with three mates as bridesmaids.

Pat was still serving at H. M. S. Medina and always getting into some sort of trouble, he was a lovable rogue and what a dancer he was, I will never forget when him and his mate Max dressed in hula skirts with their trousers rolled up and did the hula dance while singing the Cow Cow Boogie at the weekly talent night up at the Commodore Cinema.

Although the War was dreadful, you could still have a laugh because if you did not you would just end up depressed and crying.

My own dice with death came during the last few months of the War in 1945, it was when the Doodlebugs were in full flow and causing untold mayhem. I was in bed in the last stages of labour with my first baby ,there was me mum and the doctor all hovering around waiting for me to deliver when we heard the unmistakable sound of the Doodlebug getting closer and closer and as it came nearer the engine stopped and we knew it was coming down .

I laugh now but I swear that was what pushed my baby out because there was no way I could of moved out that bed with the crown of the baby showing. God once again must have been on side that day because it should have been a direct hit but of course it missed us by a house. My luck was in but my next door

neighbour's was not and that I will never forget. My daughter Rosaline was born on the 23rd January 1945 but sadly died last year, but I always told her of her lucky escape that day,

I worked hard during the War working very long hours and work I might add that a man would have found hard. I lost all my teeth at 21 due to white lead poisoning and other conditions I had to work in, but despite the hardship and sadness of loss, I would not have missed it for a moment. We all have sad memories of all loved ones that were lost in those years but also happy memories.

Maisie Smith

This house I live in was the first one to be built here as before it was all fields here. My granddad had it built in 1893 for my mother to be born in and that was the year 1894 and ever since then the house has been bursting at the seams with family up till the last twelve years where I have lived here alone.

My name is Maisie Smith and my maiden name was Rowe and the house is in Thorncroft Road which is situated in Fratton, but it can be difficult to find because it's a corner house and the entrance into the house through the front door is in Guilford Road. But on the deeds it's definitely Thorncroft Road.

Looking back to when I was growing up we had a lovely time because we could play rounder s outside the house on the road due to the fact there were not many cars then and all the kids played out, and we could chalk up right across the road and only really had to get out of the way really when the horses came along. It was the Greengrocer, the Baker and shopkeepers like that who done deliveries with horse and cart and it was a really beautiful time.

I went to dancing and ballet a lot but my hobbies was in music because my mother was a music teacher and mother taught me when I was about seven years old, and I surprised everybody because I sat at the piano and played through the sheets of music and mother had to get up and get me some more sheets of music and then thought "Oh well, she do not need me."

My father was a singer and used to sing in the Guildhall with a microphone and had a really beautiful voice, and mother would play for my father to sing and she would move over and let me play for one and I was only seven, and that was on the stage also and that's how it continued up until I was about fifteen and my father bought me an accordion and with that I won a championship. It was the Southern County s Championship and got the Novices prize at the same time.

I then had my Accordion Band and did talks, and when I was nearly eighteen then came the World War Two. I had four in my band at that time and was still in the last year at school and because of the War I lost three of my band. Three were light Bomber Pilots and the other somewhere else and even today I still get upset because they were only in their twenties.

I remember the bombing but we were lucky because we only had the back ceiling down and the council came and put that right, and when it was really bad like a lot of people about six o'clock at night as it got dark we would go and stay with friends just over night.

Life really began for me in the War because me being an entertainer during it I spent a lot of time with GIs and in jeeps being taken about to places to play, and of course by that time I was married but it was so exciting playing the accordion to them all up there on front stage .

When I was twenty they came to see me to go to France, it was a Major that came and my mum and dad said "No" and I didn't really want to go, and thinking about it if I had of gone I probably would have been at Dunkirk with that lot at the start of the War so it was just as well I never went.

I did play all around them, ACK sites, all around here and really tried to play against all the noise of the guns, I did keep the troops' spirits up and enjoyed every minute of it. I married at twenty two and my husband also worked with the American GIs teaching them to build bridges at night in the dark, so when I went around he was busy doing that until I lost a baby, then I had a month off from the work and followed him around for a little while and stayed in the hotel with all the GIs which was quite exciting for me.

I will jump a bit and tell you that when the War finished I went into Band work mostly and played Saturday Nights but there was always an atmosphere being the only woman playing in the Band and I never really enjoyed it, but needed to be there for the money.

I also done all the clubs in Southsea on the piano, in the War people was so nice to each other and I worked for the Town Clerk then and up Mayfield Road was all the Deputies just in case the Guildhall went up, which it did so everyone was right away from it all which made it more of a pleasant job.

Life was so different then though people was different, and one of our deputies used to go out cycling with the boiler man, just a thing in those days you would do.

After the War though things changed, we started travelling around by train but never knew where we was or what station we was at because all the station names had been removed during the War, and that was done in case of an invasion, and even for my wedding I had to go with the bells because that would of meant invasion and yes, I would of loved to have had the bells ringing on my special day, still it wasn't to be thanks to the War.

Regards to clothes well, that too was coupons but my mother let me have her coupons and she poor sole made her dress out of curtain material and net curtain over it, but she was a dress maker so did a wonderful job so that's how I ended up with her coupons. In them days you would say I have to have some 'going away' shoes that of course was for the honeymoon and I was very lucky because a friend of mine gave me a pair because you just did not have the coupons' that's why she gave me a pair of hers so I could say I had a pair to go away in.

People today just don't know it was very strange the day when the War ended it was so nice to see the lads again and after all them years of darkness it was very nice.

My mother was still trying to get over the First World War when the second started. Mum was always crying over her people she had lost, but I did notice that when I was fifteen things started to improve, there was dances on 'til about one in the morning all these little church halls, my mum was only forty and this was the second War for her in twenty years, both very young because dad was only thirty eight which I think must have helped a bit.

I was saying how things had started to get better and I do remember going with my boyfriend and putting up the pictures and looking up seeing the search lights up on the planes crisscrossing practicing and I will always remember that but had no idea at fifteen that there was going to be a War. Such a shame because people had only just started being happy and laughing and getting over the losses from the First World War when the second came.

The 21st December I was born 1919, and I am bursting with memories.

Leading up to the War with my Accordion Band I used to play at Charlie Hurdles' and on the day he opened me and my band went around the town on this lorry we drove all round Portsmouth advertising the opening of Charlie Hurdles'. I must have been seventeen then, Charlie's was on the corner opposite Bransbury Park, it had a lovely little Ballroom there.

I married an Army Lieutenant and his home was where Dorothy Paget lived, she was a well-known horse woman. She had a big estate and my husband's father was the gardener, well he was the only one that was left during the War and we were right out deep in the country in the woods. We had the lodge there and what a beautiful place it was with beautiful gardens, that was my first marriage.

My second husband was a Royal Marine and I met him in the bar at South Parade Pier and we were together really for about fifty years, well we didn't quite make the fifty years before he died.

I must tell you about one of my shows with the Accordion Band I did, it was out in the middle of the Solent on one of the Forts and of course we had an Air Raid and the Dockyard would not let us come back in because it was Red Alert so we was stuck out there in an Air Raid, and I laugh now but not at the time and there we had to stay until the Dockyard would let us back in again.

Like everybody else we had an Air raid shelter in our garden, mind you it couldn't have been very safe if the house had collapsed on us but we didn't think about it because we were quite young and didn't imagine things then.

When the Air Raid was on and we were at the Dance Halls we never thought about it, and when Hilsea Barracks was there and I was sitting there waiting to do a show for the soldiers I said to the soldier, "And what are we sitting on then?" he said "Oh don't worry, its only shells, live ones!" which I cannot think of the name of at the moment but will do.

We never worried and same as the food, we didn't worry about our one rasher a week but the one thing I did like that you could get after the War was dried egg, it was lovely. But I tried whale meat and that was vile, I just could not eat it but we never had anything that was out of season so we didn't lose a lot. Now you just get strawberries in the winter but we never had a banana or anything like that but you didn't miss it either.

Just leading up to the War when I used to have my band practice indoors, and because then there was no television, people would sit all along on the garden walls listening and nobody grumbled.

There was another thing I just remembered was when I was in this great big army lorry, I had at that time a room out in Drayton just while the bombs were dropping everywhere I had a friend's room and this GI was sitting on this big lorry playing on his guitar playing 'You are my Sunshine' and my mum came to the door and said "Oh isn't that beautiful, oh I love it" and a man along the road came out and shouted to him "Shut that f...... row up!"

But there again you did have different people.

When I got home from work one day I got this call when I worked as the Town Clerk at Mayfield School. This call was from an Officer to do with Americans asking me to go to this party because this Colonel wanted me to go, and being naive I said "OK" because it was an English Officer that had telephoned and asked me, and being as I was married would be picked up, this American Sergeant about my dad's age came and got me in this jeep and must of thought of me like he would of his daughter I suppose, and he was very nice and when it got to about ten o'clock and couples started pairing off he came back in and said "Come on I am taking you back home" which I thought was strange because I was very naïve, and I think he could see what was going to happen at this party and again must have been thinking of his own daughter. He was in his forties and very handsome but he could see what was going to happen with all the drink flowing and people pairing off, he knew what was going to happen and me being so innocent did not, but home at ten I went.

I was very lucky we didn't lose any one in this War but my friend lost a brother, lots lost people if they were pilots. One of the men in my band went down with his submarine and lots got caught up and cut in half by our own boats, and I remembered him saying to me,

"I got this feeling this will be the last time I will see you" and I said,

"Don't be silly, you're too wicked to die." And at twenty six that what he was, I thought him quite old.

It was strange really because in the braver days when we were young we could just walk through the park and knew the bombs were around but you just did not seem to worry, and I know several houses around here went. And I can remember before I ever married I had a Naval boyfriend who went away to see and I never heard from him and his mother came up to Mayfield Road to me where I was working because he had three letters telling him that the house were destroyed and he had sent it further down the road where the houses had took a direct hit and were destroyed, and that was why he got the letters back again and that happened on the first day of the bombing where the Prince's Cinema where all the children was and killed.

He must have been very upset but of course I was alright as his mother saw and there was me thinking that because I had not heard from him he did not want me. When things were heading towards D Day for three days you could hear this continued noise of these lorries going along the hill nonstop, and then at night I used to do fire watch with my tin helmet and it was the very day of D Day and you would of thought it was going to be all hell let loose, but when I got back in the morning for some breakfast before having to go back again my father said to me "That Poor boy" (that Poor boy meaning my husband) "would be landing on the beaches over there." but what happened was the night before my husband, being an officer, had slipped out and we spent the night at the Regal Palace Hotel, and of course he couldn't tell me anything but he was going out on one of the boats that was bobbing up and down, but everything was secret but my cousin was a WREN up in Eisenhower the American place over the Hill when she got this phone call asking her, her name and she said, "It's Beryl, Ron" and she was my cousin and recognised his voice, had only been to Devon that week, she again said, "It's Beryl, Ron" but she could not tell me 'til after the War, and the times I would often say to her, "I wonder how Ron is, I wonder what he is doing?" and my cousin knew but could not tell me, but it must have been nice for him to have heard that familiar voice knowing he might not be here after the landing. But of course he did get my letter when he was on that beach telling him that I was expecting, I expect he thought "I got to get through this now."

I had a Canadian girlfriend during the War and she came over with her mother, father, brother who came to see the grandmother, and as soon as they got here because the War started they were stuck here for five years, and when they went back she, of course the Grandmother, by then was dead, then her father because he had heart trouble, and her brother died on the submarine, and she married this Canadian chap in the services here and had a baby here and they went back. It was just her and her mother, husband and the baby five years later because there was no ships to get them back.

Another thing I just thought about was along at the Strand in Southsea on the corner there was Speakers' Corner and they would hold concerts there and would have two great big furniture vans and one would be the stage and the other for dressing in, and we were very lucky because we were the first to have a microphone and they could hear us play the Accordion Band right up on the Pier, and hundreds of people would be up there. And I think I went out with the first ever DJ and up around the Band Stand, he used to put records on so they could dance around and when the shows finished on the pier he would get to pick what records he wanted, they were very old records but we used to have fun dancing around the Band Stand every Wednesday Night, and for us this was quite exciting in those days.

On one night, which was a very bad night, it was my father's night off and the air raid shelter at the top of Arundel Street took a direct hit and the other things I remember about that raid was on Fratton Road was that there was a lovely wool shop there run by twins, grown up twins, and unfortunately they took a hit to which was a terrible shame because not only were they nice but everyone who was expecting would go to their shop for their wool for knitting sets.

Another thing came to mind was when I had rooms at the bottom of Cornwall Road, not for long, but there was so many people living here in the house we needed space so moved into the room, but Palmer's Brush Factory was there then and one land mine went off and them things just didn't go into the ground and the shelter and everything around it went demolished just like that, and they would say when a land mine came down it was like a fluttering of silk, and the nights I was in the shelter I used to think "Oh my God, is that silk I can hear fluttering?" It left you with a funny feeling.

I remember when I was expecting my son, being at the top of our stairs there with my dad we saw one of them Doodlebugs and it cut out as we were looking out and dad saying "Come away from the window, come on, get away from the window." Yes, I remember them well.

It was high up in the sky and a man across from us would drive the air balloons around and they were made out of silk, and I remember we had what we called a bomb bag made out of it with all our documents in so as soon as the siren went off you would grab the bomb bag and take it out with you. Mum probably made my wedding dress out of it because it was very nice.

These houses are newer ones now and that big house along the road was three houses then and the man was called Gordon Brown that built them but now it's one big house.

On a Saturday night before I got married we would watch the Brown Shirts' March - it was Oswald Mosley and they would march along Commercial Road and then end speaking at the Speakers' Corner, I think that's what they were called the Brown Shirts. During the day we were dispersed from Mayfield Road and my father was called up because he was still young enough, and he went to work as a night telephonist at the GPO and was fire watching at the top of the GPO and was phoning the Guildhall telling them that the bombers was coming down and they never responded and the Guildhall went up. The Germans used to put like a circle of fairy lights around where they were going to bomb and this is what they did when they bombed the Guildhall.

I was a shorthand typist and would work for the committee clerks and would take notes for them and that was a nice job because they were away from the top ones, and the next time when I went to work private for a solicitor just after the War was totally different from the War.

Money has never meant anything to me because I never really had it and was lucky my granddad built this house with a bathroom and always we had two families living here, and of course all around us was the same but there just isn't the houses any more to go around. Everybody had tenants and people didn't get a house of their own 'til they were in their forties because they never had the money, and we were very lucky because my dad and granddad built the bathroom inside. But we never got rid of the one outside 'til my mum died, she always said she didn't like the inside toilet because it was dirty, not meaning it wasn't cleaned.

When I was a little girl Tuesday night we used to have to go over to Gosport to my dad's work and it was so exciting going on to the Gosport ferry, chug chug along and on the way throw money to the Mudlarks. And then 1952 the last day of the car ferry I went over to Gosport in my friend's Jeep to Lee Tower which is not there now, and it was quite exciting going over on the car ferry. I'm not sure if we were pulled with chains or what but it was lovely and so easy, I don't know why they stopped it really.

Just before the War there was big bands on South Parade Pier and it had a balcony then and you could walk right around the pier on it for one shilling, and it was really nice and some of the bands there which was the Squadronaires, and Joe Loss and people like that. And when the War came we would go to the Ambassador Ballroom up in Cosham and the bands used to play there. The Squadronaires used to play in their uniforms and the lovely bands would play the jive, and the GI s would throw us over their shoulders and we would have a real good time, and having been to the hospital one day had a walk along the High Street after forty years and thought, "Where are the Jeeps and GI s and the Ballroom?"

A memory away but still what memories I have.

Jenny Clark

This is Jenny Clark speaking and I would like to tell you what it was like for me in World War Two when I was a slip of a girl of sixteen. I worked for the chemist called Timothy Whites then which got bombed out on the 10th January, that was a Friday and on the Saturday I went along to Commercial Road and got a job in a shop called Evelyn's and got the job and started there on the Monday as a packer.

Evelyn's was a toy and paper shop and Mr Tremlett came running down to the shop one day and said to me "Quick Jenny, get up on to the roof as we are going to take your photograph and send it out to your boyfriend."

In my job I would get to pack all the toys ready for the Royal Marines and because of this I would get to go to all their ballroom dances which I loved because I was only fourteen then and this remember was before the War.

From Evelyn's at the age of nineteen I got called up and went into the A.T.S. and what we called ACK-ACK which was behind the guns and feeding the guns with ammunition which they would then fire on enemy planes. We moved so many times at one point, about a dozen times, and I was also moved over to Ireland which was classed as overseas in them days and I have a little book here that I have kept when I was in the A.T.S. because I had to put the dates down so my mum and dad would know where I was.

I went in to the A.T.S. on November 27th 1942, I then moved to Northampton on the 11th 1942 and on the 12th I moved to Oswald Street. On the first month of 1943 I was moved to Anglesey then on the March 1943 it was Scotland. When I say I, I mean the regiment moved, then it was Manchester 6th March, then Ireland on the April, then Bristol Aug 1943, then Weymouth October 1943, then Romford and Rowners Park for a night only, it went on and on. We were actually called a relief battery so people only stayed in

London for three weeks and then was moved to Epping Forest for at least three weeks rest because of the amount of work we had to do. There was no such thing when you went into the A.T.S. about it being a twenty four hour a day

because it was a thirty six hour a day and they made sure we worked the thirty six hours as well.

Let me take you back again to before I joined the forces.

I was born in Cottage View in Landport and there was five of us in the family, that was four girls and one boy and that meant five of us in the one bedroom three of us in the one big bed and two in the little bed which was a camp bed, and my brother had to sleep on the floor because there was no other room.

My father was in the Royal Navy and would be always away at sea for either over night or months at a time, and a two and a half year commission every time.

I went to Arundel Street School to start with then went on to Besant Road before going on to Omega Street. Before I left the Omega Street School I already had my job at Timothy Whites and when the War did start we knew all about it because myself and two sisters was going to work walking along Arundel Street and was machine gunned, and the pub in Arundel Street called the Claxton which kept the doors open, thank god because we would have to run all the way up the passage way with the green wall tiling, and if the council had not pulled the pub down the machine gun bullets would been seen today. Every shop and pub in Arundel Street would leave the doors open so the factory girls could run in when being machine gunned.

My boyfriend went away on my eighteenth birthday and came back when I was twenty three and we went and got married on a special licence and everybody in the street rallied around and gave me their ration coupons for cakes and everything else and once married within seven days he would be sent back abroad and me sent back to the Army.

I'm going to jump a bit here then go back because we both came out of the Army both invalids and was just used as gun fodder and that's all I can say about the Government in those days because he never got a pension and neither did I.

Going back again the food in the Army was terrible and the three to four years I spent in there I never had decent food but the one good thing I can say was that you did not get fat in them days and there was no fat people about we were all skinny.

When we came out and my husband came home we had two lovely children, a boy and a girl which I am very proud of and I went to Bournemouth to live but because we were both ill the climate there did not agree with me and if my husband had not got me out within the month I could have been dead so we came home to Portsmouth.

My mum and dad, as I said before, was in the navy and my mum was a great mum because dad was always away so mum brought us up on her own. My dad was in the First World War and was on the Cyclops and another ship that we thought was lost, but he came home and mum said when she had us kids "Thank god I only got one boy and all you girls." But of course two of the youngest got called up which was myself and my sister who were the youngest of the five.

Just before that I had just left school at the age of fourteen and just starting to enjoy life going out dancing up to the Pier and the Marine Barracks and the Naval Barracks with the Green Jackets, and of course the Army Barracks up at North End. Yes and I did really have a good time for two years before the War came on. I loved dancing and danced with every nation going I think that there was and went to every dance that was going, but then at eighteen it all stopped.

When I was working at Evelyn's I had to do fire duty in the War because of the bombs dropping and from there I more or less joined up to the Fire Brigade and was with everyone else that was digging out, and from there I got called up to go dig out the people from Arundel Street shelter because it took a direct hit, and we pulled out two young girlies that had laid on their babies and the mummies was dead but the babies were still alive and one ended up crippled, and I do know the names of them babies but I will not mention because that would not be fair on the family.

There would be big craters left by the bombs that had dropped and in Chandler Street when I was in an air raid shelter minding my two nieces they dropped a land mine and it blew the whole of the side of my sister's house off and of course you had to have a laugh or you would be for ever crying. And the day the side of her house got blown out all her clothes were left hanging outside and we were so lucky because my brother in law said "You hang on in there a bit with the kiddies" and of course he got blown back in where the bomb had gone off. We laugh now but at the time we didn't but he was still alive and so was he and we all laughed our heads off when we see all her clothes because the tree looked like a Christmas tree decorated by her washing.

We had rationing and nobody had chocolates or cigarettes and also clothes were on ration. Eggs you could only have if you were expecting a baby.

Everybody just pulled together. If you had your back against the wall we would all pull together and when the War was over we made our generation as it is today because we didn't want the kids to go without like we did, my kids had no chocolate or sweets or pocket money because wages was so small, my husband's wage was three pounds a week and by the time we paid for rooms that left us two pound a week to live on for the four of us and I wonder how many of you would do it today.

To get bedroom furniture together we would go down to Charlotte Street and the Charlotte Street boys would give us an Orange box and we would take it home, rub it down, clean it, paint it and polish it and that would do for a bedroom cabinet. And we also made, if we could get a big chest, a small wardrobe for the kiddies' clothes to hang in our little girl's bedroom but of course she would be lucky if she had many clothes to hang in it.

I laugh about it all now but let me take you back to the dancing. It was beautiful especially if you went to the Marine Dance, they would give a lovely Ball. Then I would go up to the Hilsea Barracks as I said before we were bombed, when we were in there dancing and because it was blackout you just could not see a thing, and of course I was running across the parade ground and fell down the crater and they could not find me because it had been pouring with rain, and of course laughing again now if anything happened it was always me getting into trouble.

When I got called up but at the end of the War I used to be a driver and drove great big lorries, small cars and the funniest bit was when I was called to drive on a long journey. My father always brought us up to have good manners and always drummed it in to me not to forget, he would say if I was going out, "Now don't forget Jenny, if you go in a car then the man has to step out and open the door for you" and the first time this came back to me was when I had to drive a Brigadier. I sat in the car and he said to me, "Have you forgot something my dear?" and I said, "No Sir, I have brought you to your position and destination you wanted" and he then said, "Well you now have to get out and open the door for me" and I said, "My father said if there was a gentleman in the car he would open the door for me so sorry Sir no."

And once again I became the laughing stock of my company in the Army when I went into the Officers' Mess but I didn't care a dam because there was a War on after all and as long as I got home to see my mum I couldn't of cared less about anybody only all of us.

When we came back to Portsmouth to live because we couldn't get a house to live we got a house in Deli Street which was beautiful houses and I don't care what anyone said I thought it was lovely, and all of us that had came back from the forces made our little sculleries into bathrooms. We also made our houses look as good as we could but the Council under their wisdom decided that they had not had enough bombing and decided on the mudflats with the little houses down there and all along Queen Street to flatten all the houses along and pulled the lot down. And if you had bought your house you only got what was ground rate so you could not afford to buy another house and therefore put us all into these council flats that they built, and that's why today you see people walking about with miserable faces instead of being in a house and having little smiles on their faces because they don't live in a nice house where they could talk to their neighbours because it's like a little prison living in a flat because you don't see a soul and have no communal room and its worse than being in the Army I would say.

Let me go back again to when I worked at Timothy Whites on a thirty hour a week and picked up a whole six shilling and sixpence a week and would take it home to my mum put in on the table and she would give me back two shilling, but by the time I had to pick it up she would take another shilling and that was for my winter shoes and coat so my other shilling was sixpence to go to the dance on the pier and if I was unlucky I would have to pay to go to the pictures, but if I was lucky I might of got somebody else to take me .

I could not afford stockings so it was the old black pencil out for the back of my legs for the black line to go up to make it look like a seam on stockings because I would have already of put the Bisto on to make them look brown just thinking I had a lovely pair of stockings on, and after the War I remember I bought some cami knickers and I had just met my new boyfriend and was going across Jacobs Ladder in Somers Town and what happened? the button broke and he said to me "Pick 'em up you silly b" and I put them in my pocket and all I hoped was that my father didn't come along and find my knickers in my pocket, but we did have a good laugh over it over the years. You had some fun in the War as well as the tragedy and if you didn't laugh you would have cried, and the motto was "get up dust, yourself down and get on" and have a good laugh and because that is the word in life laugh and everybody laughs with you and cry and the whole world will cry.

Cyril Jones

I lived at number eleven Lake Road which was then opposite the Salvation Army.

As a child of two and a half I noticed a man pushing his cart down to Charlotte Street that was full of rocks and me running out of the house and my sister who had noticed I was running out into the road with traffic coming down and the Tram coming, ran and pushed me forward and got caught into the cow catcher herself. Then I heard someone say "Get her to the hospital first" and looking down I saw what looked like a baker's van so to speak which took me to hospital as well, and my dear sister who was tending my very sick mother upstairs in the house.

Someone had ran into the shop and said "Mrs Jones! Mrs Jones! Your daughter and son has just got ran over by a Tram!" and with that my other sister went to run down the stairs from mum who she was tending and tripped and fell and the shock killed her. My mother passed away a few months later.

Because of illnesses like bronchitis I did not start school till I was five nearly six but did go to Church Street School 'til I was aged about nine, then I was transferred to Arundel Street School. At the age of nine though I sang on the Strand Theatre which was situated in Lake Road Portsmouth and this I did for charity. This I did for a young girl who worked in Woolworths who had a boyfriend who chucked Vitriol on her face after a terrible argument that scarred her face she was rushed to the Royal Hospital.

I remember a gentleman came into the shop to see my father, he was called Mr Horus Wheatley who was a Producer in Entertainment and asked my father who he knew very well if I would mind being trained and going on this Charity Show at the Grand Theatre which I did. He was a good friend of Bebe Daniels and Ben Lyon and I sung two songs which was the 'Last Round Up' and 'When I Grow Too Old Too Dream' and the proceeds went to the girl up at the hospital who I told you about previously.

My father's shop in Lake Road was a shellfish shop and he also had a stall along at Clarence Pier in a Brickwood's pub and was run by Mr Padbury where my sister Dorothy worked as did my other two sisters who also worked in pubs too, one worked in the Golden Fleece and the other in the Swan, both in Guildhall. My elder sister Phyllis worked in the pub in Regent Street along by Sultan Road for a short period that was another Brick wood pub.

My mother had ten children and it was very hard for her to bring us up. I remember her bathing us all in front of the fire one by one and when it came my turn I didn't like the water so when she held me in her arms it tired her out, so my sister Phyllis that passed away would take me from her. She then asked mother if she should have me but me being so small I screamed and mother took me back again.

Come the War years I think I was getting on ten and we had the Anderson Shelter put in and I would enjoy many a day playing with my tin soldiers on top by myself as my other two brothers by then had grown up.

I had three brothers, Ned who was a twin but sadly his twin died at birth, George and Jim. Jim was a boxer who used to box down the Connaught Drill Hall with all the boxers down there like Archie Hannon, Terry Lynch you name them and they was there all having a boxing tournament each night.

War broke out and I was due to go to the Prince's Theatre who at that time was showing Mr Wrong when it got bombed, I had already seen it about three times but pictures was that cheap in them days and this day it got bombed whatever changed my mind I now thank God that I did .

After a while as War went on I went down to Sussex in an apple packing shed with my sisters. In 1942 my sisters then left and went up to Litchfield where my would-be-wife was staying with the Fosters and I decided to quit my job and go with them and met my wife as I did when I was nine years old, but I jumped a bit then so will take you back .

I then got a job at the chemical works which was exempt from the Army, but this I did not know. I went into the iron foundry which was making grenades and then found that too heavy expecting to heave the heavy sacks and load the truck up, so left that one went to the Doctors to be excused but he said I couldn't because I had to go into one of either Army or the mines so I volunteered for the Royal Artillery. So there, if I stayed at the chemical plant I wouldn't have had to go services, so there I put me foot in it so to speak. So had no choice but to go back into the Army which I laugh about now.

In 1945 I married my dear wife Isabelle Norma Foster in October 9th and had a daughter on the 15th Oct 1946, we were married sixty years very happy but going back to the War, the bombing and the life we had was very tough and the first bombs to fall was the one that hit the Blue Anchor Pub in Kingston Crescent by North End, and this we watched from our air raid shelter and as time went on there was raids every night and fires would be raging and lucky for us we could go over to my father's place in Cowplain as he had eight acres of ground with a nice hut, and if we had been terrified at the bombing and was lucky enough to get a bus out of Portsmouth this is where we went to spent the night.

This particular night my sisters and brothers, when we lived in Arthur Street which was another property my dad had, was when the terrific bombing started we were going off to fathers hut and I remember hearing the Kimber's were killed by a bomb. Me and father at this time was staying at Auntie's house in Jubilee Road Cowplain had to walk from there to the top of the hill hoping to get back into Portsmouth but the sky was red with the raging of the fires and we was not allowed to go any further than the top of the hill and watching it was terrifying, and had to walk back to Jubilee Road and listened to the raid going on till early hours of the morning. And then we managed to get a lift from a gentleman to the top of the hill then we caught the bus back down to Buckland where the fire was raging and where my brother was helping at the Stewart Pump to put out the fires.

My sister who worked at the Swan was under the Pearl Building and it was the Landport Drapery that had got bombed and luckily enough survived. The things I have seen I will never forget, bits of bodies being thrown across the road when I went round to Sultan Road to my other sister where she lived, they had dropped a land mine and a horse and everything and people were just lying there, it was awful and it's so difficult to explain the sights I have seen and believe you me I have seen many and never wish to see them again.

The law in them days was very harsh and either you respected it or people of the law and if you see a Policeman you respected them and if you did no wrong you was alright, but I remember seeing a sailor frog-marched down Queen Street by six naval Provosts to the Guildhall and no doubt charged and thrown inside.

You did have your good times though, at Christmas we would cut out decorations for Christmas and hope Father Christmas would come along but the only stocking I had or rather in it was an orange, a shiny penny, no doubt a King Arthur or someone, peanuts, apple, orange and a banana and maybe a comic if I was lucky. But I will say this you were far happier in them days than you are today.

Going back to my school days we had a musical teacher there called Mr Parrot and in them days you done as told or you would get the cane, and he would fetch us in for an hour of singing every morning and would have a big brown paper folder and each one had a song on it, and his favourite one was 'When I was Walking to Strawberry Fair' and he would thrash the cane at the blackboard and would start with him tapping the board with the 'Strawberry Fare' which we all knew off by heart.

> "As I was a walking on to the Strawberry Fair
> Singing fido fido monkey doodle dee"

He would look and then shout at them, you didn't open your mouth then they got the cane for not singing

> "Doodle ildo
> I saw a fair maiden with gold in her hair fiddle dee
> Her eyes was blue and gold in her hair
> As I went walking on to Strawberry Fair
> Fido fido monkey doodle ildo
> Fido fido monkey doodle Dee."

Before that song had finished he would slap that cane down and shout "Come out here!" to someone and as I laugh now I remember his mouth being wide open and I think that is how I learned my singing that way.

We were taught to sing 'Doe Ra Me Fa So' and we appreciated that a lot because it did help me to sing and enjoy it.

Going back to 1935 when I was nine years old, I was rushed into The Royal Hospital that stood proud top end of Commercial Road with acute appendicitis. Lucky for me I got over that and as all eight of us did was able to go and help dad in the shellfish shop he owned as I said before in Lake Road, we cooked all the shellfish in the back of the shop as well as live up above the shop, I think I said we had a stall on Clarence Pier and dad's brother J Jones had a shop in Charlotte Street.

We were a very musical family and I told you about the customer who was friends with Bebe Daniels and Ben Lyons who were a very popular musical hall act who later had a very popular radio show and got me singing at the Strand Theatre and the whole show was transmitted to the Royal Hospital for the patients to listen to on the ear phones.

I remember so vividly and will never forget the day a German fighter pilot opened fire on me, I heard this plane when I was between Smart's the ladies shop and Beaumont's that was opposite the Royal when the plane came swooping down and opened fire, boy did I run. I first took shelter under Beaumont's shop front and when I thought it clear ran to the top of Dickens Road and into Manners Road and I remembered the sweet shop on the corner where an alley way lead into Arthur Street. While running through the plane came swooping again and one bullet hit the side of the alleyway and ricocheted into the stone path which was made up of old diamond shape stable bricks, god what a sound that made, and a again I thought thank God I made it back to the shelter and when the all clear came I went back to the alley way to retrieve the bullet and found it was bent and showing the lead inside. Thirteen then I was - phew I wouldn't like that to happen again.

I remember a lovely street party that we had in Cosham Street that was opposite the Salvation Army in Lake Road, lovely time we had.

My cousin worked on the railway, she was one of the war time team train cleaners who worked day and night through the Blitz, climbing on top of the railway carriages in all weathers to make sure the tanks were full of water so the toilets and wash basins always had water, she said it was very hard work.

"When the troops had to go overseas us railway girls would put some coppers in a kitty to buy cigarettes for them and always tried to wave them off with a smile" she said because they knew a lot of them would not return, and she said about the children with their gas mask tied around there necks being evacuated from her station.

My parents' names were MaryAnn and my father was Arthur Jones.

Sadly out of us ten only two of now remain and our Ned is now a young man of Ninety and of course my good self.

So many different memories spring to mind.

Phyllis Maple

My cousin Phyllis Maple remembers war-torn Britain well and said Richard Blackman was the foreman when she worked at Portsmouth Railway Station. I am sure I will not be the only one to remember him as he was a very kind man and always had kind words for everyone.

She told me she worked day and night through the blitz and remembers having to climb on top of the railway carriages in all weathers to fill the water tanks so the toilets and wash basins always had a good supply and she said it was a very hard tough job.

Phyllis told me of the Dieppe raid when a Red Cross van caught fire after taking a hit.

We got to know all the regulars and we loved the children, they used to be evacuated from our station, bless them with their little gas masks.

Southsea woman talks of Blitz

"Smitten City," the television programme which featured the 1941 blitzes on Portsmouth, had News reader Mrs. Phyllis Maple turning out her war-time photographs.

"One of the people in the programme was Mr. Richard Blackman, foreman at Portsmouth Railway Station during the raids," said Mrs. Maple.

"I am sure I am not the only person to remember him and the kindly words he had for everyone. I was one of the war-time team of train cleaners at the station."

Mrs. Maple (pictured right), of Stansted Road, Southsea, well remembers those days of war-torn Portsmouth.

"We worked day and night through the blitz, climbing on top of railway carriages in all weathers to fill water tanks, so toilets and wash basins always had a supply. It was a hard, tough job.

"When the troops had to go overseas, we railway girls would put some coppers in the kitty to buy cigarettes for them. We always tried to wave them off with a smile — bless their hearts — because we knew not all would come back to the station."

Mrs. Maple remembers that, at the time of the Dieppe raid, a Red Cross van caught fire after being hit.

"We got to know lots of the regulars, and we loved the children — they used to be evacuated from our station and always went off carrying their little gas masks.

"Maybe some of the other girls in the photograph will recognize me and themselves and perhaps get in touch."

Phyllis was featured in an article from The News

Yvette Myriam Pearsey (nee da Gama)

I was born in 1923 in British India, an area known as The North West Frontier Province. I was born in Murree Hills in the foothills of the Himalayas and my father was a Doctor in the British Army. He was of Portuguese origin and my mother was French, born and bred in the north of France. The First World War had brought them together; my father had been sent to France by the Army and they were married in Boulogne in 1920.

My mother came to live in India and she loved that country. My only sister was born seven years later in Southern India. When I was nine years old I was sent to a boarding school, to a French convent in the Nilgiri Hills. The place was near to Ooty, a famous summer holiday resort known to many British people who came there to escape the heat of the Plains! I learned English and continued with my French with the nuns.

148

When my father was posted to Central India I was sent to another convent in Nagpur, closer to where my parents lived, in Ahmednagar. I soon made new friends and enjoyed life as a boarder. My third boarding school was in the Western Ghats, that high range of hills in western India 70 miles from Poona and 180 miles from Bombay. The Station was called Panchgani and it was home to 11 schools. I was first a pupil in St Joseph's Convent and in the years

to come I taught in the Convent; then in the Church of England Girls' School called Kimmins and was a teacher at St Peter's C of E Boys' High School! Incidentally, St Peter's was the school in which Freddie Mercury of the band "Queen" was to be educated years later, after I had left and come to England . There is a reunion every two years in the Bombay Brassiere in London of former pupils and staff of these three schools in Panchgani - the numbers from my generation are now dwindling, alas! But the new members are young girls and boys who are sent back from the UK to India to Panchgani for their education, and having heard of the Panchgani Reunion have been attending this joyful social event.

The Second World War started in September 1939 when I was in Karachi having enrolled in D.J. Sind University. I had completed my studies in French, English, History, Geography, Maths, Hygiene and Physiology, and passed my Junior, Senior and Higher Cambridge exams by the age of 15 years. I had the advantage of speaking French and English, and I loved learning for the sake of knowledge. I added Business and Commercial Studies including Pitman's Shorthand and Typing to my university course.

My father was sent to Iraq (Mesopotamia) in September 1939 and we little thought France would fall to the Germans in May 1940. When this happened my mother was completely cut off from her dear family and she was devastated. I wanted to look for a job in Bombay; my sister had met some boarders from Panchgani Convent and was happy to go there with them. I would be graduating at Christmas, so we decided my mother should go up to Panchgani and we would rent a house for her and Gislaine, my sister.

I looked for adverts for employment in the "Times of India" and saw that the French Consulate was seeking a secretary preferably bi-lingual, English-French. I travelled down to Bombay and had an interview with Mr Papousamy, the Consul; he offered me the post! He was a kind man and the pay was good, but I worked in a big room, on my own, translating letters all day, English into French and vice versa, then typing them out. I had learnt touch typing on the "QWERTY" machine but when I had to use the French "SDFGA" I made an awful mess of the letters! I soon discarded the French machine but had lost my 'touch' knowledge. When I received a telegram from my former Headmistress Sister Mary Alban offering me a post as a French and Geography Teacher in the convent my mother was overjoyed – she would have her two daughters close by. Sister Mary Alban offered me 100 rupees pay per month plus my sister's board and tuition free; 150 rupees per month. I didn't like to tell her that I was earning 450 rupees at the Consulate because the money would not compensate for the boredom!

Panchgani is a picturesque Hill Station, beautiful walks, breath-taking views down into the valleys below from the heights to Tableland! Ideal for elderly holiday makers. But there were <u>no cinemas</u>, <u>no cafes</u>, <u>no dance halls</u>; there <u>were</u> male teachers in St Peter's School but they were all either married or engaged! We played cards and indoor tennis but thought of the Tea Dances in Bombay, at Green's Hotel or at the Taj.

This photo shows Yvette in Panchgani in 1941 looking down into the 'Devil's Kitchen'; a big hole in the ground where a massive rock had fallen and rolled down the plain killing several people at a wedding in the valley.

The war with Japan had started up but in Panchgani there was no evidence of it. One evening a teacher friend, Joy Walker, and I were on our usual walk in the Hills, talking as we always did, of our families, when suddenly Joy said quietly "Gama, don't turn round! We are being followed!" My blood ran cold. We must have disturbed the home of panthers and they had cubs. They only attacked people if their cubs were in danger. Then Joy said "We will both turn around together, when I say 'TURN'" – and she said "TURN" and we swung around. I couldn't believe my eyes! We were facing two khaki-clad British soldiers who looked as bewildered as we were! The only regiments we knew were stationed in Poona or in Bombay, and in barracks!

We were to learn that a unit from their regiment was in Mahableshwar in training for jungle warfare. They were camped in the jungle and didn't think there were other people around in the jungle. We could see that they had no knowledge of India, as they didn't know at which country their boat had docked! We told them we were teachers in a Hill Station not far from Mahableshwar where the jungles were, about a mile away from us in Panchgani. We showed them the way to the road from which they had strayed, pointed them in the right direction- they had to look at the setting sun and that was 'west' etc. etc. They came from London, they said, and one of them asked Joy "Where <u>was</u> you during the Jubilee?" We guessed he meant King George the Fifth's Silver Jubilee about seven years before. We thought their English was strange – but they were young, maybe as young as Joy and I were, and they had left family behind. Anyway, we watched them walk on the right road, back to their jungle camp, and Joy and I rushed to our teachers' quarters, a huge house called Mount Echo, to break our news to the others. It so happened our Head Mistress, Sister Mary Alban, was visiting so she too heard our news.

"These men have left UK to come and fight for you" she said. "We must do something to entertain them!" (I must say here that my generation was naïve) We discussed various distractions; tea dances, opening a café and putting on concerts. It was decided to put on the play "Peter Pan" and invite the whole regiment to come and watch it. Rehearsals began that Monday. My sister, who was a good little actress, was Peter Pan. We would get help from the regiment to fit harnesses on the Darling children and Peter Pan and teach them to fly.

Excitement built up in the school. Even our Headmistress asked if she could be in charge of Tinkerbell! The fairy would be tied to the end of a broomstick with a long elastic, and dangled over a screen and made to dance by Sister Mary Alban. A doll was produced and became Tinkerbell. A letter was sent to the Commanding Officer of the unit, inviting him, his officers and all the men to the play.

Came the big night! We had borrowed chairs and benches from St Peter's and Kimmins High School, and the Hindu Boys' School 'til we were sure everyone would have a seat. The soldiers poured, literally, into our Assembly Hall, ushered by our Prefects. We, the staff, were busy behind the scenes getting the cast ready. Then came that moment we had sort of dreaded … Tinkerbell, the fairy, was dying as no one believed in her, and I heard my sister's voice pleading, with a break in her voice, "Please, please say you believe in fairies? Say 'Yes – yes'". We held our breath, there was a moment's silence and a split second and then came that shout, that collective shout:

"YES, YES WE BELIEVE – YES, YES WE BELIEVE IN FAIRIES"

The hall shook as the shout echoed and re-echoed. These grown up, hard-bitten soldiers were not going to let down the children! Then Tinkerbell, held aloft at the end of an elastic, began jiggling about!! Our Sister Mary Alban, our dear Sister Superior was doing her bit with gusto! We were laughing and crying – and so were many of the men who were probably thinking of their own children.

These units would do their training and leave for Burma, and new units would follow. St Peter's and Kimmins High School followed suit and organised fairs and football and hickey matches, and more plays. But I will never forget "Peter Pan"!

There was one unit, trained in Mahableshwar, who were ambushed at Kohima, in Burma, and not a single man survived. There is a big stone monument in Kohima in their memory, which reads;

WHEN YOU GO HOME

REMEMBER US AND SAY

WE GAVE OUR TOMORROW

FOR <u>YOUR</u> TODAY

As the war progressed, more and more of us young teachers were leaving the profession to enlist in the forces. I, too, left teaching, which I had enjoyed, but I was drawn to doing something "for the war effort". Many of my friends were joining the W.A.F.I. (Women's Auxiliary Force India) so I went down to Bombay to enlist, early in December 1942. I was allocated to the Censor Department. We wore a Khaki uniform and a green beret. It so happened that the Parachute Regiments wore green berets too and were called 'The Airborne Commandos', or the 'Green Berets'. We were called the 'Chairborne Commandos'! Another name we had was because someone asked our girls "Are you from E.N.S.A. (the Entertainments National Services Association)?" and the girls answered "No, we are from CENSA".

Our job was interesting – we were each given a pile of letters from one unit in Burma and at the end of the day we had to write a summary on the state of the morale of <u>that</u> unit and specify complaints made by two, three or more men of the same problem. I would like to think that our summaries were taken seriously by 'Upstairs'; that is the name we gave to the faceless persons to whom we would send our summaries; and something would be done to alleviate the problems of these brave men.

When we were being trained for our work, we were given <u>strict</u> instructions <u>not</u> to open any enclosures we found in the letters 'til we had <u>first</u> read the letter. Whatever was in the enclosure, unless it was revealing <u>where</u> the unit was stationed, had to be re-enclosed and sent on to the recipient. One day, there was a piercing, hysterical cry from one of our young girls. We rushed to her chair to see what could have produced this reaction. With shaking fingers she pointed to an open enclosure, stammering "I tasted it- I tasted it!!" Then, she had read the letter. The sender wrote "I am truly sorry; I could only save some of John's ashes, which I am sending to you"!

Many a time there would be small packets of chewing gum with "3 for you, 1 for the Censor" and there would indeed be four packets. We never accepted this gift. We would also record the 'enclosures' in a big book, and whether we had destroyed them or sent them on.

The war in Japan ended 14th August 1945 and the Censor Department had another job to do. We were sent bags and bags of mail that had not been delivered to the British prisoners in the hands of the Japanese. They were postcards containing not more than 15 words. It was heart-breaking – for years these cards had not been sent to the men! Obviously many of the writers had given up hope and thought the men were dead. We had to sort them into tragic piles under their names. Then we heard that the prisoners of war from Burma and Japan were returning to UK via India. Our Head of Department asked for volunteers to meet them from the boat which would dock in Madras on the east coast; we were given talks about what to say – I cannot even remember what the talks were about because we didn't expect to see what we saw.

Many of our Censor Department colleagues had to leave the office as their husbands were returning from the different theatres of war. There were about 12 of us volunteering to go to Madras. We knew there would be volunteers from the Q.A. nurses; St John's Ambulance; Red Cross; the Salvation Army and church leaders and other kinds of societies – which there were. We waited at the quayside and watched this Royal Navy boat docking. We waited for what seemed a long time but wasn't really. Down the gangway came the first stretcher surrounded by two or three nurses and then we saw the first living skeleton, his gaunt eyes staring into space, expressionless. The silence that greeted the first stretcher case was palpable. These men were the real victims of the war. Allowed to live, but only just. We had been told to expect men who had had no human contact and had probably lost the power of speech. We were told that Japanese culture was different from ours. To the Japanese 'Death' is an honourable way out, so they would not confer this honour to their prisoners. They would allow these men to starve slowly to death. It was true that there was a great lack of food in the whole country and that was one of the reasons they had capitulated. We needn't have Atom-bombed Hiroshima or Nagasaki. We should have left them to die of starvation.

Yes, we were told these things but we still couldn't believe what we saw – I didn't count the number of stretchers – and what can you say to a man who has faced such horrors? "Are you glad to be free at last?" or "Are you happy you are going to see your wife?" Probably that wife had given up hope of ever seeing her husband again and had possibly married again? The religious leaders had the task of preparing these men to face there problems.

We became tongue-tied. Not only that, we couldn't approach these stretchers – we stood there, trying to smile at them and they wondered what on earth were we girls doing there? Even now my eyes fill with tears when I remember. War brings out the inhumanity in man towards his fellow humans. I think of the camps of Jews in Germany and Poland; the same inhumanity was rife in the West as in the East.

We realised we would never really get a chance to talk to these poor men. They had so many other people trying to talk to them. We were all silent; I tried to reach out and touch the clasped hand of one of these men. I wanted him to know my heart was bleeding for him.

I often thing of them and wonder what life had in store for them.

The war in Europe ended on 8th May 1945 and my mother sent a telegram immediately to France. It took her two or three days before she got a reply: "Maman, morte avril '45", "Tout le monde sauf." My dearest grandmother had died in April – a month before the war ended! True, she was in her 80s. The rest of the family were alive. The details were to follow, first by mail and then by word of mouth when we came to England. My Aunt Helen was in a Detention Camp in Belgium, and her husband, Uncle Paul, had been sent to Germany, also to a Detention Camp. My cousin Yvonne in her 30s had married an English Airforce man who came from Portsmouth. His name was Jack Diamond. He and a mate had taken a wrong turning to get to Dunkirk Beach and had hidden in a field of a French farmer all day. The farmer knew someone was hiding in his field. He only knew one word of English, which was "English", and waited until dark to go out to the spot where he knew they were hiding and said "English? English?" They shot up and he motioned them not to talk and squat down again. He walked into Boulogne where my cousin Yvonne lived with her parents and asked her to take these Englishmen off his hands as the Germans came every day to inspect his farm for food. Yvonne went with the farmer at midnight and as she spoke some English she managed to bring them unseen to her house. They hid the men in their attic and shared their meagre rations with them. To cut a long story short, they were led by Yvonne on foot from village to village to Free France. Yvonne and Jack had fallen in love, had two sons and when the war was over they went into Spain and returned to Portsmouth. Another two sons were born, I'm not sure where – in Free France or in Portsmouth. When my parents came to England they could only enter if they had an address and someone to vouch for them. They came in January 1948 and stayed with Yvonne and Jack and their little family of four boys. The house was small so my parents went house-hunting and found a house in Queens Road not far from Yvonne's in Lynn Road.

Meanwhile I had married my first husband Peter Smith in 1946 and my daughter was born in 1947. I came to England in January 1949 and stayed with my parents. I had a legal separation from Peter Smith as our marriage had not worked out. I married my second husband Brian Pearcey in April 1969 and we had a very happy marriage for 38 years. I was and am still heart-broken now that he has died. He died in October 2007.

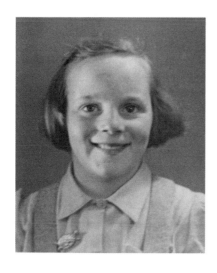

"You got over it in the end"

Doris Leggett

I was born in Commercial Road in Portsmouth but because of my father's work we had to move away and I did not return to Portsmouth 'til I was twelve. We then lived in Brompton Road in Mile End and my school then was Church Street with my two brothers.

Once I left school I went to work for Sara Harrington's which was a lampshade factory which was situated in Hay Street Portsea but is now known as Beck Street.

I then met my wonderful husband and married and went to live with my in-laws and what they done was asked me to stay for two years because if I did they then got rid of some of their furniture, that way they would not have to lose their son and in the end I stayed like twenty two.

We had not been married long before War was declared and the first raid I can remember was July the 11th because it was my husband's birthday and a girl I had been working with had called in to see me, and I said to her stop have a cuppa tea as its Eddies birthday and Eddie had already gone round to the first aid post.

I was asking after the girls we had worked with and I remember asking how Nesta was and she told me she was an Ambulance driver at the Penhale Road post and as she said if the warning siren went off and I said, "I must go down to the shelter" and the dog kept barking as we went down.

My father in-law was quite a genius. He had put a record on and it was a Salvation Army Record and the band was playing 'In the Firing Line' and at that moment the bomb had hit Drayton Road Post and Nesta my friend was killed. When we were at work she would say to me, "Tell me what Eddie tells you about driving and I can practice in the garage. That way I will be more knowledgeable when dad takes me out." But that morning she was killed and only recognised by her ring and her watch.

The Blue Anchor at Kingston Crescent took a direct hit and my bother saw the Policeman that had been on point duty because he was a messenger and it was not very nice for him. The Drayton Road Post was the school and after being hit it went out of the town that way.

The warning went off about six or seven and we went to the cellar and my father-in-law said "We got a bomb upstairs Doris" and at that time we always kept a bucket of water on the stairs in case of emergency along with earth, and he threw the earth on my dining room table into the doorway to the two rooms as it was ablaze there like a torch twelve inches high and around the same wide. We had our tin hats on still so he threw the earth and I said "Should I throw the water?" and he said "Go on" and both at the same time threw and my water hit him and nearly pushed him down the stairs.

There was a quiet spell for a bit and I was worried about my parents in Brompton Road and my father-in-law said "We will all go together" so we went and got to the end of Besant Road, it felt all squashy and soft under foot like a cushion and a warning went off so we retraced our steps and all of a sudden the shelter there took a direct hit in the school in Besant Road killing so many.

The fireman had come to our house a short while after and told us there was thirty major fires and at the end of the road the shelter should have held fifty but had over seventy that night with just one survivor who was brought out with a broken back and died on the way to hospital, but a baby survived.

My brother told me he had walked through Baker and Church Street and through to Besant Road and only had dim torches but on the corner was Samuel Knights Bakery on the corner and they saw a leg and an arm hanging from the window so they came and stayed with us in the shelter 'til the all clear came. It was a night you would never forget the sky was blood red and the majority of the people that night went out of the town and slept on the hill and the next night, but we were lucky to have got ourselves into the Devlin Hall in Purbrook and slept on the platform there with lots of other people.

I remember one day we were down in the little room down by the cellar where the coal was shoved, my brother made four bunks down there so we could sleep down there and this night suddenly the door flew open, the shutter came down, the pots flew off the shelves and we had a job to get out and we were worried about father-in-law as he came in and said,

"I was in the Coliseum I was in the circle and didn't feel anything but when I came out and walked along Arundel Street and looked back the devastation was dreadful."

One Monday I was in the house on my own but had always been told to go down the shelter as soon as, which then was an Anderson Shelter beneath the Co-op wall, it was a tall wall and me and my little dog with my tin helmet on went down and in there we had an armchair so I crouched behind that cuddling my little dog and was singing hymns at the top of my voice and I thought I was the only person alive in Portsmouth. But had I stepped out I would have seen the houses was still standing and after my neighbour s heard said I must not go into the shelter again alone, I was to go in to theirs with them.

My father-in-law was an insurance agent at that time and cycled all over the town and of course he was always out on the bike and looked in the shelter and oh how thankful I was to see him. I asked where Eddie was as I knew where he should have gone had been bombed but Eddie didn't go there, he must have come back and put his clothes on and gone round to his post in Penhale Road, the school there.

I will tell you an unusual sight. There had been some damage round that way with the bombing and I went round the school and an ambulance had been blown upside down and just like it had been posted through a back bedroom window.

Houses were damaged everywhere and a relief had the baby in the cot in the front room and the baby was covered in glass but he was fine thank god, I was lucky I didn't lose any family.

My friend lost a work mate from McIlroy's in the Besant Road shelter.

We are Salvationist and they used to have a house in Alexander Road and this night this woman wished her husband didn't have to go fire watching and he was standing beneath the British Home Stores talking to two young girls and pushed them out the way and lost his own life .

Saturday afternoon Blitz was in 1940 and I was in the town for that and it was in the August. I did go out of the town after the big Blitz on January the 10th to the country and my mother-in-law used to go to little restaurants and have a cup of tea, my father in-law and my husband was delivering bread to a restaurant and my mother-in-law had just heard the news about our Major from the Salvation Army and stormed into this Restaurant to say "Harry the Major is dead."

D Day we would have to go round to the main road to the shelter, and by then I had a baby Marilyn who was rolled up in a dressing gown and a dog who was tied to my husband's leg, and we went to the shelter and the soldiers were in there and they were waiting to cross over and Horndean Road was packed with lorries and men just lying all over the pavement, even taking the dog for a walk for something else because he would want to get near the soldiers lying on the pavements and even in the gutters and it was dreadful to see them go and we would wonder if they were going to come back .

Some of them would come over to the Girl Guide hut and ask if we could sew a button on or cook, me in my early twenties stood and cooked a pile of bacon about six inches high or even more than that. We had two tents then in the grounds and one outside but Keydale Lodge had a good name with the treatment of the soldiers which was told to me by the girl who was looking after the big house and worked for Heath the milk people, but she was in the Land Army and her boss in the Navy.

I was sort of living in this Guide Hut at Lovedean when D Day was announced and we heard the War all night long when the planes were going over. When the War was over we went back to our flat in the town and at the end every one amalgamated in Guildhall.

Going back to January 10th when we were walking around the streets we saw the Fratton Hotel ablaze on the bridge and a doctor's house in Somers Road and that's when we knew we had to get home because the city was ablaze and the Guildhall, and as I said before the fireman said thirty nine blazes and we have not got any water and that is when we decided to go see my parents in Brompton Road and went home.

I also told you how my brother worked for the bakery but didn't tell you how he had to get all the vans up to Alexander Park as fast as he could which he told me after.

Our Major was Mrs Woods who was a Major in her own right whose husband was in the fire watch who lost his life that night at the British Home Stores I mentioned earlier, she did carry on for a few more months then dedicated my daughter in the junior hall in Lake Road because the main hall had been blitzed.

The War was terrible but you got over it in the end and went back to as normal life as you could.

We are still Salvationist today.

Pam Webb

My family life was very happy my sister myself and my mother lived in Nelson Ave in North End. My father was in the Merchant Navy and often away and on these occasions it was mum who had to play the role of both parents and it was not easy on her because sometimes I was very naughty and of course in them days we got a good hiding if naughty but my mother did give us a very good home life.

Everything in our lives was very happy till the War started then it all changed. We went to Gladys Avenue School in North End and it was from there arrangements were made to evacuate us children out of Portsmouth.

I can clearly remember being giving my gas mask and having it fitted on me and I must say I hated that they were horrible things stuck all over your face but of course we had to wear them. From there on we had to carry these Gas Mask cases over our heads where ever we went at all times.

Then the time came when it was decided that we had to be evacuated, and I don't think for as long as I live my mother standing on the station waving goodbye when it did occur with tears falling down her cheeks with me and my sister both crying but there was nothing we could do about it because we had to go.

Eventually we ended up in Eastleigh and disembarked from the train and all us children with our gas mask boxes slung round our heads on our shoulders were led into this big Drill Hall where all these people came and select and take the children away.

It was very frightening for us children not knowing what was happening to us because it was almost like a slave market really.

Slowly all these other children were taken away and there was only Jacky and me left in this big Drill Hall holding one another's hands absolutely scared of what was to come because nobody wanted us, and this was because my mother refused to have us separated and she stipulated that where ever we went we had to be together.

A lady then came in who didn't really want to have evacuees but was told she had to because she had the room, well she did take us away. So we went back to this lady's house and our first night there was horrific for us because we missed our mum so much and I could not forget standing in that Drill Hall crying with Jacky clinging to me .

No cuddle or kiss to go to bed with before we went to sleep.

The next morning this woman said, "Your job in the mornings will be for you to do the washing up before you go to school" so of course that became my job every morning. If anyone was late because of breakfast then when they got to school then they got the cane, and because I was nearly always late it was me who got it but this woman did not care about that.

From then on things just started to get worse, we ended up cleaning windows, bedrooms, the whole house, Jacky and I was like little unpaid servants.

Sorry but it is still quite painful for me to remember this but it must all be recorded so not forgotten what us children of the War had to endure as well as the bombing.

Jacky lost a lot of weight and myself because this woman did not feed us properly and there were a couple of times she put dinner up in front of us and it would be crawling with maggots and I looked up and said, "I am not going to eat that" and she said to us "Well I will put it up in front of you till you do." It was horrific and till the day I die I do not and will not ever look at a maggot again. How can one human being do that to a child, I suppose it was because she was forced to have us but didn't want us.

That became our life while there, two little servants and of course would get a good hiding but at least it was not sexual only physical. That episode in my young life made me what I am today, bolshie and fight for what I believe in.

After we had been there for about a year my mother had noticed that I and Jacky had lost an awful lot of weight, she could not get to see us very often because she had a very important job in the Admiralty and asked the lady why we had lost so much weight and of course that is when I stood up very bravely and when you think about it, I was being very brave telling mum because the woman could of taken it out on us when mum went, but tell mum I did all about the maggots and the lack of food and how I would sneak down to the larder and take a little slither of cake and share it with Jacky because we were always so hungry and anything else there in the larder I thought I could take and not be missed I would take .

After I told mum all what was going on she immediately packed our clothes and took us away. Luckily we had a very supportive family, aunts and uncles etc. and we were allowed to stay with them for a little while.

That was in Portsmouth but of course we had to get out so mum in her great wisdom, or so she thought at the time, sent us to the Convent in Alton. That was like jumping out of the frying pan into the fire because it was a dammed sight worse than the first place.

We slept in dormitories and because I wet the bed every night because I was home sick and hated it in there, it was all polished and austere and not homely and out of all the nuns there, there was only the one that was kind and really lovely and that was Sister Madeleine and she was really beautiful inside and outside.

But the Mother Superior was a disciplinarian and of course as much as I tried not to night after night I wet the bed and in the end they used to put me down in the cellar with a bar of soap and make me wash the sheets. Can you image I was only a little girl with a bar of soap left to wash a great big sheet and it was dark and very damp down there as well, but that's what I was made to do every single morning with a bar of soap, wash the sheet and of course the very night after washing the sheet I would wet the bed again.

I think because I had it on my mind before I went to sleep worrying I would do it again.

It was a Roman Catholic Convent and we were Church of England but still had to go to church and wanted mum to change our religion but of course she would not. Monday, Wednesday and Friday we went to church three times a day and Sunday to a little girl seemed like all day and we had to endure all these old men, well to us they were spouting a load of rubbish we did not understand.

The one thing I do want to say though is that we had the most wonderful education because there was only twelve of us in a class not like today.

But of course there was no love there at all, we didn't get none in the other place but this one was a darn sight worse, I don't know what happened but I told you mum was high up in the Admiralty and we had to move from London back down to Portsmouth but before that I passed my exams in the Convent then I went on to pass the Civil Service Exam and went to work at the Admiralty with mum as I was near or sixteen by then but it was so boring.

We had to leave Jacky behind in the Convent because Portsmouth was being bombed.

We came home from work and there was a bundle of clothes in the doorway and when I moved them it was Jacky beneath them asleep and there were tears still rolling down her cheeks and she had a half-eaten bun clutched in her hand because she had run away from the Convent. She could not stand it without me being there looking after her. I have buried a lot of my memories so don't ask how she got from London back to Portsmouth back living with her family because I honestly don't remember.

Going back to the first lady in Eastleigh, she had a son and he was learning how to play the accordion and every night we were made to sit and listen to him practicing and it was horrific, we were never allowed to go out to play whilst there or play with other children we just had to sit there and listen to him.

I must say ever since then I hate the accordion I hate it, can't stand it, I shiver.

When we lived in London with mum it was then that the Luftwaffe attacked London and that was the first time in the War and I can see it right now in my mind, a blood red sky and buildings went up in flames and us running down the street and mum holding on to our hands trying to find an Air raid shelter, and I remember this Air Raid Warden picked Jacky up and she bit him. I have to laugh at that memory.

When I watched the programme on television 'Mr Tom' it really did annoy me because they had glamourised evacuation and evacuation was not glamour at all, and I am sure other people out there went through the same as me and Jacky. Children that had been plucked from their homes to people that did not want us.

I must have been ten and my Jacky my little sister must have been six, when I think how they made her clean windows when she could hardly reach the window sill was beyond belief and I was always worried because to reach the windows she was always on this step ladder and had to go to the top to reach the top of the window and if she had fallen off she would of definitely killed herself because of the height.

But they didn't care because they just didn't want us and that was fact.

That's what annoyed me so much in that film Mr Tom they glamourised it too much, people just didn't want you but you were still taken from a warm loving home to the unknown.

I told you I had the most boring job in the Admiralty and needed stimulation in what I did to be able to do the competitive work I had to do which drove me mad, so I went to the recruitment office and joined the Air Force which was absolutely wonderful, lovely people and the love I had missed over all those years I got when I was in the Air Force.

I signed on for three years at a time and we were what they called in the WAF S but the government brought it through that it would be called The Woman s Air Force and then had to sign on for nine years, and nine years I thought was too long so I left and it was the worst thing I ever did because I was a sergeant and I was going through for Warrant Officer. Why on earth I made that decent I just don't know.

But in the end it all worked out well because I have always liked helping people and I suppose it is because of what I went through during the War when I was desperate for help that now I feel I want to help other people so I started to help different individuals and because I was so well educated I could fill in a form for them or give direction and what to do, and one day went into the Civic Offices one day to enquire about a problem for a lady I was helping with a problem and spoke to a couple of very nice chaps which was, I hope they won't mind a mention, Cllr Pope and Cllr Burnett and they said to me, "For what you are doing, always helping people, you should be a Councilor" and I said, "Don't be silly," but they said, "No you work hard for the people" and I then said, "When do you want to know?" and they both replied, "Five minutes ago!"

So in time I became a Cllr and enjoyed it and went on in 1999 to become Lord Mayor of Portsmouth and I suppose in a funny sort of way what happened to me during the War gave me an insight as to how other people must be suffering with no one there at times to help them, and I must say I enjoyed every minute of it.

So you see little children that suffered grew in to good adults with a story to tell.

Peggy Jean O'Mara

My name is Peggy Jean O'Mara and I was born in Portsmouth in 1935. I and would like to recall and share with you some of my War time issues.

First of all I would like to tell you what it was like being an evacuee. It was a terrible time for families because the children had to go away from their family packed up with a case, a gas mask and any other little bits they had and had to stay away for the War.

Unfortunately I had to stay in Portsmouth because I had to go into hospital, but two years later I was sent out to an evacuee station out in Petersfield where I ended up staying for three years. I lived there on a small farm holding and had to walk three miles to school and three miles back to come home but I loved it very much.

I came back to Agincourt Road in Portsmouth when I was eleven years old and then the War had nearly ended.

I am now going to tell you about the two times I was buried in Landport Street, opposite us was a big clothes and corset factory which was bombed. Let me go back to the beginning because I didn't tell you my maiden name which was Peggy Jean Todd. I was born in Arundel Street number 14 and that was next to the Labour Club which is still standing today.

I started to tell you about when I got buried when a bomb exploded near us. I lost my little brother who was then two years old when the bomb fell and exploded, we were walking down the road one minute holding hands then the next I was buried alive and my little brother was gone.

We did have a little bit of hardship in them days but not a lot because my dad was a Sergeant Major in the Army so we sort of lived Military style indoors but apart from that everything was just normal .

The school I went to was in Arundel Street which is now Tesco car park, then I left that school and went to Agincourt Road well just along from there in Seymour Street.

When I came back from being evacuated it was really awful, all the bombed out derelict buildings and still we thought we were going to hear the doodlebug bombs. It took quite a long time after the War to get back to normal life.

Going back to when I was buried alive, I was in hospital at the Royal for three months and after that things did get a little bit better. I remember what a lovely day V. E. Day was, War was over and every one was singing and dancing there was celebrations going on everywhere.

Two years I was in the War from nine till eleven and sometimes we would go to Portsdown Hill to the shelters which was underneath the Portsdown Hill. Lots of other people from Portsea and other areas would go up there and was known as the 'Yellow Convoy'. I will say no more about that as I was a little girl at the time.

When the War started it was really very frightening and we had an Anderson Shelter out in the garden and we would all have to go there at night and just sit there and listen to the bombs drop everywhere which was very terrifying, and my mum, my brother and myself got buried and mum ended up in hospital for a couple weeks and I was in hospital too, but I already told you about my young brother who died who would have been about seventy odd now. It was a terrifying time so you could only eat what stuff you had indoors or if you were out and all of a sudden the sirens went off then everybody had to run where ever you could get in. My brother's name was Billy and when we got buried unfortunately his little insides got crushed.

A coloured man dug us out and this is why I have never been colour prejudiced because that man dug me out with his bare hands and so did several other black men as well, and we will always thank that black man for it and I wouldn't even know who he was and wish I had of found out, but of course he might of got killed himself. I would of liked to have found out to have thanked him mind, he was very good as were the others.

My mum worked for the GPO on the Milton Locks on the Boat Houses. One of my aunties looked after me while she was a work and as I said we were not really poor because of me dad having such a good job. When dad came home from the War my mother met someone else and moved on and that was another disturbing thing but it was just one of those things that happened.

That was my years not many in World War Two.

Coral Smith

My name is Coral. I am one of Molly's sister and born after the War but mum would tell me lots of different stories about the War that I would also like to share with you.

I was born four years after the World War Two in number eight Hanover Street Portsea. My dad was in the Navy and was well in with the cook on ship at that time and the cook would thieve bits to give to my dad and my dad would then throw them over the wall for my mum to collect when the rationing was on, sometimes salmon.

Another story mum told was when she went to post a letter on the Hard, after dropping the letter in the postbox and leaving a couple of minutes later a bomb dropped and destroyed the post box. After that mum got a bit nervous and was evacuated because she realised it was too dangerous to stay in Portsmouth.

I do remember very clearly when my brothers went Mudlarking and of course mum would tell them off but would take the money they offered, and also when they took me as being only small they always got more money. They also took me carol singing because they got more money me being with them.

My best memory was the Street party after the War, the Coronation because I got a prize which was chocolate money in the street party because I came second in the fancy dress. There was a photograph taken that day and our picture was in the Evening News and most of my family was in it at the Street party.

I remember playing on the bombed buildings and mum cooking late at night if I woke up because we had a big family, and of course she used to take lodgers in and we had the Irish staying in our house. Another thing mum would do was to go round buying second-hand clothes and wash them up and iron them and take them out and sell them for a bit extra and that would help to substitute feeding the family.

Dad never got high wages in the Navy but mum did get allotments sent home to her. Did I say dad was also in the First World War and joined up when he was 14 and when he finished his service in the Army that's when he joined up in the Navy? 22 years unbroken service and he did not get a penny pension. When he came out of the Navy along with my brothers he worked in the Dockyard.

Going back to the clothes mum bought and sold I must say a lot of people done that in Portsea to help ends meet. I do remember we had a Muffin Man that used to come round on a bicycle and used to sell iced buns, and another thing I remember well was this bloke who we called 'He No Me' and lived with his old dad and lived down the other end of Hanover Street and he was a great big bloke and everyone thought he had a learning disability, and now I think it was a bit cruel really but all the kids would chase after him because rumour had it that he carried children in his sack because he always had a sack over his shoulder but apparently it turned out that years later we heard he was a millionaire, but he was dead scruffy and all the kids used to walk behind him shouting out "He No Me!" and he would turn around eventually and would chase us and we would all run down the street screaming .

Molly Smith

My name is Molly Smith and sister to the other three Smiths obviously. I was a War baby and my earliest recognition was at two years old but I can recall some of the After War years, we were evacuated to Dummer to Kettle Farm and I was just two at the end of the War

I do remember though when we moved from St Georges Square we had this big kettle and we moved to Hanover Street to this huge house and it had three flights of stairs, and the reason for remembering the kettle is because we had this great big range and seeing this kettle sat there on it and it was a lot like the 'Upstairs Downstairs' - not like the kitchens you see now. It had flag stones on the floor and the little cook's kitchen was under the pavement and a coal hole with meters that you had to put a penny or tuppence in to pay for the gas or electric. I also remember there was only three houses and the rest was bombed sites and a great big gap which was being filled in daily, and every night we used to have great big bonfires. Best of all was bonfire night when we all shared and mums used to light all the fireworks, we used to get up to all sorts as youngsters and would go what was known as 'guying' with our stuffed guy and we would sit outside the Naffi Club and some of us, if we didn't make a guy, would dress as one and the Sailors would come along and give us money for the guy, and if the police came along we all got up and ran. It must of looked funny when the guy got up off the floor!

I remembered going to Beneficial School then St Georges which still remain in Portsea today and I still remember getting hit there with a ruler because I did not know my times table and having big welts up my legs from it. I remember the Headmistress Mrs Powell who was a lovely lady and I remember reading to her, so I could read when I left the infant school which a lot of kids couldn't. I remember going on to St George's School and having to walk down this alley, and there used to be what was known as a doss house not far up the road and we would see a couple of the shell shocked men there and it was quite sad when I think back now because as kids you used to take the piddle out of them. I remember though on the way to school in the morning we would go to Champions Bakery and they used to give us all a handful of crumbs and sometimes it had bits of cake in it as well so that was nice. I also remember when St George's Church got bombed and going in having a look around, but they did start to rebuild it not long after and they used to have a church social club in the halls, and we hid away in there one night and we got locked in but we had some great fun playing around in the hall but we didn't do any damage, just thought it was fun being locked in the hall.

I do remember mum used to take in lodgers as well which helped her as well as them and the workman. We stayed up the very top of the house a room with four girls and across the landing the boys shared the other room, and down on the next landing was the best room for the lodgers who used to come down from London. Mum and dad had the other room and we used to have a toilet outside but we all had buckets on the landings to save us coming down in the middle of the night and it saved us going down to the bottom of the garden, and I do remember the first high rise block of flats being built and also climbing over the wall to go to the Co-op or the other shops.

Best memories I got was when we used to build dens on the dumps and some of the bombed houses still had the cellars so we would build a brick house from them ,we also did concerts at the top of the house and charge ha'penny in the bombed house and our Sylvie doing one. I also remember Mr Norris who had the warehouse that supplied food to the Navy and shops that was in Queen Street, he also did the illegal bookies in the back room and my brother used to have to go down and queue up with the Dockyard mates and used to get his papers, his betting papers, then I had to do it for a couple of days and would get half-crown for doing it. Our Barry would be down the Docky Mudlarking and was good at it and would come home and share the money with mum, our Sylvie used to go as well but always shared the money. Best time was when they were at Sally Port beach and found a bag of money under the stones, they ran all the way home with it and gave it all to mum. We did all sorts to earn a couple bob, chopped wood and even going to the bombed site in Old Portsmouth by Sally Port and picking up bits of copper wire and mum, who knew the Rag Man, used to give her a good deal for it.

We would also go carol singing to the posh area of Milton and we had a lady chuck her cat out the window and say to us "Here is my cat to join your choir!" You remember Portsea with the bombed sites and scruffy kids with patches on their knees with affection. We also got sweets on our ration books but they were happy days.

We had a great big Queen's Coronation Party in Union and Hanover Street and they dressed my sister up as 'Miss Coronation' - she was the baby of the family and she wore a Union Jack dress and I hated dressing up but they bought me a slave girl outfit. I ended up getting clouted because I did not want to go in the line-up because they didn't want me to wear my glasses. The one that won it was dressed up as the Queen with all her flowing robes.

Oh God, when the Yanks came in we would go ask them if they had any 'Gum Chum' and they were kind and gave us loads, and still today I got the autograph book and I used to get loads of autographs from all the foreign sailors. My sister even went out with a yank called Bob. I still got the bracelet he bought me, I was four then - lovely man. He would take us to Victoria Park and in them days they had a Parky and was not allowed on the grass because he would shout at you to get off, how times has changed. They used to have a small area with swings where you could play, coming down from there in North Street was the fish chip shop, gone now, and seeing the ladies of the night in the doorways waiting for the punters and one was called Pompey Lil. The kids used to follow her up the street and take the mickey out of her.

What about this then? Me and my young sister was in bed at the top of our house and I was reading and there was this blue eyed, blonde haired man looking down at us and I still, to this day see his face, and I said, "What do you want?" and he said, "Sorry I'm in the wrong room" and me saying, "Shush" to my younger sister thinking he might come back and kill us. And after a while we walked down the stairs and a head poked round the corner and it was him, and we screamed the house down and he vanished. Everyone came running and a matelot came running in after hearing our screams and seeing the bloke leave, but he watched where he went. He hid in the Co-op door way and the sailor wanted to thump him but he was stopped, it turned out he was a petty officer and got fined ten bob for being drunk and disorderly. We were told years later that the house we lived in used to be a brothel and he was looking for one of his ladies!

We knew a lady called Dixie Dors but don't know if it was her real name but anyway, she had a swimsuit made out of parachute silk and when she went into the water it left nothing to the imagination. Mum used to take us down to the Hard some evenings and there was a jacket potato place down there and we sit down there with half each of this jacket potato. Never tasted any as good as them they were really lovely.

They had really happy days in the War my sister Kath just said, and she saying she had a coat made out of a blanket, a skirt made from black-out material and my dad went abroad a lot and brought back silk scarves, and I had blouses made out of them and I used to feel like the cat's whiskers. I also had a top made from a parachute and you had to wear something under it because it was see-through. Then nylons came out and the shop would mend them when you got a ladder, nothing like the old days in this day. Yes we had the War sad times and happy, but memories that will stay.

Part Two

Its Molly again now and it just came to my mind how when we lived in Hanover Street, well you have heard the old saying how something 'fell off a back of a lorry' if it was knocked off, well this really did happen. A big box of margarine and mum sold this margarine for a tanner and another day this really did happen, a box fell off the back of a lorry again and this time it was monkeys on a stick and I remember taking these out and selling them for a tanner each. It's so funny when you look back, with the margarine which I think might have been Stork but I am not sure about that, I remember it was unsalted and we had never heard of unsalted butter at that time.

The Camber in Old Portsmouth was a place we loved to go because we got mum all these new potatoes and the men that worked there would deliberately drop a box of potatoes on the floor so us kids could pick them up, and my brother Barry was brilliant at it, clever he was. He was always the first one there and would come home with cauliflowers and stuffed coco that they used to make the chocolate with we would get little chunks of that, and I remember get little bits of that because the blokes were brilliant down there and would always let us have these potatoes and bits and I remember mum always had this tub in the corner of the larder which was full up with them that lasted all through the summer.

We moved at one time to St Georges Square in Portsea and there was a nurses' station and a bombed dump next to that and the girls found a kitten there buried all under the stones and we took him home and we had him for fourteen years and he stayed with us till we moved up to Wymering, and somebody had put some poison down and killed him. But we also had a grey hound and my brother really loved this greyhound but they was running up the road with him because you didn't bother with leads in them days and for some reason he carried on running because he couldn't stop and got knocked down by a Post Office van and died.

My mum used to do washing and cleaning for a lady who lived over Gosport who was obviously quite well-to-do and mum would bring these lovely clothes back that belonged to the girl there and I can remember this really nice mac coat which was really posh which must of belonged to one of her girls, it was really warm which became mine, and she was very generous to mum and became a friend as well. My mum would do anything for a bob our mum would and we never ever went hungry and there was plenty of people round by us that did, and another thing was mum was very house-proud as well and dad would always repair our shoes so we never went without anything really. Some kids did go without shoes on their feet but not us.

Some kids also had to go around with patches on their trousers and we never had that we were very lucky out of most of the children down Portsea.

Happy days.

Kath Smith

My name is Kathleen Smith and I came from a very large family of nine and we lived in various locations of Portsea. I had five brothers and four sisters and when just before the War started there was my three brothers and my sister who was born in St James Street, and then there was me who was the eldest of the girls and children came after.

As I said our Joan was born in St James Street and I was born in Union Street at the top and it was rooms we lived in, then mum had my brother so from there we moved and stayed with my grandma for a while because my dad was in the Navy. We then moved to North Street and that was when the War first started, well talking about it anyway.

I was eight years old when the War actually started and remember Lord Haw Haw talking on the radio and would say "This is Germany talking" and this caused me to have a little break down and I started to walk in my sleep because they were all talking about War.

Then the gas mask came out and we had to go down and get them and I really did not like it but we had to have it I knew, and then they started to evacuate the children and I went with my brother Reggie and brother Georgie along with cousin Natt and a friend of the family Charlie Peacock who was the boys' mate. We all went up together on the train to Basingstoke and I remember that train ride, it was packed full of children and I think they all thought we were going on a holiday.

We had carrier bags with our sandwiches in and when we got off the train at Basingstoke we had to walk through this like cattle market and were each given a carrier bag and inside was a tin corned beef, bar chocolate along with other bits and pieces and everybody was watching us and they took down to this Drill Hall and they all got going and we got on the wrong train. I think we should of gone somewhere else but they didn't have our name down so we had to wait till everybody had gone and then it was just us going to Pambry or somewhere like that in Basingstoke, and I stayed with my brothers and the others a bit further down the road. Charlie had these two kids he would have to take out and the lady that took us had a little boy and was quite young and she had this bicycle that she used to put the baby on the back of in this little seat.

I do remember when we arrived she was going to put me in the same bedroom as she and her husband slept and I didn't want that so I begged them to put me in with the boys, and I remember going in the same room as they slept in and me sleeping on the floor. I also remember how the boys didn't want me always with them but if I sang 'Popeye' they would let me go with them.

Reggie was the one that used to hold me and they used to run off but it was good and the lady was nice but of course I got a bit homesick and wanting me mum, but we were there for several weeks then a car turned up one day at the bottom of the drive and who was it got out? it was Mum.

She too had been evacuated because she had such small children and our Joanie was one of them and they come and got me and I went with mum to Mrs Coalman who became a Lady. She took me to where mum was staying and it was a beautiful house, it really was a big house and we had a very big nursery and best of all they were really good to us and after a while they got us a cottage on the farm and they all came to stay with us but not the boys, just me Joanie and Sylvie my other sister, and it was a good while we were there but nothing came of the War so we had to go back, mum kept in touch though with Mrs Coalman for a long time after that.

Then I was evacuated again but this time to my Aunt Elsie and Uncle Jack but I was not very keen on them. She was quite nice but he was very strict and I don't think he liked me very much. Mum in the mean time had come up but was staying at my cousins who was like a brother to us and mum had to sleep on the floor.

I remember their place was called Chestnut Court and on my way to school which was a temptress hall just for evacuees and I remember going in there one morning, but I didn't know anything about this but Uncle Jack told mum I was not to go there no more. Why I do not know but I did go there and then mum went to Oakley and stayed with my uncle there because they had a family and mum stayed to look after them, Sammy I think his name was.

I forgot to give you my name in the beginning, I am Kathleen Smith but of course it has since altered and one of the places I lived was St Georges Square in Portsea and mother had a big house and used to take in lodgers to help out. I went to Kent Street School as an infant and remember us all in the afternoon laying down on our beds having to go to sleep. I also played in the band, I had a triangle and every time music played I had to ding the triangle and I found it funny but I was really young then.

I do remember when I stayed with Aunty and Uncle Jack because I used to save up farthings and I recall Uncle Jack must of shouted at me or something. Because of this I was determined that I was going to Oakley to try and find her but I didn't know where it was so I went down to the bus stop which was around the corner and my brother Donny started crying because he wanted to come, he didn't want to be left and he was only five or six. And here we was stood at the bus stop and when the bus came we got on it which took us to Basingstoke and I had to count all my farthings out to pay the driver, and of course once off that bus we had to get another bus, I think I was very wise because I had the sense to ask what bus to get on but of course I did not have enough farthings but he said alright I will let you off and he dropped us off at the top of the road and we had to walk down this lane, but of course we soon got to where we were going and of course mum got a shock, but after we got a house on the farm and Aunt Lil had her baby.

That was some really good times. Let me go back to before we were evacuated when our shelter had not been built, we would go into two of our neighbour's' in Union Street and I remember the house now with a big smile because they were all drunk laying on their sides. I also remember going into my friend Dolly's shelter and the dog barking and her dad shouting "Shut that bloody dog up, he will give the game away!" I can laugh now remembering it but not then when we were all so scared. We all started laughing after though we see the funny side to it.

I then went on to tell you about how mum nearly had a fit when we knocked on the door because it was such a very long way, think about it a youngster of nearly nine and another one not six going all that way, we did get a good telling off but that's all.

On the farm we used to help with the hay making. I remember the church down the road from the farm having bombs dropped on the room and my brother George up there chucking them off after along with cousin Frankie, then my Granny got bombed out in Bishop Street and they were running through the streets to Union Street to where we used to live. When we were on the farm we got bombed, there was two or three houses bombed.

My brother George then joined the Home Guard s and they had these rifles but they were not allowed to shoot them and of course he was standing by the window with his rifle and mum was standing with the little ones in her arms next to the window too and Georgie was mucking about pointing the rifle and pulled the trigger thinking it was empty and it whizzed past her just and went into the wall. When the Home Guard heard about it they took his rifle away from him and he had to have a broom handle.

I did enjoy some of the years but we didn't suffer because we went backwards and forwards but I was in some of the bombing. I remember going upstairs when the air raid went off and Joan and Sylv who was only little, no one heard it so I woke them up and took them down stairs and trooped in to the cellar. Mum of course was expecting Terry at the time and it was Union Street and a time when mum used to pass out a lot.

I also remember the rations but because there was a big family of us we did quite well.

Our boys used to go Mudlarking down at the Hard and I remember my father when he was in the Navy walking across the bridge and was looking at these children and our George saw dad and stuck his head in the Mud dad went off but still recognised him so he got a good telling off when he got home. I used to go watch them but never went myself.

Mum would use the local pawn shop a lot too and when the house got bombed so did the shop and our dad's suit was still in it. We all laugh about it still today because mum would put it in every Monday and get it out every Friday.

Dad was on a reserve and one of the first to be called up.

Terry came along, then our Molly and there was a lady that lived across the road who had the big farm house and spoke with a plum in her mouth and said to mum she knew how to deliver babies, but it was our Aunty Beet who brought our Molly into the world.

I came back to Portsmouth before the War ended and was coming up to fifteen by then and mum got me a job in service back up in Basingstoke so I stayed up there for a little while and mum came home to Portsmouth, but I couldn't stay up there on my own so came back as well and a couple months after that the War finished.

I was then working in what was called the 'Box Factory' making boxes and when it came over the tannoy we were told we could go home because they were expecting Victory over Japan and said if it happened we could all have two or three days off. It was smashing though towards the end of War, I just got in and everyone was outside banging their pots and pans, people were out in the streets singing, pubs were opened up, we went up through the Guildhall, it was marvelous just seeing them. It was crowded and everybody was marching around singing, then they all marched up to the Dockyard gates and I don't know why but we all followed, it was just a beautiful sight seeing people up lamp posts and in the Guildhall beforehand, people climbing all over the lions and the soldiers that had a gun in his arms which are still there today.

Then came the street parties which was good but I was too old for them and too young to go into the pub, but of course I did have a sly one.

The pub which I think was Stockers (White Hart) in St Georges Square even brought the piano out on to the street .The box factory was down School Alley, the old John Pounds' School was nearby in St Georges Square along with the ice factory which we got the ice from and of course there was Campion's Shop which sold cakes, and there used to be a man that used to come up he was manager or part owner and would give us kids that stood there a cake each, they used to sell thruppenny bags of cakes and mum always sent us down to get a bag of cakes.

When I left the box factory I went to work at Flemings the hat and coat company in Lion Terrace, Portsea.

"It was very scary at the time"

Dean Clark

My name is Dean Clark and I was born in Merton Road in Portsmouth. Dr Clarke was meant to have been in on my birth but he did not turn up. His clinic was on the corner of Shaftsbury Road, the point is I was very privileged because my father was not full time working before the War, he was the Secretary of the Portsmouth Camera Club and Associate of the Royal Photographic Society and he was around a lot of the time.

We lived in Kent Road Southsea in a nice big house because they bought it on the corner of Sussex Road in 1934 when we moved to Portsmouth.

One person who was in involved in photography with my father was Charlie Fry who became a very significant person who was a key friend and a Chemist in Albert Road, Southsea. Later on in my story you will see why I have mentioned Charlie it is because he came to our aid.

I do remember as a two or three year old walking along the road with my father in Old Portsmouth to go to the Butchers in the High Street which was called Pullins. Also the road to the shops where my father would stop and chat to many people on our way.

I recall that one day as we walked along as I was looking up in the air an Airship was moving by and I believe it to be a German one but I could be wrong, I just can't remember but I did have a very vivid memory of that occasion.

I was then very interested in cars and the like, like the Worsley car and I was very interested in photography.

Then of course the War came along but before that I recall my parents saying to me would you rather have an Austin Car or a baby brother and I replied I would rather have the Car but it turned out I had a brother Trevor instead who was born just after the War.

I do remember the day War broke out because it is a very vivid day to me because while my mum was cooking the Sunday lunch my dad had taken me down to the Kings Bastion Old Portsmouth.

This we did most weekends but on this occasion as we crossed from Kent Road to the Common, that is the road that leads from Western Parade opposite the

Wheelbarrow Tavern through to Clarence Pier which was still there in those days, as we were going through there past the greenery we actually saw activity on the green, the area adjacent to the pier. There were lots of people in uniform standing around and there were barrage balloons being erected. I thought that was amazing and proper impressed by it, then we bumped in to a friend that was coming back from Clarence Pier and told my father that the Band had ceased playing and there would be no more Bands to be played on the Kings Bastion.

My Dad in his spare time was an ARP man and of course I went everywhere with him and his ARP Post was in Castle Road which, if you knew it, was Flemings for a while, and we would have to go to the cellar under there for all the ARP different mask that we had to put on, and I think I had a Mickey Mouse for my age and I believe my younger brother, who was just a baby, they had some sort of contraption for him.

That was the beginning of the War and in the May the following year in 1940 my parents, along with Charlie Fry then a Chemist, decided to pull out of Portsmouth and where we went my Dad was friendly with another camera man by the name of Doctor Blumenau who was a Dentist who had his practice at the end of Palmerston Road and on the corner of Clarence Parade. He was a great friend of my Dad who was German.

Soon after the War had started he was taken away with his wife to the Isle of Man. But before he went my father being a very kind man said to him, "All your dental equipment which you can't use I will have taken over to mine and will store in my basement in Kent Road."

So we had one room that was given over for Dr Blumenau to store his equipment before he went. Then we moved out to the Course Way in Petersfield which was a good few miles from our house.

In 1940 we moved to a brand new semi-detached house, it was on the way coming out of Petersfield and could be identified because Petersfield School stood directly behind it.

There myself, my little brother and Charlie's two children, his daughter Gill and son called Michael, all lived there together. We were all very young and I do remember the next door had not been built and a pile of bricks were sitting there and Michael said to me, "I bet you would not throw a brick at me," and of course I did and it hit him which was difficult for me and my mother then said I will have to give him a present because he was hurt. It was serious but it was a bit embarrassing so that was that.

Occasionally my dad would take me with him on the Southdown Bus which was just across the road so I would jump on the bus with him which was an effort for a four year old boy but I did manage and enjoy it.

Petersfield was pretty safe in those days because the enemy wasn't too keen to drop there bombs in that area. We was all warned as children that we were not to go into Petersfield by ourselves because the Luftwaffe did tend to straddle machine gun and people who were out in the open were shot.

But life wasn't that dull then but I remember the shelter and corrugated roof on it and if weather it was rain or hail it was very noisy.

My parents with myself and brother lived in one bedroom room. I remember waking in the middle of the night and heard explosions, Boom! Then another even louder, Boom!! which was fantastically loud and the windows rattled and the roof shattered. It was very scary but at the time I properly didn't make any comment being just four.

The older girl Jill started screaming so I copied her and the next morning we went out to the fields where the school and railway lines are and to see what damage. A German Bomber had actually discharged three Bombs in a line trying to hit the railway line at a right angle it was very close to it, and the second one was very near our house and the third one was almost at the end of our garden. The actual land there was full of clay good, brick clay and the impact of the bombs I recall made three big craters like, and looked like you could fit double decker buses as I remember it.

Well that was that for Petersfield.

I have a really happy memory in 1940 when my mum took me to the shops in the market place. There was a private place rather like Handley's in Southsea which was a general shop which had a colouring competition for all ages and I was the lucky one to win a prize and it was fun. I also went again on my own accord to the Abattoir which was very gory detail with all the blood going down into the drain and I can still remember that quite well as I didn't like it.

In September in 1940 I have a most vivid memory of that stage of the War. It was late afternoon and it was in fact the Battle of Britain. It was a very clear afternoon with the family standing on the patio outside on the windows facing west to the railway line and towards the hills beyond over in Stoner Hill, very near where Bedales is. Looking up into the sky there was five or six fighters in the sky, three British Hurricanes or Spitfires with German bombers attacking one another going around in circles, around and around in a circle and one by one they were shot down, the German ones went one, two, three, and one of the planes that came down came quite near the house and crashed on the east side of the A3 in the suburbs. It was either the next morning or even later that day, I am not sure which, but a large transport trailer which lorries are transported on had the crashed aircraft came down the A3 with a Messerschmitt on the back of it Prang. Well soon after that my Grandmother, that's my mother's mother, came down from London and actually lived in a little cottage across the at the cross roads which was on the end of Sussex Road and then would visit us a lot in our cramped situation and it wasn't at all comfortable and we had the opportunity to move across the border to West Sussex.

Incidentally, but not part of the story, my parents when they came back to Portsmouth after the War met Mr and Mrs Marsh and we called him Bobsy Marsh, and he reminded my mum that he worked for the Dockyard as a Dockyard Worker that when the War was on he moved from Portsmouth and lived in a chicken hutch on this side of the Horndean road on the East Side, and every day he had to ride to work to the Chemical factory on the bus and it was very grim.

We then moved to a country house called Little Green because my great aunt was house keeper and there was no servants left so we lived in the servants quarters and we were very comfortable there, but of course by the time I was six and a half it was time for me to go to school, There was a village school but for some reason my parents thought I would get a better education if I went in to Chichester.

So I would walk one mile each day with my dad to catch the 8am bus it was a Southdown bus number 54 into Chichester and my dad then was working for the Admiralty at Leigh Park and he would get off his single decker bus at Rackton where the 43 bus would stop and he would go on to Havant and I would go on to Chichester, then in the afternoon I would leave school and make my way to the bus stop and catch the quarter to three bus back to Compton for the half mile journey in the front seat because I was a eager little beaver and there was lots of exciting sites on the way. I used to see cattle going into front gardens and in 1943 saw the advanced Air Field being built at Huntington. I then transferred at the age of eight to boarding school in Ipswich. By the late 1944 things were settling down again and I came back to Portsmouth.

I recall that in 1941 it was February and my dad took me into Portsmouth on business and we went into Woolworth which was then in Elm Grove opposite a church that was between Yarbough Road and Castle Road, typical Woolworth with slated floors and we ended up in the toy section and there was a Jack in the Box which was about six inch square and the jack popped out of the box. He didn't get me it but said to the lady there, "This is very amusing" and she said "Yes but one popped out of somebodies hat but we daren't of asked for it back" which we couldn't understand and to this day still don't understand. The point of this little story is because this was the night before it got burned out in the big raid and we were the last ones to go into that shop.

Well we came back to Portsmouth and it was a state and there was only one room in our house that was useable. I was able to help my parents at stages to decorate the building and the conservatory had a tree going up through it and the Victorian tiles had been pushed up by weeds and the garden, which was very large, was just full of knotted weeds so the next spring we had to get shears and cut the grass to get it back to some sort of state.

But my biggest sorrow was the fact that there were no motor cars and of course I was then attending the Grammar School and it was a bitter winter with no heating in the school and it was very cold and you could go in school uniform and Portsmouth Grammar School playground had in it an SWS tank, a static water supply, a big round one and many days there was ice on the top of it, and we would be taught with our coats on and it was all very grim, a very difficult time and generally it took us some time to get back to normal. There was a shortage of food but at playtime we would go out in playtime we had a supplier and had milk bottles each at the School. Sometimes they had ice on them and we push it up and a third of the school was unused because of the damage and the junior school which was across the road was barely damaged. Opposite the junior school was just acres of demolition, and temporary fences had been put up around the edge of it which was on the corner of the road, St Georges Road which lead down to the Dockyard.

Most of the High Street bombed areas can been seen in Mr King's extremely good oil paintings in the Museum, he was in St James' Hospital and brought up by the nurses to do these wonderful paintings .

It took some time for things to get better but after the War I remember the Billet down by Alexander Road hidden behind the metal railings, very tall railings with a long corrugated fence which behind of course you couldn't see anything at all. They had the Italian prisoners of war chatting away and putting up wooden fencing all the way down the road because you could see right through to Elm Grove all the way to Kings Road along.

I do remember going past the burned-out church coming home and seeing all the wooden mosaic and seeing different breeds and plants and buddleia, and we went into play and came across a Policeman who had his tall helmet on the ground and we asked him what he was doing and he said he had actually captured a pigeon which he was going to take home to eat. That gives you some indication on how hungry we were and how difficult it was to replace the damage done in the War.

I remember three years later going with friends to Chichester and finding a bowl which was about twelve inches across and it was for mixing up flowers and things like that and I knew my mother didn't have one so I managed to grab it and buy it and bring it back on the bus.

The things I did was always by travelling around on a South Downs bus. I used to go in from Compton to Chichester and a Mr Peters used to run the bus and coming in to Portsmouth the later part of the War sometimes, but my parents on the 43 and the GUY bus with seats across, but I would come in sometimes on the Utility bus and we would stop at Kimble's in Osborne Road and my treat there was to have a cup of Bovril which was great fun.

Pauline Scutt (now Pritchard)

I was born in 1927 and I lived in Common Street when the Second World War broke out. I think I must have been about twelve then but still very petite for my age. I stood about four foot and a bit.

I clearly remember one day when my aunt came to take me out, she was in the Royal Navy and served as a Wren so she was either stationed here or on leave, but she always helped mum out with me because I was such a very naughty child. Why I do not recall but I was always in some sort of trouble for being naughty.

This day she came to mum's and said to me "Do you like Shirley Temple?" and I replied "Yes, she is my favourite" not knowing that would be the last film there I ever saw. Well, off we went to the pictures and while we were inside the bombing had started in Lake Road, so out we came and she said, "You get off home" because it was just to the top of the road and she said she would get back to the barracks. Just in time we got out the Princes Theatre, as a bomb fell on it - a direct hit. She shouted back "Get straight back home to your mother!" I was a little bit scared but aunty knew I would get back home safe.

I can't recall if she was married at the time but I do remember her having a son and she was very friendly with Father Persil at the Royal Naval Barracks in Queen Street, Portsea. I was half way home and the next thing I heard was that she was blown half way up Lake Road and ended up in The Royal Hospital, but lucky for her she got away with it and just had bad injuries, and that was the last I saw of my aunt Dolly because mum wouldn't let me out and told me straight I was not going out any more that day.

It came as a shock to mum when I got home by myself and asked where Dolly was and I told her she had to get back to the barracks. With that we went to the Air raid shelter. That day was a terrible day in Lake Road, because they bombed it very badly. Aunt Dolly as I said did not die then through the bomb that blew her up Lake Road, but she was in a very bad way. After a long time in hospital, she did die of the injuries caused through that day, which was a very sad occasion for me because she always found time for me.

Mum told me about the funeral and when it was going to take place and that I was allowed to go to pay my respects. I was given photographs of her and when

I looked at them it always brought back memories.

I got caught out by mum one day because she said, "Have you been to school?" and I said, "Yes, of course" and with that she said, "Yes, you leave but you never get there, do you? And I want to know what you do when you are meant to be at school?" which wasn't very often because of the bombing. I made up one excuse after the other, but I used to go to the shops, just to look. With that, she said, "I won't let you out on your own any more then, if that's what you are doing."

I will always remember the night time Air raid shelter we went to, because we had to catch a bus, if it wasn't too dangerous, to the Hill. Portsdown Hill was where we went, because it was underground and safe. It didn't have beds or anything, so we all huddled and cuddled up. Mum was very in with the Nuns from the Convent in Old Commercial Road and they was always on hand to help her. When our house in Common Street got bombed, they helped her get another place and at that time it seemed we were always moving. I said to mother: "I don't want to move." and with that she said: "I know why and what you want to be doing, you want to go Mudlarking." (Because my brothers were going.) "But," she said. "I'll be putting a stop to that young lady."

Of course, we moved, but still I went with my three brothers or even met them down on the Hard but said: "Don't let her know, because I will be in deep trouble as usual." I did not realise what danger I was putting myself in at times, especially when the Dockyard was getting bombed and the streets surrounding it. Us kids that were larking just carried on until it was ablaze, then we dived for cover under the Rammy, until we could come out, wash and get home.

When mum found out, she said: "I think I will have you put away for your own good, because you don't do a thing I tell you to do and don't take no notice of me." With that, the next thing that happened was the Nuns came and took me. I can't remember where they took me, but it was a long way away in the country. Lots of us kids were evacuated there. I liked the Nuns and they treated me well. I got fed well to and was even allowed to sit and write my mum a letter.

When I was allowed to come home it was a shock to walk down Lake Road because there were big craters where the bombs had hit and half the shops and houses were raised to the ground. I stood crying looking at all the devastation.

We moved back to Common Street, I was still a Convent girl but I was OK because they liked me because I did a lot of sewing, which I enjoyed doing, as well as using a machine. The Nuns were very good, they looked after a lot of children and helped to feed us. They kept a good eye on me because I was very naughty, but I would ask what I had to do for that day and they would let me do the sewing.

It seemed to us that the Germans wanted to bomb every bit of Portsmouth because of the Dockyard, but of course it was us that they were bombing and t was very frightening seeing dead bodies by the side of the road where they got caught when the bombs dropped, and the aftermath of it all just made you cry seeing it.

I used to think what a lucky girl I was, and I said to the Nuns as I was older that I would like to do my bit and join something to help, so I went in to the ATS. Even mum said that would be the best thing you could ever do, so off I went. I was about fourteen when I joined but because I was so small I would still go Mudlarking with my brothers down the Hard and when people came across from Gosport or trains or the Island my brothers would sing to them. When I was younger and my Aunty Glad used to come over from Gosport where she lived they would shout "Quick, here comes Aunty!" so I would get under the ramparts where she could not see me.

One time when I came home on leave I found out dad had left my mum for another woman but once again the Nuns said "You will be alright, we will look after you and your mum." So that was that, it was very tearful.

As youngsters my brothers would go out and collect shrapnel, but me I only wanted to collect money because mum was so poor. Even if I picked up anything, the boys would say "Put it down", even though I would say I wanted to keep it, but of course, they said "mum won't let you keep it". But I was the one who always had the good hidings, because I never done as I was told.

My mum never went out to the Dance Halls, she always stayed in even after dad went off and left us.

One of my brothers went into the Army and when the War finished my brothers formed a singing group called the Scutt Brothers, and was well known and even sang with Tommy Steele and played all over the city and halls.

I left the ATS in 1946, when I fell pregnant through being a naughty girl and I had a son called Barry and once again the Nuns came and rescued me and helped me while I was pregnant and the after care, and I was glad of all the help they gave me.

My younger brother would sing and by then I had a little brother and I said, as he got a bit older, "If I make his clothes can he go along and sing with you" because he had a lovely voice, and after listening to my brothers sing he had the knack for it. I did embroidered shirts and made trousers for him. They were very well known in the end.

When the War was over it was very strange, everyone partied and went back to normal life, if you could call it normal. I had Barry by then and went on to have my Jenny, and still the nuns helped me and mum out. Even today, I still feel lucky that they did because I was so naughty in childhood and as a young woman not doing as I was told, if they had not been there for me I don't know how my life would have turned out.

Did not tell you about when I came home on leave from the ATS went Mudlarking and while in the mud with others the bomber places came over and bombed the Dockyard and we just carried on until it was ablaze. Then we dived for cover under the rammy. I didn't care if any of my fellow ATS workers saw me or not, because to me at the time it was an easy way to make a bit of money to help mum out.

The War years were very sad and very scary and I thank my lucky stars I was able to get married after everything settled down.

Eddie Pritchard

My name is Eddie and I was raised in Heverstone in Surrey and I know that I was adopted at birth by two lovely people and have two brothers. We were brought up near a farm and would play in the field at the back of the house and sometimes venture in and pinch the farmer's eggs for the family.

All I can remember is the desolation that was around us and was told it was caused by the War. It would need to be built up again, but in 1951 we decided we would move, so we moved to Portsmouth to a street called Dover Road which was in Copnor and we lived there for two years. Then it was upheaval again and off we moved to Eastney where we lived for the next forty years.

In the forty years I see Portsmouth how it was destroyed and damaged by the War, bombs had fallen all over the areas and was being cleared and rebuilt up. The Guildhall was very badly bombed and the roads and streets that surrounded it. Schools, shops, factories all over the city lost parts or all of its building so there was plenty to do after the war and plenty of jobs but we still had ration books for different bits and pieces, but on the whole everyone was thinking they were lucky to survive and got on with life, and now when I look back I know I was one of the many lucky ones.

Barry Brett

I remember my father telling me that in World War Two our King arrived on the ship the Aurora in August 1943 in Malta.

There is a photograph of my mother aged around fifteen walking her dog Nell outside Portsmouth and Southsea Railway Station.

This photo is showing the King in white in front of the bridge above the second Gun Turret.

This photo is of the King on board the Aurora in Tripoli in August 1943.

After the War my father worked at Brickwood's Brewery in Portsea where he drove the lorries among other things, and my father stayed for many years until he retired. That was in 1986.

Cyril Tutte

My name is Cyril and I lived in Garnier Street and went to Besant Road School which is no longer there now and in its place stands a petrol station next to Asda Stores in what is now called Holbrook Road.

I was born in 1928 on the 14th January and was one of three, and I was five years old when I started in the Besant Road School but for some reason we moved house round to Arundel Street, number 238, and I am pleased to say both addresses still stand today. I then went on to Penhale Road School and was there when the outbreak of War was declared.

I had a very happy childhood and played a lot around that area and Fratton Road, but I was approaching ten by the time the War started and didn't take much notice of it in the beginning but of course now in my older years I know what it was all about.

We were kept up in the night with the air raids and having to go to the shelter but during the day like the rest of the kids I was out looking about for shrapnel from the shells that came down from the aircraft.

A lot of Arundel Street has now changed and been replaced with flats and different buildings but going back I had an aunty who used to be a tailors and worked for Herrengburg which was in the middle of Arundel Street which then widened right out before going straight, and my aunty worked for this Jewish shop that made uniforms and things for the Royal Navy. She sewed all the pieces together for the uniforms for the sailors and I would have to go down there with the cutting that Mr Herrengburg had already cut out ready for aunty to sew together. It would be a big brown parcel but once finished they would come back as uniforms ready for Mr Herrengburg to press up and send on to the Navy.

That was part of my childhood but the main day I remember was the day of the Blitz which was the 10TH January 1941 and I was twelve then, nearly thirteen because my birthday was only a few days after.

I do remember that day and going to the shelter, and it was around about eight o' clock and was next door to the one that took the direct hit. We all piled in and it was meant to hold only seventy or maybe eighty people but by the time every one pushed in it was more like a hundred, but it was a very long one with benches along. It was a big conning-type tower at the other end so if the entrance got blocked up we could still get out at the back as it was like a submarine conning tower with ladders so we could get on to the top, and it had two steel doors up top but not locked. I do remember a big explosion and a big draught coming right down the shelter and the steel doors of the escape tower banging up and down but I don't know what sort of time that was, but the noise it made and it was several times because of the blast banging up and down.

From then on I do not know how long it went on for but when the all clear went and we finally came out the shelter, instead of steps going down from the shelter it was just like we were walking on Portsdown Hill and that's the part I remember the most, not the debris or anything else because we were all ushered away and unfortunately our house had the back half of it separated from the rest of it and also another bomb had dropped in Besant Road, so I think it must have been sticker bombs dropped, and in parts of Arundel Street you will see where new houses had been built where the other bombs had dropped and these sticker bombs had come through and cause a lot damage and it might have been a few seconds away and I might not have been here now to tell my story.

We heard that there had been about one hundred and one killed that day.

We did go back to the house that day but the next day we were ushered out and sent over to Waterlooville to spend the nights in the Hero of Waterloo which was at the crossroads in Waterlooville. It was several nights we spent there up in the Buffaloes room which was a big room at the top of the pub which had mattresses laid out not only for my family but several families. and the second night there we had a big land mine raid so Waterlooville had it then and they were very big ones which made huge craters around Denmead and all around that area, and in the end we ended up in cottages on the Havant Road. There was about six of them and they were two up and two down and they had been condemned before the War to be pulled down but because of all the buildings and houses that had gone in Portsmouth they opened them up and we had number seven and stayed there for the rest of the War.

Mum did quite well with rations and we didn't go hungry.

Being on the Havant Road we saw a lot of the troops coming from the Leigh Park area because it was all woods at that time before the estate had been built and on D Day it was the American troops with Captains and tanks and all that going past down to the Dockyard or to Southampton to de-embark there, and I can remember chaps singing in the back of the lorries going along, all the old tunes like 'Tipperary' and that sort of tune and some of the lamppost being hit in the narrow road by the tanks.

After the War my mum unfortunately died, but the War ended in 1945 and in 1946 I was called up to do National Service and I went into the Air Force because down in the recruitment bay they had Army, Navy and Air Force and it was Air Force day. So I went in the Air Force and went up to Liverpool and got kitted out then come back and done some training in Melton Mowbury, then went down to Compton Basset where I done a signals course for the Air Force and then shipped out to Germany where I served two and a half years in a place called R A F Cottesloe just outside Hanover. After that I came out of the Air Force and once mum died I went to live with dad but he couldn't take care of me, so I went to live with my sister in Stanley Road and my dad went into a little flat in Charles Street off of Lake Road and that is where the War ended for me.

Gillian Gemmell

My name is Gillian, Gill for short. I was born October 1934 to parents who lived in a modern house on the Highbury Estate which had a proper bathroom, so having to use a tin bath in front of the kitchen fire with the first family I was evacuated with in Horndean in 1939 seemed alien to me.

When I was born my widowed Grandmother was already living with my parents. My mother was a district Midwife in Portsmouth and my father was a Telephone Engineer with the General Post Office and because they worked full time my Grandmother had a lot to do with my upbringing before I started school.

My mother also employed a young girl by the name of Daisy Collier who had just left school to help my Grandmother to look after me on the week days and I believe the three of us got on very well.

The Second World War started in 1939 and to be evacuated was a daunting experience for children of any age so little ones like myself had no idea or understanding as to why we had to leave the security and comfort of our own homes and family in such haste.

I was not at all happy with the first family I was placed with in the country, the main reason for this was because when it came to bath time I was expected to undress in front of the whole family who was strangers to me and I was expected to take it in turns to use the tin bath. Tis tin bath was brought in from the back garden and placed in the kitchen in front of the fire and filled with warm water and my parents realised this upset me greatly and found another family to evacuate me with.

This family lived in Purbrook which was just outside Portsmouth which meant my family could visit once a week. Purbrook at that time was very countrified with woods and fields close by.

My new family was Mr George Snook and his wife Olive and his daughter Dolores and they lived at St Johns Avenue. I was made very welcome and allowed to call them mum and dad, Dolores was just a little younger than me and even though we are now into our seventies still remain good firm friends.

Dolores went on to have a sister by the name of Barbra while I was still living with them in 1942 and of course she naturally assumed I was her real sister. Being eight when Barbra arrived I enjoyed helping out with bath and dress, Dolores on the other hand much preferred looking after animals than her little baby sister.

Of course the War brought about a significant change to everybody's lives.

Dolores' father and mine were both in the Home Guard, this was addition to their day jobs but there was a notable spirit of hope and optimism that united people during the War years. We were all in the same boat we all had to make do while enduring the air raids, blackouts and rationing and of course we all had to carry a gas mask at all times.

My parents owned an Austin which was a small boxed-shaped car in the 1940s and drove over once a week of a Friday to fetch me so I could spend time with my own family in Portsmouth. If the sirens went off to alert of an imminent air raid then I would be bundled back into the car and quickly returned to the country to my foster home.

Daddy Snook was a builder by trade and worked locally and I recall one day he came home from work with a pint of cream he had been given when working in a farmhouse, what a treat that was because neither of us had seen or even tasted cream for a long time.

Certain foods were scarce but people managed as best as they could and I remember I didn't like the powdered egg, but mummy Snook did wonders as a cook and she always made something nice for our meals even though everything was rationed and I never ate greens up 'til I was evacuated.

As the War started just before my fifth birthday I began school in Purbrook which was not too far from my foster home. Mr Twigg was the headmaster and could be very strict at times and we would have regular drills in the playground and if we heard the Sirens whilst in the classroom we had to get under our desk 'til we heard the all clear and one of the family came to collect us. Usually though we were allowed to walk part of the way but mummy Snook would be waiting for us at the top of St John's Avenue.

Daddy Snook was also an artist and at weekends, if the weather was fine, set off to his favourite places to paint, bluebell woods and sometimes to the fields that were in bloom with poppies and corn. He would also go to Bosham Harbour near Chichester and he would take us to if we were good and mummy would pack a picnic basket and we would get a chance to paddle in the small harbour. Bosham also had a small Saxon church where King Canute's daughter is buried I believe. The little boats bobbing about on the water always made a picturesque scene as did the Windmill.

Times like those made the dark days of war for children as happy as could be.

I experienced a couple of near misses by Hitler's Luftwaffe myself when early on in 1940 mummy Snook, Dolores and myself were walking along St John's Avenue when suddenly a German plane came into view and it was flying so low I could see the pilots face grinning as he opened fire on us from his cockpit with his machine gun. Mrs Snook's swift action that day saved our lives when she grabbed my hand and Dolores and fled into a nearby garage for cover and us thank God the garage doors were wide open.

I recall a second scary moment when the heavy night time raid was over Portsmouth, my home Town a few miles away. In Purbrook we used the underground shelter Mr Snook had built in the back garden, it was quite habitable inside with bunk beds, a lantern and we also took board games, colouring books and pencils and such like.

In the house, however, Dolores and myself had to share a bed and some nights mummy would have to wake us to go down to the shelter, Dolores was always reluctant to leave her warm comfy bed in the middle of the night but I didn't need telling twice, was up, had my dressing gown and slippers on and teddy tucked under my arm. I was usually the first to get into the shelter trying not to be frightened of all what was going on around us.

The noise of the gunfire Bombs exploding and the droning sound of the planes overhead that was hoping not to be detected by our search lights sweeping our skies.

On one such night I was on route from the house to the shelter and had just stepped outside the back door and into the garden when a house brick came flying through the air at such speed and just missed my head by a whisker thus landing at my feet with a thud on to the grass and that fright made me run faster to the Air raid shelter.

I told you my own mum was a District Midwife J. F. Gemmell who during her thirty years delivered more than three thousand babies into the world and at the end of her career was delivering them in their own homes, and in time more and more babies were born in hospital. I think my mother was very brave during the War to risk her own life and drive through air raids which were plenty in Portsmouth to reach her patients and deliver their offsprings, I do recall seeing mother's little car with lots of shrapnel sticking up from the car roof.

Some pregnant mothers I was told by mother chose to have their babies near Winchester, supposedly a safer place during the War.

Part Two

Nurse Gemmell, my mother, was well known and respected in Portsmouth and when she died in 1971 she had wonderful tributes paid to her.

Did I tell you my dad was in the Home Guard as well as working for the G.P.O.? In the photograph of me at the age of five and a half I am wearing cream and tan lace ups of dads and of course his tin hat. I also appear to be holding his walking stick, this photo was very rare and taken in my parent's garden in 1940 when we lived on the Highbury Estate during a day's visit to see my family.

One of the local places that was earmarked for protection was Wymering Manor which is believed to be the oldest house still standing in Portsmouth.

I had already mentioned that I was evacuated with Mrs Snook and husband from September 1939 'til May 1945, and 'til 1950 Purbrook was very countrified and had bluebell woods and fields so nothing like it is today.

Another thing I remember is, as I said, my mother worked as a district midwife and hired a young girl to come every day of the week to help my grandmother look after me and this was to be the young girl's first job after leaving school and her name was Daisy Collier and Daisy belonged to a very large family and when she got married I became one of her bridesmaids.

One dark night during an air raid on Portsmouth my mum and grandmother made their way down to the Anderson Shelter and called for my dad to hurry up and join them, and in the effort to hurry to join them tripped over a cat, lost his glasses, when they came off and had to wait 'til daylight the next day to find them which he did in a bramble bush.

Margaret Cook (nee Warren)

My name is Margaret Brenda Joan Cook and my maiden name was Warren. I was born in Sussex Street, Portsmouth and my date of birth was 3rd May 1926. I was the only girl and had three brothers, my parents were very loving and kind and my father worked for the Portsmouth Water Company. I said that I had three brothers who were called Bill, Arthur and Bobby and eventually we had to move from Sussex Street to York Street because my mother bought a house there and it was a really nice house.

My older brother Bill went on to join the Royal Marines and two years later the Second World War started and I was then evacuated to the Isle of Wight which I did not like because I missed mum so came back, but by this time my other brothers, one Bobby was in the medical core and all three were abroad. We of course got bombed out in August, it was the 25th 1940 and mother had to get us out because it was inhabitable so we then moved to Telegraph Street, number 24 and then after a while my mother was taken ill, very ill with cancer which we didn't know till the last.

We had to travel all the way to Southampton by train, dad and myself because of this, and my brother Arthur was allowed home on leave but Bobby was too far away and we could never get in touch with Bill because he was always on the move and my mother was just hanging on for him to come home, but unfortunately he couldn't so the only one that came home was Arthur and the only son to attend the funeral once mum passed away.

Before mum passed away I met Cyril who used to go in to the pub and used to talk to mum and dad and then he was stationed in Belgium and when he came home on leave would bring my mum a great big box of grapes. Mum got on really well with him so it was a good job when I married him.

Going back before that mum was only forty seven when she died and of course my life changed then as I said. When Cyril came back and we got married I then moved out of dad's house and moved in to number 24 Telegraph Street, that was the first house my mum had gone in the first place.

When I was small I went to Swan Street School, that was when I was four and a half that was off Russell Street no longer there, that was near the Guildhall and from there I went to Cottage Grove School, then onto Omega Street School. I was thirteen when I was evacuated to the Isle of Wight, we went by ferry across and got to Ryde, we had to go and see a film there and of all things it happened to be a war film and we all started crying because it was one with Anton Walbrook in it and they played the Warsaw Concerto. It wasn't the type of film we should have been seeing really and that's why we were all crying.

After we all got on a coach to St Helens on the Island, it was only a little village and as I was having a look around there was a bungalow there and I had never seen one before and it had an orchard and I had never seen apples grow on trees before either not being a country person, so that fascinated me.

It was an elderly couple we stayed with, it was me and Mavis Woods and we had had the same initials MW so we had the front bedroom with a big bay window. They were a lovely elderly couple but unfortunately the man died and we had to go somewhere else and of course that was not the same.

After I came back to Portsmouth I heard that there was a bomb there and I remember saying to my mum that was a waste of time, meaning the Island got bombed as well as Portsmouth. So once back I worked in a little factory making like test tubes with a Bunsen burner and I got like half-crown a week in wages, plus I used to make the tea.

Then I went on to work for Cox & Co the bottle people and that was washing bottles and from that job went to another factory in Kingston Road. My mum was in charge of me and Betty Glue because we all worked together, and me and Betty would josh with my mum and say "Tell us about when you were younger" because it gave us more time to have a cup of tea and that. It was really nice that was, and mum also had a job at the Apollo and was a cleaner there and of course then she became ill and then everything all happened at once, then I worked at Chapman's Laundry in Kingston Crescent and because it was all Army stuff, had to work from seven in the morning till eight or nine at night. It was just long hours in them days so I was exempt from the Army and everything.

Then they said I could work out at Elm Grove area it was just actually a little shop by the Kings Theatre in Albert Road, and from there a bit later on I was allowed to own my own shop which I ran myself out in Palmerston Road so that was nice. I used to do the big ledgers, do all the money and then you used to have the War charge which was like our VAT. It was a big thing and I used to have to use my head to work out the prices and that then once done would then have to go put it in Lloyds Bank. The bank used to have that little safe in the wall and you would just put it all in there. I left that job when I got married.

One time when the old Doodlebugs started dropping we were in bed and my mother pushed me down the stairs, god I could of broken my neck but she pushed me down because we had no shelter so had to run a couple of doors away to their Anderson Shelter .

Before I got married and while at home my dad was very strict and I was never allowed to talk to any Americans or Canadians or any service men like that because he kept such a firm hand on me. I would have to be home by ten at night but other than that, up until he got remarried he was OK, then when he remarried he just changed. Before that though him and John Bull, who was aunt Tootsie's husband, would exchange light bulbs and things like that so we never went without food and of course when mum died and I used to come home from work he would have the dinner already for me and looked after me well.

When we got bombed my mum sent me over the road to the Bones' who was a family of about seven or eight children, and when I went over I went down to their Anderson Shelter and the first thing the mother said was "Oh my god look at the state of you, you look like a black person!" because I had soot all over me, funny because my mum sent me over to see if they were alright. And then when I came back there was a lady next door that had twins and a little girl called Shirley, and her husband who then worked in the Dockyard had made a thick brick shelter but they wouldn't go in it so they went under the stairs which was down the stairs because they had a different house to ours, and of course when the bomb came along and dropped on the house the rescue couldn't get in through the door and it ended up that Shirley ended up with a broken back so they made me take the twins out, and I had to go to Copnor Road School and stay there with them over night till a relative came along to take them off.

But down the bottom of York Street there was a fire Station and all the fire men took a direct hit that was in the building that day.

My friend who was … Jones, her mother-in-law died because the blast had knocked her false teeth down her throat. Haverford her name was, they lived just down the road from us and of course the Cathedral in Old Portsmouth took a direct hit as well and all of St Paul's Road, but of course when you're thirteen you don't think too much about it and all I was worried about was the new coat my mum had bought me. It was a mustard colour which was hung behind my bedroom door and she had only bought it the day before which she bought for five shillings from McIlroy's which was a lot of money and that I'm afraid was all I was interested in. But I do remember looking at the house and seeing all the nets in shreds and the windows blown out and glass everywhere and bullet holes in the sofa, even the phone my dad had to have from the Water Company was all ripped off, my mum just stood and cried and now I can understand just how she must of felt but not then.

It was such a lovely house as well, me and Bet Glue used to go around all the air raid shelters to watch all the entertainment that was there and we would go to pictures because there was never really anything else to do really because we worked long hours, but we did also go to the sixpenny hop over at Twyford Avenue in Stamshaw to do a bit of jiving, but of course my father was so strict that I was not allowed to wander very far.

Rations, well I only ever had to queue when I was married and pregnant with my first which was Steven, and I would queue for sausages which when fried in the frying pan would come out these really little tiny things because they were mostly made with bread, and being as you were pregnant you were allowed to go to the front of the queue but my dad mainly did all that because he knew what to get.

We spent a lot of time in the air raid shelters because bombs mostly dropped at night, we had a brick air raid shelter next door in St Luke's School and I used to go in there with a woman who had a couple of kiddies and would sit there talking to her and sometimes you would have to stay in there all night. Mum would also come in with our two dogs, one was called Peggy and the other Bonzo, and she would bring her little brown case with all the insurance policies and all that in it because my dad would be out with the Water company, and one time down Queen Street in Portsea he said there was this loud bang and where he should have been there was a great big crater there so he was very lucky he moved. It was a very dangerous job that he was doing with all the broken water mains and I will always remember that because he nearly got killed.

Then my friend Bet Glue lost her dad, the shelter he was in took a direct hit and it was on my birthday that was 1940 or 41, it was one of them time 3rd May which was very sad.

Another place we would go would be Verrichia's which was Italian ice cream and we would sometimes go and have one at the Guildhall that was once, another place we would go was to have a Primrose milk bar but I can't remember the street but it was just past where the Hippodrome was and pictures as I said earlier. We had to go out with torches in the blackout and of course there wasn't many cars on the road then in them days and the ones that were had their lights half way across.

Mum got fed up with all the bombing so we then moved to Petersfield - that was an experience and I got a job in the rubber factory there and made rubber soles and heels and nearly every weekend I would cycle from Petersfield to Portsmouth with a friend, Butser Hill was Butser Hill in them days and my friend was Queenie Biles and that's what we did every weekend then because my mum trusted me to go with her, sometimes we would catch the bus as far as Clanfield but that was as far as it went.

On that time we had to walk from Clanfield back to Petersfield and on this night walking along on a moonlight night you can imagine it would be very bright so we would walk along with a couple of Squaddies soldiers, I was about fifteen then I suppose maybe sixteen but what an experience that was and I often think of that. I loved my bike and would cycle everywhere from Portsmouth to Fareham, then go on the ferry other times to Gosport because you could then because there was hardly any traffic around then.

Some times when in the cinema if the sirens went off they would say you can go if you want to but that was rare because the raids was mostly at night so we were lucky really because it wasn't so much during the day.

The Guildhall took a direct hit and when the War was over and by this time I was married and had gone to see my sister in-law Ivy and cycling down to the Guildhall got as far as the station and everyone was saying the War was over, so I took my bike home in Telegraph Street then just up the road and went back into the Square where people was collecting all the wood for a big bonfire, I stayed out all night with the celebrations because it was such an experience.

I went down to the Gunwharf recently and in there is still an actual building that was then in the War, a waiting room which was then in the middle of Guildhall Square and when I think of the Guildhall Square it was lovely in them days but now it's nothing really, it's been spoilt like I think they have spoilt Portsmouth to be honest. We used to sit in that shelter out of the rain, it was a very, very wide road the Guildhall was, you had to cross three parts to get to the other side. I must say I never found it very scary but we were in them air raid shelters too much and once you were in there you couldn't get out. I was lucky though because I never lost anybody so the only bad experience I had was when we got bombed out.

When they first started the bombing it was up at North End and Bet Glue and I walked up there and realised what it was like then, houses gone to rubble but when you're teenagers you just don't think too much of it really but we were shocked to see all the houses gone. And of course there was another time when a family I knew, Peggy Byng, got bombed as well and the father had gone to the pub the Queens Head and bought some beer and when he came back his house had a direct hit and the mother Sally and the brother were all killed and Peggy Byng was the only one to survive, and she had to stay there for several hours with her family and dead mum beside her. She was screaming, it was a terrible time for her and she was a nervous wreck after that.

I didn't know what happened to her after that but it was the only tragic one I saw or heard of, terrible, he only went up for a jug of beer came back and had lost all his family, Sally was a beautiful girl with her long ginger hair, Peggy was a few years younger than me.

The gas works took a hit as well, lots of places went but I never saw it, but I always think of Peggy Byng because they had a basement they went down and they were trapped for quite a few hours, it was in all the newspapers, and I wonder if she is still alive today because she was a little bit younger than me.

Moving away from Portsmouth you lose all contact.

When over the Isle of Wight we went to school and I remember there was a big green in front and a grocer store where I would spend my money but mum would come over with a tin full-up with sweets so that lasted me a week. I wasn't over there that long as I went in the September and didn't spend Christmas there so was back by October, November time because I was always crying every time mum came over, and I think she got fed up with it in the end and thought "right, I take her back". They were a lovely old couple and we used to have a cooked breakfast which I was never used to back home, we had fried potatoes with it, really nice couple, but the second family had children of their own so I was never happy there because I didn't get the attention because the elderly couple before was good and we had our own bedroom. But it was her daughter we went with up the top of the road but we felt that we were pushed out and felt like evacuees, and that's when I said to mum "I want to come home". I wasn't happy there

I came home from there though because I was lonely and missed my mum and of course by then the boys had come home on leave and I can remember one time your dad Bill took me to the pictures it was either the Regent or the Chiverly it was called something like that up in Elm Grove.

I hated the gas mask and remember when we first had to try them on they smelt of rubber and was not very nice at all, but we had to carry them always with our identity cards all in a little box.

We also went to the British kitchens and get cheese rolls, think they cost about tuppence in them days they had all them British Restaurants around then. We also went to the Dockyard to watch the Mudlarkers which in them days were different, I used to stand and watch and think "oh they are getting all muddy" but they looked quite happy they enjoyed it and so did the people throwing money in, it was nice.

Our Bobby took me into the Dockyard and we went all around and it was very interesting in there, our boys used to go Mudlarking and I love that book you wrote.

Going back me and Bobby would go to the mission St Luke's and dad would stand on the door step to watch us go in to the mission, and Arthur would always run away and my dad would say "What lesson did you have today?" and of course when you went they would give you like little tickets which were pictures with Jesus on it, but of course he never had one so he used to get a clip around the ear.

Mum was very strict that you had to go to Sunday School and of course when

Bobby and I got a bit older we would go visit aunty who wasn't really our aunty but we called her aunty, and she lived Brompton Road which was off Albert Road. We would go for tea and the grandmother used to be there who was very tall and all in black and always smelt of blancmange which we always had on Sundays which was made in a proper cast. In the evening we would walk home and past a house that had a sweet shop in the front room of the house and aunty Marg and another aunty that really wasn't related that lived in Lake Road we used to visit on the way home.

As Bobby got older and went in the Army of course that all stopped and we sort of drifted apart.

Our Bill always took me pictures when I came back from being evacuated, then of course he was sent abroad to Germany and France, then after he joined the RAF then was dated Stella Farwell and was given her allowance of five shillings a week and I would have to take it up to her to Lake Road because they were saving up to get married, and when he came home on leave would take me out with them. Then all of a sudden something happened and she got pregnant by somebody else and it all fell through but she was a lovely person but unfortunately he didn't marry her so it was a very sad time for him.

Then after a while he came home eventually and by then he was with your mum so we would all go to pictures together and of course they would come and see us, then of course we all started our families and then of course you drift apart a bit because you're so busy getting on with your own lives.

"I remember all too well"

Maureen Grady

My name was Maureen Grady and I would like to share some of my memories with you of the Second World War

I was born in 1939 in Clarence Street and our house got bombed when we were either in the air raid shelter or when I was evacuated to Basingstoke. I remember all too well the sound of the siren going off as a warning we were in for an air raid and if it was evening time how the search lights would beam across the sky, and also the big air balloons that would be floating over Vernon Barracks.

My dad, who was in the Royal Air Force, was somehow involved with the air balloons but I don't know how as everything was secret. He sent me a letter when he was stationed in Brussels and it had a picture of a beautiful peacock on the envelope. I remember my dad telling me later on in life that he signed up to the RAF while he was celebrating my birth.

When an air raid siren went off mum would take us to the one that was in St George's Square where a playground was built after the War and a newer stands there today. Sometimes if it was packed we would catch the bus and go to the Portsdown Hill shelter by bus, but my older brother Frank would never travel by bus so would walk all the way there all on his own. My aunt Pat told me this long after the War and said he was a little *** at the time.

The shelter on the hill had bunk beds going up the wall and it had lots of tunnels and it was very noisy, and I remember when the city was getting bombed how they would sing songs and I thought that was very jolly, and after the War told my aunt Pat that my favourite song was 'Roll me over in the Clover' which she told me was a very naughty song at the time but it had such a catchy tune and everyone laughed when singing it.

Once again we got bombed out of the house in Clarence Street so we then went to live with our grandmother who lived in Aylward Street in Portsea. Her friend Mrs Pagden that lived upstairs kindly stored what furniture we had left which was not a lot but at least we rescued some, so mum was glad of that because not long after mum was given a flat in St George's House which was situated in St George's Square and it was only a two bed roomed flat and there was mum, dad, uncle Hedley and us three kids, and one day my mum took in a woman who had a couple of kids as they had been bombed out and had lost everything. Mum didn't even know the woman but that was what people were like in them days at such a terrible time. I can only remember her name being Rose and don't know where they moved on to.

I went to Beneficial School that was situated in Kent Street and the Headmistress was Miss Hickish and the two teachers were Miss Powell and deputy head was Miss Husher, then eventually Miss Powell took over as Head Mistress after Miss Husher and ran the School for many years after. I can name every one that lived in St Georges House at that time and most of them went to the 'Benny' as it called.

I have given lots of photos for the book which lots of people will recognise but there is a copy of the Foden Steam Engine that belonged to Brickwoods Brewery and pictures of the Carnival they would hold every year, a photo of the Coronation Street Party as well as a photo of my uncle Hedley when in the Home Guard when King George came to Portsmouth. Brickwoods always put on outings for the staff that worked for them.

There is a picture of my sister Edna at four years nine months old just before she died of septicemia standing in the house in Clarence Street which I think was just at the back of where Argos Stores stand today. There is also a picture of St George's Flats with Fremantle House sat alongside it, but the White Hart public house looks like it is gone unless it was stood back a bit.

When Brickwoods did the Carnival everyone made the effort to join in and in the photo you will see they all dressed as Pirates that year. Today Brickwoods Brewery no longer stands so proud as it did along Cross Street and Bonfire Corner for so many years, in its place now stand the Admiral Quarter which is a very grand selection of private flats with Tower on Queen Street and underground car park.

Sidney Adlam

My name is Sidney George Adlam and I was born in 1923 and lived in Cosham, then in Albert Road Southsea where I started work there as an apprentice and was there for three months, then World War Two broke out and the Air Speed, which was government, commandeered the premises and of course we had to move out.

We then went on to Old Portsmouth to work because they had a private car department and the cars we worked on were in the commercial department so we had a big contract for RAF Vehicles. That's where I stayed until January 10th when we had the big Blitz. I used to ride my bike from Cosham to work but after the Blitz it was very difficult because of the craters and debris everywhere from the bombing, and on this morning when I arrived for work there was no garage left, it was burned out completely, everything gone, nothing at all left, so we had half of Gordon's Motors in Castle Road until after the War.

Actually when we were working in the High Street, Old Portsmouth one of our chaps would go up on to the roof with a pair of binoculars. When the siren sounded as he could see the Semaphore Tower in the Dockyard and when danger was imminent they would hoist a red ball. He used to clap to warn us and we would rush out the garage, down the road to the shelter or the basement of what is now called today the Lemon Sole Restaurant, and one of the funny things that happened there was an air raid siren that was 'Danger Imminent' so we all had to leg it down to the shelter along the road, and me being a bit slower was that when I got there I couldn't get in because they had put the mesh over to stop dogs from getting in and there were so many people inside the shelter was pressing outwards. I was panicking but they let me in just as they dropped two bombs in Pembroke Road. It made a direct hit on the corset factory and completely destroyed it and that was on the 10th January.

I didn't get called up because we were working on a War contract on the transport but twice I got called and then a third time for the RAF but by then the War had finished. After the War we went back because we had new premises built at Cosham.

I was very interested in athletics during the War and would go to Court Lane Athletics Club there in Cosham and I think it was run by Brownie for the Council but he's dead now. But he lived in Drayton then and one day I went down there and he asked me if I was interested in joining this Auxiliary Services and we would wear Home Guard uniform once you joined and we would have to use explosives and grenades etc. It was a secret services and we had a hideout which was hidden in Albert Road which had been built by the Royal Engineers in the woods there and I've tried to find it several times but it must have been built on.

When I lived Cosham I had a part-time job as a Warden fire watching and had to spend alternate nights doing fire watch and we would have a bucket of sand and a stirrup pump, and if an incendiary bomb had landed we would have to cover it with sand, and up the top of road we had what was called a static water tank which had a fence around it. One day a chap came running down and said so and so had fallen in the tank. He must of really squeezed to have gotten in there but when we got in and up top he was floating on top of the water but we managed to pull him out then. He was ok, he survived and would you believe when I got home my mum moaned at me for getting my clothes wet!

I remember the end of the War clearly because we all went to the Guildhall and I ended up sitting on one of the lions and we were all rejoicing.

Getting back to the Home Guard bit we would go out all night on Patrol and do exercises. One night in Leigh Park there was a little bridge by the cross ways you had to cross to go into Barton Road. One side of crossing there used to be a gravel pit and the other side would lead you on down to Funtington, but in the Gravel Pit they used to put old cars in there and we would have to get some explosives down there on them and blow all the cars up, and one night after laying the explosives and coming back up again we noticed one of the chaps missing but didn't know if he was still down there or not so had to call the whole thing off till we found him.

I give you a run down on what the Auxiliary Services stood for because after the War there was never any records to show that I was engaged in anything, but we were told in the War if we had an invasion we would have to go as Resistance and was also told the longest we would live would be two years and I still have my Badge - mine was Auxiliary 602. Years later going to a jumble sale we came across this book called 'The Last Ditch' which tells you all about the Resistance which I bought.

Going back to this organisation I was in, we had a Captain Browning who lived in Burrell Avenue, we had to go to his house at night in the kitchen and learn and be shown about how to use the explosives. Lots of people belonged to this organisation, it was not until after the War that I met his wife because he had died and learned the house opposite had the secret radio transmitter, and she asked if I knew but I told her I didn't because no one knew about it.

When with these services we went to a place called Cold Hill in Yorkshire, I think it was to the Head of Resistance because we used to have training up there only for two or three days using the old camouflage and all that and being shown all the explosives, and it was also where Anthony Quail was an officer.

I remember also that Elm Grove in Southsea was just a pile of bricks from there to the Guildhall through the Blitz and there was quite a few people killed in the War. One friend of mine who was in the RAF got killed, and what about the air raid shelter in Besant Road that took a direct hit? That was bad with a lot of lost lives.

Didn't tell you that at the back of our garage in High Street was St Thomas Road, I think it was, had a lemonade factory at the top of the road. I remember all the lemonade bottles exploding, I can laugh now.

This is my missus, now she said she can remember when she was about seven or eight reading a story in a newspaper and there being a picture of a Australian serviceman that had been beheaded by the Japanese and it terrified her, and another story about some boys that had to go to a goal post and if they did not reach the top they would be killed, and I would look at my brother who was five years older who was thirteen, and would be so frightened they were coming to get my brother because we lived the nearest point to Norway up in Arbroath and were told if the church bells rang then we were being invaded. And there I would be lying in my bed worry that they might ring and how I was going to be able to save my brother, always worried and frightened for my brother but never for me but luckily he survived.

Even today at the age of seventy eight I still remember it and think about it, it goes to show just by reading something you can be traumatised by it. Another thing I remember was when we came back from Arbroath after the War we got out at Fratton Station, walked to the top into Fratton Road where there had been a beautiful tower with green tiles - there was just a bit of a shell left remaining and we stood there horrified. Everywhere was gutted and all over Portsmouth to was the same and for years after the rubble remained until the Council decided to rebuild, and in Stamford Street where my mum's mum's house used to be they had prefabs, and a man used to tether a goat on the rubble and I laugh now but he stank every time you went by him and you had to hold your nose because he really stunk until you moved right out the way, and do you no he was there for years.

Going back I remember we never had any fruit or anything like that but up in Arbroath in Scotland they had prunes and mum brought a couple of tins and even though they had prune label on, when we opened them they were Victoria plums and they were gorgeous, and when mum rushed back they were all gone.

During the war my grandmother and aunt came up and the bunch who lived in Netley who was expecting another baby and who cried for two weeks because she was scared for the children because the raids had got worse and worse, so they came up and we managed to get paid accommodation for all of them in the same tenement block. And they stayed for a very long time and even had the baby up in Arbroath, and everyone was so kind to her because she was suffering nervous exhaustion where she could not sleep worrying about her children.

When we did come back to Portsmouth we never saw any fruit at all and wondered how we all survived it but I think because we had none of these things we did survive it for years. The corner of the road one day opposite the Co-op in Fratton Road was the fruit shop, and one day you never see a queue like it and we ended up queuing too and about fifty yards away we saw these bananas but we never got any, I didn't even know what a banana looked like to be frank with you.

We moved to another house in Clifton Street which was better than the one we had and stayed in that for two years, but then it had compulsory purchase put on it to build ghastly flats on it that are there now, Albert Court, so we moved again.

My mum used to turn coats inside out and do them up because we had no boot sales then you had to get what you could and make something out of it so you could wear it. My sister had a lovely coat that mum turned inside out that she bought from the second hand shop which my sister wore for years. Really funny things you remember.

Its Sid again now and I can remember when I lived in Cosham there was an Anderson air raid shelter in the garden which I only slept in once because it was so damp and smelt musky so me and my brother would sleep under the table.

Yeah, I can really laugh at that now.

[Here Sidney was talking about an exhibition he had seen at the Museum] For fifty years the Auxiliaries went without recognition but now more than forty audio tapes have been complied along with pictures and exhibits. It is also possible to see photographs of the officers and men that served in the Auxiliary Units along with information of their weaponry and the original examples of fuses and crimping mechanism etc. of the explosives in which they were all so familiar, the Museum displays examples of dead letters boxes and intelligence instruction dossiers employed by the special duties section and practical details of radio communications. A few books has now been written about the Auxiliaries, some has donated money from the sales to the book to the Museum.

This was a secret British Resistance Organisation from 1940 till 1944, with stay behinds highly trained up who stayed in undetected, carefully built bunkers (OBS) secretly guarding our lands from the invading German Army.

The general public did not know that we had a Resistance movement and was training ready for the unthinkable that never happened. Major-General Sir Collin Gubbins was the man said to have created The British Resistance Movement and a photograph was taken of him in 1967.

During the day you could be a normal hard working citizen but by night a highly trained Auxiliary who went about their business quietly setting explosives where they were ordered to. For me this was something in my life I was proud of and not discussed much but through the years as I said, before many books has now been written and Museums have open in a lot of places we trained, we remember with pride that we, that I served as an Home Guard, an Auxiliary.

Gwen Weeks

My name was Gwendolyn Mary Weeks. As a child at school which is now a secondary school but wasn't then of course, as a child it was an infant school, I was an evacuee and was evacuated to the Isle of Wight from St Luke's School. My mother went as a helper for the older boys but not the boys from the infant school. When we arrived we went to Newport into a big school and when we got there we went into a big classroom and lots of the mothers who were helpers came to see their children because we were only five.

I was born in May 26 1934 and when I started school in the Easter it was 1939, so when we were collected that day from school for evacuation I was five years three months and as I said lots of helpers and parents came to Newport to see their children, but sadly mine didn't come for whatever the reason I still don't know, but I started to cry and spent the whole lunchtime there sat on the Headmistress' lap and her name was Miss Joyce.

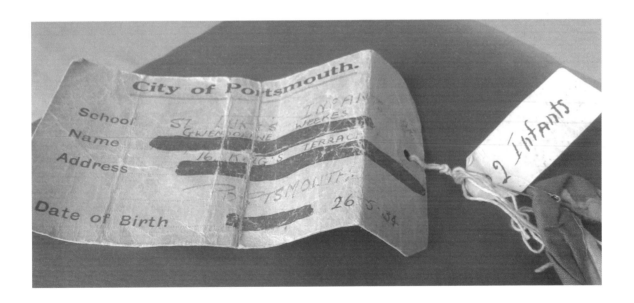

Must say, funnily enough at the end of the War I meet her and she remembered me! Anyway going on from that we were then evacuated, me and another girl, to a couple in Newport and my mother wasn't so she didn't know where I had gone so it was a worry to her as it was a bit chaotic. So of course what happened was she was trying to find me.

The evacuation officer was Mr Knots and clever clogs here remembered my home address which was 16 Kings Terrace, and I wrote home to my dad just to say I was safe and that the lady and gentleman that we lived with was very very nice, and he then let my mother know and they came and collected me. But she was evacuated to a family called Mrs Butler just outside Brading, and when they came and collected me this is where I also stayed in 1944.

My father was a bit of a what name and he said her place was with him and not with me, so after a week mum went back and I was left alone at Jolly Down Agistone, still on the Island at the age of five years and four months and I regret. Any way I started school in Brading - it was the Elementary school and I absolutely loved school and luckily the evacuation officer was Mr Knots and things jogged along, and where I loved the school I started to do very well but Mrs Butler who was in her sixties was at the old school, but she was very kind although she didn't give you any cuddles or love or anything like that, but you felt safe with her. She was very kind to me so the months just went by and mum used to come over to visit me once a fortnight on the boat, and at a later date one of them ferries was hit by a mine and the boat was carrying a box of oranges that went down with the ship, but as a kid all I was worried about was my oranges not the loss of lives, but I was only five.

In 1941 the powers to be decided that the Isle of Wight was no longer safe in case there was an invasion because they thought it might have been the first place to have been invaded, so they had to re-evacuate us to Petworth. Well I didn't know anything about it only that I had my little bag and my gas mask and was trundled on to a train, well the boat first then the train and I didn't know anybody and unfortunately as said before my name was Weeks - almost the last letter of the alphabet - so when we got to Petworth we were taken to a church hall and people came along to claim the children, but because of my name being Weeks I was one of the last ones. I can remember sitting in that hall thinking to myself "What about my life?" but lucky enough this young couple came in and picked me up but sadly I wasn't very happy there and I hated it. I hated the school, hated the people there, they both worked and they didn't really want me. And then I got nits in my hair and having got nits they really didn't want me and for one whole weekend they washed my hair in Der Bac soap with a nit comb about seventy times, but after that they didn't get rid of them so they got me transferred over to an old couple of ladies Miss Pembleton and Miss Radcliff, and I think later we found out they were quite somebody in the County at that time.

When I went there it was a huge great big house and they had a Pug dog, a maid and a Gardner and all their other servants had gone because of the War. I used to live with the maid and my bedroom was right up the top of this huge great house, but to cut a long story short I didn't like it there but one good thing was that I joined the Brownies and got my uniform and I was so chuffed with that. They were very strict and we always had a bath of a Saturday and hair washed of a Friday, and I used to have my meals with the maid and the only time I was allowed to eat with the ladies, and the dog who sat at the table on a cushion, was a Saturday for tea and the rest of the time was spent with the maid who was very very kind to me. But eventually she sent a letter to my mother saying "If you love this child you will come and get her", and in the meantime Mrs Butler had written to my mum saying after the bomb - which I hadn't mentioned earlier. We were sitting there having our sandwiches lunchtime and a bomber leaving London going back down to the coast had a bomb left and dropped it and it landed on the boys part of Petworth School, and quite a lot was injured and killed and one of the teachers was also killed, and some of them boys were evacuees and had been re-evacuated so hadn't been saved at all. After this my mother took me away and took me back to Mrs Butler over the Isle of Wight, and that was a strange thing really that I had spent the whole four to five years with Mrs Butler and I ended up marrying a Mr Butler and I was called Gwen Butler before because of staying with Mrs Butler which was all very strange, but there you go.

It was so lovely me being back with her and school and such familiar surroundings, and in all this time my mum would still come over once a fortnight and I would have a day off school, and my dad had only made it over the once in the whole time I was over there and then he went to bed and said he had been on nights but it didn't matter because it was mum the one that I had loved so that was ok.

Lots of different things happened to me but we were very lucky over the Isle of Wight because Mrs Butler had a chicken, old Agatha, and she managed to lay an egg nearly every day and the powdered egg we were given everyone loved even me, but we were very lucky because Agatha used to lay a fresh egg and perhaps I would have the egg every other day and Mrs Butler would make cakes, but of course there was never any fat but I liked them but when mum came over and tried them. She said they were pretty awful but I thought that was a bit unkind because she did the best she could.

Mind you, when I first got there and didn't eat my dinner, which was a Sunday dinner, she would not let me get down from the table and said "You will eat it because if you don't eat it you don't have your tea" which was cake. I sat there and sat there and the afternoon went by and tea time came and she got the table cloth out ready, and there was still this horrible-looking congealed dinner looking at me on the plate and of course I did in the end eat it, and fortunately now I can eat anything and not finicky in what I now eat so in some ways it was a good thing but not very nice at the time.

We had to carry our labels and gas mask at all times and we would have lessons on how to put your gas mask on quickly which was hilarious because we were only little and in the infants and only just five. It was a lot to take in at that age and to do it on your own like I had to. Eventually in 1944 when the bombing stopped mum decided that perhaps it was okay for me to come home which was a bit ironic because when we got home the Doodlebugs started, so we would have to go down the shelter to sleep.

I told you how I loved going to school over the Isle of Wight and done good by doing so because I passed my eleven plus which I took in 1945, so hadn't been back a very long time and went on to Southern Grammar School for Girls that was in Fawcett Road which is now the Priory. I made lots of friends there and remember one day all us children were in the playground watching a dog fight which then was aeroplanes, Spitfires and German bombers and our Hurricanes all over the skies and all us kids looking at it. Well anyway one of them got shot down and a German parachuted out and then the Headmaster said "What are these children doing out here? Get them down the shelter" so we all went to the shelter as there was a big one in the playground, and when it was time to go home I used to walk alone and it was about one to two miles and I was really scared this German was going to pop up from behind the hedges and grab me. Why I thought he would want to grab me I don't know, but I thought he would and when I reached home I said to Mrs Butler about this plane crash and she said "It's all right they captured him as soon as he hit the ground, you didn't have to worry yourself " so that was ok.

Another thing she told me was that they were having manoeuvres up on the Downs and I was not to go up there, but of course if you're told don't do something what does a kid do? They do it. So I went up there and picked some wild orchids and of course when I came home I put them in a little paste jar and was thrilled, but of course when she see them she said "I thought I told you not to go up to the Downs" in which I replied "How did you know?" and she said

"Because the wild orchids don't grow along the hedgerow only on the Downs" so I wasn't so clever after all.

I was never really accepted, I was always known as The Evacuee in the school, and another girl that was there in 1939 only stayed a couple of weeks then went home to Portsmouth. Mind you Mrs Butler said after she moved from Southampton to the Isle of Wight she never felt accepted all the years she had lived there even though she had her children, because to them she was an outsider. But as a child you long to be accepted but you was always on the outside looking in. I was never unhappy but just wanted to be one of them.

Mum used to send me all her chocolate rations and also sent me Mars Bars which wasn't very many on the monthly sweet thing, so Mrs Butler and I would cut the Mars Bars into slices and we would have a slice each every night and that was all as we didn't have much chocolate or anything like that. But once in Brading they had ice cream in the middle of the War and the next day I said "Can I take my money in with me?" and she said "Yes if you want to" because I had one of them little silver things that you kept your sixpenny bits in. Anyway I took it in but they had sold out, I should of known they wasn't going to have it there very long. I'm afraid to say I didn't get my ice cream.

They used to have these manoeuvres on the Island, and sometimes I would walk to school on my own or with others, but there was this soldier one day who was billeted in Brading that came up to me and said "Can I walk to school with you?" and of course being innocent said "Yes" and he said "Can I hold your hand?" and said "Yes", but somehow someone had written about this man holding my hand going to school which when mum heard made her frantic. Every morning he had met me and said "Hello Gwen, off to school?" and never did anything horrible or anything, just used to talk to me and of course mum had got over by the early boat and came to meet me on the way to school when he popped up and said "Oh you're Gwen's mum". He also said "I hope you don't mind but I have a little girl about the same age as her and I just like to talk to her and walk her to school because it reminds me of her." I often wondered as I got older if he got killed or went home to his little girl. I never knew his name I was just a kid and we took people how they were.

I used to go to Sandown every six weeks for a haircut on the bus but toward the end of the War, the time I was there they ran taxis for children to bring them in to school or I would have had to walk in on my own but just caught the catchments so was very lucky to get the lift.

When I came back to Portsmouth my mother had had another baby, Lesley my sister, and when I got back she was about a year old just under '43 she was born, new baby and me coming back thinking I was going to be everybody's apple of the eye. I wasn't because the baby was and my dad had been sent to Bermuda because he had a Front Line job he was there for eighteen months. Lesley was about fifteen months when he came back and the first thing she said to him was "Hello daddy" and he absolutely loved Les, she was his little girl. I was OK once I got used to it, but my home life wasn't very happy. My mum and dad didn't get on and in the end got divorced when my sister was old enough and was at school. It just wasn't a happy home but as I said over the Isle of Wight there was never any hugs or kisses but you felt safe. I didn't feel that at home, maybe that's not the proper word, it was the rows at home. As I said I passed my eleven plus went Grammar school made lots of friends that I still have today.

Another thing I remember was when mum came over to see me she would go into the Ryde cafeteria buffet and have a cup of tea while she waited for the train, and would talk to the lady behind the counter and when I got married my mother sent her a wedding invitation and she came, but I still don't know her name. My mother would of done but of course she is no longer here anymore.

In the War it was worst in Portsmouth, we had this Morrison shelter and when you were inside you could hear the Doodlebug but once it stopped you would pray it would go a little bit further, but some poor other devil would get copped, but there was I think a Doodlebug at the end of Locksway Road and also they dropped land mines and I think one dropped on Dunbar Road, and funny enough that's where we bought our first house, those that were built after the War, and that's where we brought our children up, a coincident really how things work out .

Going back to Doodlebugs, once the siren went we would go down to the shelter and sleep there that night. My grandmother had the bunk above me and she was a big lady and the bunk would go right down in the middle and I would worry as a kid that she was going to land on top of me, but of course she never did. We used to play cards, New Market and all sorts of things before we went to bed. It was an adventure and I can't say I was frightened, I was never worried like my grandad who would never go down the shelter. He would stand out and look and my grandmother saying "Oh George, come on in and sit" and him saying "No it's alright", but any way we were all alright in the end

We did however get bombed out when we lived Kings Terrace but the house I was born in is still there. The mines just dropped and they had five minutes to run in and get what clothes they could get and from there we moved to Essex Road where I went to school from after the War.

When on the Island we could see bombs dropping, they were big and black and after us kids would go out and pick up shrapnel and see who had the biggest bits, and another thing we did with the Army being over there was to collect hat badges - it was only the ones to do with the War. The aeroplanes did come very low so you could almost see the pilot's face and you would wonder how they could look at you then machine gun you or bomb you. I suppose in some ways it was easier to kill with bombing because you don't see what you're doing because you have gone past it.

It's an awful thing to say because I was lucky, I didn't have an awful evacuee time apart from when I went to Petworth, but as kids it was like a big adventure and I often think now as a parent what they must of gone through but as a kid you just thought "Something else has happened, this is good" and you just wasn't scared, that's the strangest thing. Only the time I thought the airman was going to jump the hedge to grab me, but as a small child it was an adventure but now when I think what the parents must of gone through because there was two schools that had evacuated children and some parents thought it better to keep the child with you because if you were going to die then they all die together which was a stupid way to think really because you still might not have died together. But on the other hand I think to myself could I let my five year old go off with her gas mask and little bag and label and think I don't think I could, but the two Schools did what they thought was best.

It was funny when the soldiers did the manoeuvres because half was German, half English and there was four cottages up top by the Downs and if they got killed the woman would come out and give them a cup of tea, so really more got killed through having this cup of tea. Pretend it was, but funny because they came all over the fields and once dead would walk up for the tea. As a kid I thought it was a good game.

My husband was evacuated but went with his mum to Fittleworth just outside Petworth, but he wasn't at that school when it was bombed but around that way. Mrs Butler, the lady I lived with at Jolly Dale, she had a huge garden and at the back of it and beginning of the War her sons was home and did the garden, so after they were called up this huge acre and a half and orchard she grew her own veg and I would help with my little wheelbarrow so we had plenty of fruit - raspberries, apples, pears, loganberries, rhubarb, plums and greengages like of which I've bought greengages but they never tasted the same as the ones in the orchard - most of ours now are not English, and we had plenty of milk. Things we didn't have was fat although she used to get cream off the milk and at the end of a fortnight would shake it 'til it went on to make this butter. I used to sit there shaking this container thing for hours on end waiting for it to turn to solids. We also dug the garden up, but of course she was knocking on a bit to do things like that, and we would collect it all up, sell apples out by the gate but we had so many apples, pears, plums, a lot went to waste, crab apples as well and would make jelly if she could get the sugar as that was another thing that was scarce. But we always had sugar in our tea even now as an old person I can't abear tea without sugar. We enjoyed it, collecting up, plus the egg from Agatha but we didn't have variety like today but it was all substantial, like the stew she would do with loads of pearl barley in it, almost stodgy, but you ate it and it filled you up and when I think of now as I've got old I feel it was a healthy foundation for your life really because you didn't have cream or ice cream. Today you go into a shop and all the wonderful variety in season and vegetables, because you could only have them when in season now you get them all year round but I don't think it's a bad thing.

I had a friend I played with called Gordon Chiverton who lived up the top of the hill where the six houses were. We played soldiers and I was always the soldier and he was the Sergeant, we marched up down because he was older and a boy and got the pickings and I was left to do the dirty work. They had a big garden and his father gave me a piece of ground of my own which I dug and put marrow seeds in and he gave me runner beans and broad beans. Unfortunately when it came to fruition I got re-evacuated so never saw what I got, but eventually I got a marrow and took it to Mrs Butler and she said "Well what am I going to do with that? Do you like marrow?" but I didn't even know what it tasted like but she said "I don't" but there you go, that didn't make a great success did it?

We didn't have a bathroom so had a bath by the fire in a tin bath every Saturday, and we were the last house to have a flushing toilet but not hot and cold water, but up the hill they would have to dig a hole and bury theirs in the garden but that's why they had such good fruit and veg. We were lucky though, we had gas but not electric but had a gas oven which today you take for granted. You wonder in them days how they done a lot, put whatever food together and cook. I also took sandwiches to school but they did do school dinners and the Headmaster was very kind because if it was a really cold day he would make a big pot of soup and let us with sandwiches come in for a bowl which was for nothing.

That's about it really. I came home as I said, later got married to Mr Butler who was not related to Mrs Butler who I stayed with.

Percy Baigent

At the begging of the War I was twelve years old and it was in the 1930s and I lived in a street called Abercrombie Street in Landport in a house with my mother, father and two sisters.

When War was declared it was on a Sunday and the whole of the country were put in a panic.

Later on when I left school I joined the Civil Defense and the very first bomb that fell on Portsmouth was the Blue Anchor Public House in Kinston Crescent. A lot of people believe it was Rudmore so I might be wrong, so it could have been the second direct hit. I was a messenger boy that used to ride around all over delivering messages - I was underage so lied about my age.

The Blue Anchor was a double sited building and lucky for the Landlady and Landlord that they were out because this bomb was dropped around 4pm on a glorious sunny day. The sirens sounded and about a dozen German planes came over and started to drop the bombs which resulted in a direct hit on the Blue Anchor, luckily with no fatalities.

Then the Gas Works at Rudmore copped a bomb and then another in that area landed on a hairdressers. Then a bomb dropped on the R.A.P. first aid depot and the eight people that were on duty unfortunately lost their lives that day.

Everything for a while went a bit quiet until around December 1940. That was the 15th December that the first bombs, and as I said before I lived in Abercrombie Street - that was situated outside the Dockyard. The first things that then got mentioned was about bombing the Dockyard.

On the 23rd December the sirens went but nothing was about, it was very low cloud and it had been snowing. My father who worked in the Dockyard had been working and instead of finishing at half four they didn't finish 'til half past six, and on this night of 23rd December 1940 there was me, mum, dad my sisters indoors and all we heard was a whizzing burr sound and it was a massive great big land mine. And of course where all the houses had been built in the 17th century in Lord Nelson days to house the Dockyard workers and of course they were very flimsy and small, you could walk along a few streets like Waltham Street and Copenhagen Street, even our Street you could walk along and touch the bedroom windows with your fingers.

When the bombs dropped these houses went down like a deck of cards and could be heard as far as Drayton and up on the hill, and of course us being home that day we were trapped underneath the rubble of our house in Abercrombie Street for eight hours, and when they got us out they took us round to the nearest school which was in Arundel Street where we spent our Christmas until we had a new house.

At that time there were masses of houses cheap and of course we settled in well, this was in Besant Road. Asda and the petrol station has now been built there. So many people died on that ground that a plaque of remembrance should be erected on the wall of the petrol station. We will never forget because we witnessed it, but a lot of people lost loved ones that day so it would be fitting to those men, women, children and babies.

I didn't tell you that when the land mine came down my school which was Conway Street was bombed, but that was 1940 and in that summer of 1940 we used to get daylight raids due to the Battle of Britain and of course when they came over they would try to attack the Dockyard. Our shelter was not far from the school then and my mother was a bit deaf so before the school got bombed they would let me run home to warn her that the sirens had gone off.

I actually see three fighters and bombers battling with our Spitfires and Hurricanes above Portsmouth and in among that lot they had the Stuka dive bombers which were terrible and so frightening as they would come straight down out of the sky, and all you heard was like "whiz" and they would drop their bombs again. We had two or three bad raids like that mid-week then they would proceed upwards again. It was those that bombed us in Abercrombie Street but we got out alive, we had minor injuries.

Up the top of Besant Road where we were re-housed was two air raid shelters that had been dug out underground. The first one had ninety-five people in and consisted of men, women and children and now this was in 1943 and we had a night raid about half past nine at night, they came over and dropped their bombs and the first shelter took a direct hit, it was traumatic.

Me being in the Civil Defense by then went round there, but we couldn't do anything only put lights up because there was a crater there forty to fifty foot deep and about forty foot wide, and of course there wasn't anyone left only their bits and pieces. And in the morning we went back round with lorries and traps and we couldn't find one person, only bits and pieces of human bodies and this we done for six weeks and had to put them in wicker carrier baskets that the women would use to put the washing in in those days. After we had been there for about six weeks and cleared most of the body parts we had to put quick lime down to dissolve what was left of human flesh.

At twelve when I was still at school when the land mine went off it destroyed fifteen streets and over a hundred people were killed and about three hundred injured.

When I left school, as I said I joined the Civil Defense and at that time most of the telephone wires were down hence the reason for my job as a messenger boy on my bike, and I must say it was a very frightening job indeed. I would ride round to first aid post and the Warden's post and would be on stand-by to deliver letters or attend incidents.

When I got a bit older was when I joined the Civil Defense Rescue Department and as I said previous, one of the worst incidents that I attended was Besant Road, the first shelter that took a direct hit by a thousand pound bomb.

That hairdresser's I told you about was called Tralogin's, and it had gone from the thirties fashion into the new styles of the 1940s because previous to this the ladies did not know what it was like because they be doing washing and looking after the children and all around our district was very large families so this was a treat.

There was plenty of food about but the money was very tight indeed, and my father used to earn two pound twenty five shillings a week as a skilled labourer in the Dockyard, and of course with over time would pick up more.

Apart from everything else times were very quiet. We had our Trams and horse and carts and people coming round the streets with coal and any other utilities that you needed, this was pulled along by a donkey and you would get coal delivered to the door. Times were tough though in the thirties. As I was getting older we didn't have the electricity in our house because you had to be like a millionaire to have it and it would cost you one hundred pounds just to have it installed and fifty pounds for every point socket in the house in each room, so the majority of people had gas with a penny meter, and a man would come round on his bike every six weeks to empty the meter and would put a big bag on the handle bars of his bike which he would put all the coppers in.

We now go back to the 1940s and there were quite a few air raids day and night.

Some of the daylight raids was done by recognizance planes to take photographs of the harbour.

One night I was out with my mates at The Clarence Pier in 1942 and this German recognizance plane came over and was about five miles up which was unbelievable and we had never seen a plane that high before, and outside Clarence Pier we had a gun battery with four anti-aircraft guns and four search lights and manned by ATS women and men, and also we had two gun batteries either end of the common, one by the Queen's Hotel and the other one as I said at Clarence Pier.

This night both gun batteries opened up on this recognizance plane and got a direct hit, because it exploded all over the Solent - it was marvelous sight.

We didn't know if it was a reprisal but a couple of nights later they came over and it was about nine o'clock at night and they actually came down the beams of the search lights and then released their bombs and blew this battery on the Clarence Pier to pieces and I see it, next day, when we went back to have a look. The debris and bits were everywhere and there was a lot of events the same as this around Portsmouth.

January the 10th was a massive fire raid and about four hundred planes come over that night and dropped flares so they could light up the district and then they dropped incendiary bombs and then high explosive bombs. That was a week that was because we had no water, gas, and what water we were getting was coming around by tanker and of course we had to use candles, but these things were in such a short supply that you would have to queue up for and if you see a queue you ask what they were queuing for and join because it would be for bananas or oranges or even candles.

They put everything out of action that week, but we struggled along and the only warning we could get about the air raid was the whistles from the ships in the Dockyard, but of course we got over that terrible week.

We put up mobile canteens and one was put up down at the Guildhall Square, Lyons it was called and you could get a cake or a cup of tea or whatever you wanted. There was so many shops bombed and during the fire Blitz I saw the Guildhall burn and all the copper ran all down the dome. It was gutted, all that remained was a shell, all the shops along Commercial Road, Arundel Street and other parts of the town were gutted too.

On a another night Temple Street, which is off Church Road where Tesco is sited and not far from where I was billeted as an Air Raid Defense worker, three bombs were dropped on the houses in Temple Street. The first bomb that hit exploded causing massive fires and sadly a lot of people got killed and lots got injured which was natural with the force of the explosion. I was, after the War, awarded a shield for helping a woman out of the wreckage, she was an elderly woman about sixty five but once we got her out we realised she was decapitated and that was not a nice thing at all.

These bombings by then was going on day and night and then we would also get a lot of lone raiders come over when the cloud was very low and raining and of course would drop their bombs, and that's how quite a few places in Portsmouth were destroyed.

Locksway Road copped a bomb and further down the road on Langstone Foreshore they dropped another bomb, then they went on to drop another bomb the other side which I believe to be St Cuthbert's Church which took a direct hit and was destroyed.

If you had been anywhere near an explosion you never stood a chance, the shrapnel from the bomb would of killed you and of course, as I said previously, it was one of my jobs with others to go clear away what we could.

During the hours of darkness when the moon was full the bombers would come over guided by the light of the moon, so the Ministry of Defense organised a convoy of oil tankers to come from Clarence Pier right up to Portsdown Hill so when we had a full moon and the German planes was being directed by the light of the full moon, that way they could see everything down below that was going on. The sirens would scream out and the Army would set the mobile tankers on fire to smoke all over the City to blacken the City out, it was terrible choking and you had to put your gas mask on. Blowing up all the water mains, gas mains - everything, the fire service was running out of water all over the country.

This effected not just Portsmouth but London and all over the cities, so what happened was they built static water tanks in the ground of bombed-out premises and was like a giant swimming pool about twelve foot deep and fifty foot long and thirty foot wide and that was used for emergency water supply. The sad thing was that a lot of children got drowned in these pools because they were not fenced off.

Portsmouth City Council then decided to build a water main about ten inches wide all through the City that was from Clarence Pier up to Portsdown Hill because of the mains that had been destroyed and broken. It was a struggle but as I said if you see people queuing up you would ask what they were queuing for and join the queue.

The Battle of Britain was very bad but our Boys done a very good job because we were outnumbered six-to-one, but our boys went up to Tranmere, this side of Chichester, who were in the fighter command and shot down as many jerry planes as they could, and I believe that by shooting down as many aircraft as they did do during the August and the September and October, they managed to shoot down one hundred and fifty-odd. During air raids all over the country the Luftwaffe sent over a couple of thousand planes.

At Portsmouth you could see the Battle of Britain clearly because the Spitfires and Hurricanes used to come from Tranmere which was about thirty mile away from us, it was near Chichester. They also had the Bomber Command at Thorney Island that used to go over every night to bomb Europe.

This day I am telling you about now is the most brilliant day in history. One Hundred and fifty bombers got shot down and this day certainly saved us from being invaded because Hitler was all ready for the invasion with his barges on the French coast, but he also wanted air and if he had engaged that then he would have been able to invade Britain, but with our Air Force that was in very short supply. We had Polish, Czechs, French, Norwegian, even South Africa - nearly every part of Europe including India and if we hadn't had this marvelous devastating attack on the German air force as they approached the coast, especially the South Coast, it would have been the chance for Hitler to invade. But thanks to them as the Germans was out numbered six to one he didn't get that far.

In the 1930s Krups the German Armaments, we knew they were rearming because after 1929 we signed the Geneva Convention and that was meant to suppress Germany to only a limited amount of tanks and guns and planes. People in our Government at the time had shares in Krups and other businesses of course in the country.

Because Krups was building, and building stuff like armaments, planes, tanks that in 1939 Germany had so many thousand tanks, aircraft, boats, submarines, U-boats, you name it - they had it. And of course people were getting their

233

dividends from Krups the German armory factory and didn't worry about what was to come in the future, but that was the outlet blitzkrieg for War.

And of course that went on for five years .The day War was announced was on a Sunday eleven o'clock in the morning and the paper men came around shouting, "War Declared! War Declared! Britain at War! Britain at War! War Declared!"

Then of course everybody was in a panic because they did not know what to do just like myself, but of course my father had been in the First World War 1914 to 1918, and now in the second War 1939 'til 1945 so he had had just about enough of it as he was now getting on and in his late sixties getting on to seventy, he knew what about to happen.

Mr Chamberlain at the time told Hitler to get out of Poland because they had invaded Poland in 1939. Mr Chamberlain went over to Munich to see Hitler and stated to him that they wanted a pact, a peace pact and Mr Hitler agreed and Herman Goring, the Chief of the German Air Force and Himmler, who was in charge of the Gestapo who was a very cruel man indeed, he was in charge of the Belson prison camps where thousands upon
thousands of Jews were murdered in his Gas Chambers. Well they got the Bow right and of course it saved the British nation and Mr Winston Churchill said this was the finest hour which it was, but of course we lost quite a few air men but they lost twice as many and quite a few were taken prisoner, the same as we were taken prisoner on the Continent.

The German prisoners were kept in the countryside, Petworth and places like that which were real rural countryside, Petersfield and Horndean. But they were made to work on the farms and was treated better than ours over in Germany where our boys suffered the same as in Japan as they declared War, then they bombed Pearl Harbour. Well the prisoners that were taken out the Far East were in a terrible condition and like Belsen they were like skeletons and when the American troops got there these dead skeletons were piled sky high where they had died due to lack of food, they were nothing but bones.

They then chased the Germans well back into Berlin and the Russians came in one way, the Americans the other way and we came in another way and made a pincer movement towards Germany, through France then Belgium on to Germany, and that's where the treaty was signed between Mr Churchill, President Roosevelt of the United States and Stalin who was the President of

Moscow in Russia. But I am afraid years later the Cold War started and then Russia set up the Iron Curtain and then the only way we could get supplies into Germany from our sector was to fly them over by Air.

They used Dakota planes which was freight carrying planes, and if they had not of done that the Germans would of starved or they would have been taken over by the Russians.

Regards to the bombing on Portsmouth, that went on for five years and different sites we went to all over the city, Portsea copped it very very bad, all round North Street and Queen Street. When I was down there in 1940 with the AFS and all the other Civil Defense down there, places were obliterated like Bonfire Corner which was just outside one of Unicorn Gates, Marlborough Gate it is known as today.

The German aircraft had come over by the plenty and attacked, and even though we had plenty of anti-air force guns which I said before were stationed down at Clarence Pier which was completely destroyed, and another one at the end of Clarence Pier, and guns all along the south coast right along the beach.

Eastney had the Royal Marines and they had guns as well but when they attacked during the Battle Britain in 1940, I remember this Monday when they came over with the Stuka dive bombers the Navy in the barracks which was down the end of our street had these Lewis guns they were firing and had sandbags placed all around them, and on the wall was these Lewis guns and of course these Stuka dive bomber planes were so fast, like so many million miles per hour and then back up again. But anyway we also had guns coming around the streets, big guns on wheels and when they went off it was like a BOOM BOOM BOOM and used to shake our windows out, but apart from that our defenses were in different parts of Portsmouth and the south coast as I stated before.

There was a big radar stationed over the Isle of Wight at Shanklin and we were one of the first to invent radar and we had the Germans by the scruff of the neck because at the beginning of the War this big radar station in Shanklin was manned by the Air Force used to pick the Germans up as soon as they left the French coast, and our fighters would go off and fly up and along the East Coast and intercept them, and they even tried to get across the Chanel and of course that was a great victory until the Germans found out what the secret was – radar. So then they started to destruct the radar installations but the one at Shanklin got severely bombed in a daylight raid.

They blitzed it, destroyed it completely and of course that meant we had no radar for quite a few months until they were able to re-erect the radar station again. I must say though it was more the Radar that saved the country with the Air Force otherwise the Germans would have definitely got here and there's no getting away from that because Hitler had thousands of barges all ready to be pulled along out to sea by tugs or warships, so we had to destroy the German air force because as I said before, if they had gained the strength and been the master of the skies he would have invaded and we would have been under German occupation.

But as you know the Channel Islands were under occupation but it was the water that saved us, the Channel - twenty two miles wide but it was a Godsend, but we used to go over there and bomb but during the D Day Invasion all the American troops and the other troops that would come in from different parts of the continent, even South Africa and India, they were not only airmen but soldiers as well and that's what saved us too, they were all there and in Leigh Park we had a great big massive wood which now has one of the largest housing estates in the country, I believe it to be over thirty thousand foot wide, and in 1942 the Air Defense Ministry started building these prefabricated huts and there was hundreds of these white painted prefabricated huts that were camouflaged, and this is where they accommodated the Commonwealth troops. And to try and disguise our tanks and planes the Ministry invented rubber for the prefabricated tanks, guns and planes from different places around the country to trick the Germans when they came over with their recognizance planes that we were ready at a certain place when we were due to invade from another place.

They invaded from Southampton, Weymouth, Plymouth even took off from Portsmouth, but this deception of the imitation aircraft and guns certainly fooled the Germans and when D Day arrived The General Eisenhower, who was Commander of the American forces in Europe, decided with Winston Churchill and Mr Roosevelt to invade on a certain day when it was very high tide very high, but that day happened to be very rough and very windy and the invasion had to be cancelled but they knew the Germans had these V1s coming from Europe and V2s which there was no defense against at all.

You would be sat down in doors and just blown to pieces, but with the V1 they would come over and at the back of them have a little motor and a blue light would come out of it and it would sound like a motor boat 'bru bru' something like that, and our fighters would be able to go up and shoot them down because they only travelled about three hundred mile an hour and our fighters could do four hundred mile an hour. But the V2, if we had not invaded they definitely would have brought us to our knees because there was no warnings because really they were German missiles and they would bring them on wheels on lorries and hide them in different parts of the forest on the continent, like the French and Belgium rural districts where we could not find them, and when we did go over to bomb them they had moved again and then again and so on.

But in the end with a terrible loss of men we finally succeeded and over run Germany and stopped this rocket attack and V1 attack was a great victory to us.

Talking again about the night raids the Germans would go up and scan our bombers by radar and shot quite a lot down, and also with the high altitude of the American bombers the B45 the Germans would come under the actual aircrafts, under the smoke trails coming out from the exhaust of the B45 aircraft and fire under the American plane and of course the Americans lost an awful lot of planes like that.

But of course we went on and on and we made the D Day Landing and of course we have a big D Day Museum in Southsea with big exhibitions and it shows you the actual plans of the Retreat from Dunkirk, which that was a wonderful thing because when the Germans invaded the Continent in 1939/ 40 the French had a Maginot Line which was all tunnels under the ground with plenty of guns which could defend them for hundreds of miles across France and on the borders of Belgium. But when the Germans broke through Holland and then Belgium they got as far as the Maginot Line but went around it and entrapped the French and the other forces who were fighting at the time because they had counter attacked and came in the back, and of course it rendered the Maginot Line useless. And of course there were millions of pranks but the Germans were cute and that's why they came in the back.

The French Resistance used to do very well but the only problem was like they have today in Afghanistan, the terrorist out there can see our men because they are in Army uniform, the same as the French Resistance that would see the Germans in their uniforms, or even without the uniform on they could tell by the style of the aircraft and by the way they walked, and of course the sniper had a field day and the Germans then were being shot left right and centre, and of course this is what happened in Afghanistan and that is why so many of our men in my opinion are getting shot because they can see us, but it's like fighting an invisible enemy with these Arabs or whatever they are.

The day the War was over was the Victory in Europe and everybody went berserk, they were drinking and dancing all over the country and people went to Trafalgar Square and it was real anarchy, but it was good but of course rationing still went on and ID cards during the 1950s plus, and the last thing that was rationed was bread but we could get two ounces of butter, two ounces of tea and sweets, four ounces of meat and two ounces sugar or whatever maybe in the War.

Whoever was in the family had a Ration Book and when you took it to a retailer he would cut the coupons out for that supply of meat you had that week and you could not get any more until the next week, but in between time there was people that used to buy food on the black market and they would call them 'Spivs', and if you had the money you could buy what food you wanted or what you wanted, but because of low wages like my father earned it was an impossibility to spend any more than what he was earning. But all the Spivs had extra money and they were called Spivs because they didn't go in to the services but had the money to buy all the extra food and sell to the public for twice the amount, and that's how people with money got on.

They started building again in the 1950s, New Road and up around Rudmore up to North End, and gradually came back and built into the centre of the city, so Mile End was the start of the regeneration along Kingston Road, Lake Road, Sultan Road, right the way down to the Dockyard, and of course now we are like the German cities and cities on the Continent that have been rebuilt, very nice indeed.

I did not tell you that I went in to the Air Force after a while when I finished with the Civil Defense and was stationed at Warrington where I done my square bashing, and then went on overseas and went to Germany, then on to Malaya and done about four years in the Air Force and then came out and went back to civvi street, and things started getting back to normal where people went dancing, drinking and cinema which I didn't tell you about.

When I work at the ABC Cinema in Commercial Road as a rewind boy it was one of the biggest cinemas in Portsmouth, but it used to close at nine pm at night during the War and all the buses would stop at nine o'clock at night so the only way you could get around was if you had a bike and the majority of people did have bikes. They had to have and I have seen thousands where I was living outside the Dockyard gate in Abercrombie Street. The Dockyard workers would go in to work between seven and half past in the morning, the bell would ring at quarter to seven then again at seven o'clock to warn the workers it was time to clock in, and then thousands upon thousands coming back out the Dockyard on their bicycles which looked just like Beijing Square, just like the Chinese that got thousands of bikes there. These Dockyard men would put their bikes in different parts outside the Dockyard Gates in different sheds for sixpence a week.

I have never seen so many thousands bikes in my life and never will again because these days everybody got cars and a lot of the Dockyard is now shut down and the only place that is building now is Vosper Thornycroft, and they are building parts and different parts are being built all over the country because they are building a Destroyer so they have levelled the work out. We have not got the ships that we used to have, no fleet in the port.

Years ago as kids in Wood Sea Quay in Mile End is where we would go swimming. It was full of Mud and very deep and this Woodsey's Quay at one time had a great big cemetery with a couple of thousand graves but when they built the Continental Car Port quite a few years ago, which is massive now with the PO Line and the French lines go to Calais and Cherbourg. But before they had it as I said about the quay and also a big wood yard called Woodsey's, that also belonged to the shipping company as well, this is as I said the Car Port where people go to get the ferries over to France and other places even Dunkirk.

At the back of the 1950s I had a motor bike and my first wife, who was an usherette at the ABC Cinema, would ride pillion and I would go to Leigh Park to see a mate of mine in one of then prefab huts after the Navy moved out and other service personnel, and because of the shortage of houses in Portsmouth because it got bombed so much, lots of people were moved out to Leigh Park to these prefabricated buildings.

I would ride up this Eastern Road which was built by men back in the 1930 s rather than keep them on the dole. We would come back home between twelve and one o'clock in the morning and the roads would be clear, no one else on that road whatsoever just a few lights, and nine times out of ten the old sea mist would cover all the road up and we would have to get off and walk. So different from today as you now got lights from one end right up to Drayton and it is one of the main roads into Portsmouth, and of course we only have the two main roads the other being London Road which was built in the 1920s or 1930s that would take traffic and trams through the city even up to Portsdown Hill. And there was one company called The Horndean Light Railway and the trams would run along the bow of the hill and as children we could get on that tram to Horndean for a penny, which is about eighteen miles from Portsmouth and we really had nice days there.

Also up this Eastern Road we had marshes and these marshes was full of blackberry bushes and we would go up there and mum would pack us some sandwiches and make us a flask of lemonade which was cheap from powder, it might have been a farthing or halfpenny an ounce, and we would spend a whole day there. It was then called the Farlington Marshes and of course nowadays the Eastern Road is treacherous and has seen a lot of accidents, and I can recall going to work one morning up to the old Airport Road and I saw a young man on a moped about twenty one years old when it had been raining and as he approached the bend that was in the Eastern Road at the top of Tangiers Road, it was a new bike, new helmet and he had a briefcase on the handle bars which when I passed him got caught in the front wheel and he went up in the air like a missile. Out of all the stanchions along the road he happened to hit this one and with his new helmet on, I ran across the road in between the traffic to see if I could give first aid and an ambulance came and said, "Why did you not cut the helmet off?" and I said "Well I was just going to work" so anyway they said he had a fractured skull and he died in my arms on the road. And that's just another tragic time.

Going back to the War years, I used to go to the Dockyard with my mates and do a bit of Mudlarking. I was living at home with me mother, me father and me two sisters, and one sister worked at the ABC Cinema and the other making and painting lampshades in the centre of the city with the other girls. They used to convert the lampshades but I forget what it was called. My mother was in very bad health so she could not go to work and inclined to be rather deaf so when I was at school and the sirens went off I was allowed to run home to warn her. I was at Conway Street just across the road from our house, I would tell mum and take shelter. One sister worked as a waitress in Guildhall Square, the Denmead Restaurant it was called.

What about the Pompey football match then when you could get in for two shillings and sixpence? And in those days in 1939 we won the World Cup against Wolves and of course you could get in to the pictures for thruppence but what we used to do, half would club together and the rest would go round the side door once a few paid to get in and we would open the side door and let the rest bunk in. Then down on the Hard where the ferries come in that would go to Gosport and would also go to the Isle Of Wight there was a wooden bridge and at the bottom it had a big railway trestle for the Royal Train to come in from the main line straight in to the Dockyard by the Kings Stairs and that was there for years. Well we used to get down there Mudlarking, we used to get all the holiday people going over to the Isle of Wight mostly and Gosport. We would call out to them -we had the old gramophone device and used to shout up, "Chuck a penny down to us mister or half penny" and we would dive into the mud to try and recoup it which was a godsend if we got anything decent for the hours we were Mud larking, and that was just one of the things we would do to earn a penny or two. And also when the Dockyard men got paid on Friday and outside the Unicorn Gate was a mile of pubs and we would stand there and say "Mind yer bike mister" and when he came out we would get pay tuppence or a shilling depending.

Also when they came out we would stand there and ask for lunchings and shout out "Lunching! Any lunchings?" and they would give us the food they didn't eat, then the rag and bone man would come around with this little donkey pulling his cart shouting out for rags and he would give you a gold fish in a jar tied up with string as a handle, it truly made us up. And the men when they finished in the Yard would do a lot of gambling and down the bottom of my road, which was Abercrombie Street, you had a small traffic island and all these men would get there Saturday afternoon and play Pitch and Toss throwing a penny up to see if it was going to land heads or tails, and they had men stationed at different parts of the street to warn them when the police was coming, and you could be sat in doors eating dinner or whatever and they would run in down your passage out the back and over the wall to get away, and of course it even went on down the foreshore at Rudmore. They would play Pitch and Toss and it would be quite a lot of money in them days, but of course a pint of beer was only four pennies but I can still remember when it was half that, it was tuppence and three cigs and a match for a penny and that was in the 1930s up 'til the 1939s, a penny for chocolate and a packet of woodbines cigarettes for tuppence, ten for four pennies and of course vegetables was cheap - a bunch of onions a farthing and a pound potatoes for a penny and Charlotte Street, which is now in the centre of the city, they used to stay open with long lines of fruits and vegetables and Saturday nights they would stay open and the butcher shop did not shut till midnight, and then the men would come round with the horse and water tank and wash Charlotte street down and we would wait 'til the last to go into the butcher shop and get the cheap meat. And during the week didn't butchers would sell two penn'th of cuttings for a stew as there was no money about in those days and the only people that had money was bookies, publicans and corner shops and doctors, and only a few cars and telephones. They were very extinct and only professional people had them but you did have call boxes but they used to be about tuppence a call.

To have a telephone or electricity was unthinkable, about hundred pound to have put in and my father in law had it in because he had a job as an electric plater which was a skilled trade and he would pick up around three pound a week which was a big difference from my father's money which was two pound twenty five shilling a week, and my father in law had a lot of perks with dental surgeries and doctors' equipment, and of course that pulled him in more money, so he had it all put in and he lived down a little street called Omega Street off of Somers Road. And to also have a wireless set well, you could buy one a battery one with the Home and Light Programme on for three pound fifty and you had men come round every Friday with a three-wheeled trike with these accumulators, and these would go into the back of the battery set where you had a big long battery with studs in which would cost you five bob a month so you had your accumulator battery and your valves, and to have the electric set it was five pound and of course just plugged it into the mains and would get your programmes, the Light Service and Radio Luxemburg which was a luxury in those days.

When our Queen Elizabeth the Second got crowned there was not a lot of televisions in the country and those that were was about ten inches wide, maybe a bit bigger but would cost over a hundred pound a week and to see the Coronation of the Queen Elizabeth the Second you had to go into somebody's house who was a bit better off than you were who had one to see this event.

I remember when a bomb dropped on St Mary's Road Cemetery, the New Road end, and when we got there there was thousands of bones, it was skeletons, bones, skulls it was there, and there was another time when I happened to be in our street in Abercrombie Street before it got bombed that there was a group of us kiddies and this Spitfire came over and done loop the loop and that was to say it had shot a German plane down.

On the Monday one August through the Battle of Britain they came over on the raid, about four hundred planes, and me and one of my sisters who got into a bit of a panic had run out of the house and as we were running up the road towards the nearest shelter we got machine gunned by the Stuka bomber and just about escaped with our lives. That was as I said in August in 1940 on the tenth. After all the dismantling of Conway Street and all the other streets a bomb was dropped out side Unicorn Gate and all the properties by then had already been demolished so this left a great big crater in the road.

We would have been bombed out sooner or later because of the land mine explosion that was on the twenty third of December 1940 right near Christmas. Well, as said before this happened at six thirty at night and they also dropped one on the Dockyard when the workmen was coming out and of course a lot of pubs around that area got hit and a lot of people got killed.

I think I have already said about the Anderson shelter where Asda Stores are today that took a direct hit and there was two shelters there, and that happened in April in 1942. I remember how they came over this night and dropped a sticker Bomb that landed on the underground shelter that was situated where the Asda Convenient Store stands today. There was ninety five people killed in that shelter, men, women and children, and when we got there, there was a massive great big crater about forty foot deep and about fifty foot wide and we just couldn't do nothing that night and went back round the next morning and all we could see was the remains of the bodies which myself and other Civil Defense Workers had to pick up for six weeks in the wicker baskets I said about previously. Laundry baskets they were.

When I lived in Cottage View in Landport there stood a big Leethem's Factory and on the night of the big fire blitz which was January the tenth 1940 it was stated that a German plane had come down amongst the ruins in which they bombed us with masses of fire bombs, which then scattered and ignited all the unexploded bombs all over the place, which I found one German incendiary bomb and another one which was called the Butterfly Bomb because it opened up like a bowl but with like a couple of wings attached to it and as soon as it was touched it would clamp its self together and explode.

The Incendiary bomb was found to be easily put out with sand, so what the

Germans done was put a nipper on the end with an explosive capsule so that when it hit the ground it exploded so you could not get near it and that's what happened on numerous occasions.

I already mentioned the Gun Battery opposite the Clarence Pier that got obliterated and Eastney end was the Marines with the big Radar Station and that got bombed as well, but they did have anti-aircraft Battery there and nine times out of ten it did drive the bombers away They had immense fire power them guns had.

The Forts out in the sea also had guns attached to them and they would open up and shoot down quite a few planes which then ended up in the Solent. Lots of German planes down there and no submarines ever got through either because our defenses were too strong compared to what they were down in Scapa Flow where a German submarine did get through and sunk one of our battleships and a lot of men were killed. There was a big gathering down at the Guildhall and people were drinking and dancing when the War was declared over, but around the Guildhall a lot of buildings copped it and in the Guildhall Square most of them was burned down and even the railway station Portsmouth and Southsea copped it but it was mostly the Station Master office, the toilets and the Parcel Office which was flattened.

But the lines and Platforms were OK but opposite stood a great big hotel which took a direct hit, it was called Maddens Hotel. And of course there was quite a lot of people killed there, and Old Commercial Road was completely demolished from one end from the Guildhall right up to the other end practically to the Mile End, North End and there was extensive fire damage all the way along and explosive damage as well. Because of this you could see right the way through the centre of the city where everything was burning.

People could see the flames from Portsmouth from miles away where the actual city was ablaze from one end to the other where many shops and houses were destroyed mostly by the fires and the explosions, and the fire fighters could not do anything because they had no water because the fire mains had all been broken, and that is where the static water flow came into operation.

We had the Canadian's and all the soldiers and sailors and airmen from all over the world who was all stationed at Leigh Park, which was a big estate, woods which covered about sixty thousand acres and more which was built on with prefabs to house all the service men back in 1940 to 1945. I remember the massive woods and one house that was stood there I saw when I used to go to Bedhampton in 1930s to 40s and that was just one house which was past the Bedhampton railway gate, and we would get over to there as children for about tuppence return and this big house we learned belonged to Timothy White who was the only owner and that was the only isolated house that stood on its own miles away from anybody.

This house you could say was as safe as houses because it was miles away from anything else which was a very good thing 'til they started to build the Prefabs by it for the United Nations, well that's what we called it then, but it was for all the service personnel from all over the world who was billeted there in the prefabricated huts. Well, after the War where the housing situation was so bad, so critical in Portsmouth they started to re-house the people and I had a friend over there that I would visit on my motor bike and take my wife on back of it and we would come back 12 in the morning along the Eastern Road, we were in our teens then and there was no night clubs or discos or anything then and if there was a dance hall it would be shut at nine o'clock at night, just the same as the buses and the trams that stopped at nine o'clock at night.

As we came home along the Eastern Road we would have to dismount the motor bike because of so much fog because there was hardly any lighting compared to what is up there now. Gosport got bombed but nothing like here in Portsmouth, but it did get bombed in isolated places and of course a few people got killed over there. But of course the main target for the German bombers was the Portsmouth dockyard.

After the January fire blitz a lot of people were killed and was buried at St Mary' s Graveyard in a mass grave that held about four hundred people which I attended and present at the ceremony and that was yet another tragic event I went to.

Nowadays we have flat screen televisions with hundreds of channels, multi-screen cinema which they got on The Hard and at Port Solent and the one at the Hard used to belong to our navy where they kept torpedoes and mine sweepers, and torpedo ships that could dock at the end it was manned by Wrens and Sailors for many years until they run it down but now it is Gun Warf Quays Leisure Centre with all sorts – restaurants, shops, bars and people go down there mostly weekend and have a really good time.

Myself now have a four wheeled scooter that I go around on and go along the

South Parade pier and down to the Camber then through the Gunwharf to the Hard where I used to Mudlark, then back up to the Continental Port which used to be an old coal place which is just a memory away, then back home to the modern life style of today.

"Those were the good old days"

Margaret Oram

I was born in 1945, so World War Two had ended but of course there was plenty of debris and materials left over from the War and bomb sites became the playground for all children of all ages. Much of us kids' playtime was spent on the bomb site across from our house which was in North Street, Portsea, Portsmouth. We played for hours, being shopkeepers or pretending we had our own house and would fill it with anything we could find. That was one thing, we were good at improvisation and we certainly had plenty of material too - hand bricks, slates etc. which we used to construct furniture.

An area of the site was taken up by several old wooden carts. I don't know who they belonged to, so we would clamber all over them and I remember once I thought it would be a very good idea if I looped my skipping rope around a shaft to make a swing. Result of that was the shaft tipped down trapping me right underneath. The ambulance came down Queen Street from the Royal Hospital in Commercial Road at great speed to the excitement of the crowds gathered to watch them safely get me from under it all safe and sound. Just a few scratches and I had only been winded, thank heavens.

We had with many other streets four public houses which it wasn't unusual at closing time to see many customers passing by our house somewhat the worse for wear. One time I recall, myself and my friend were sitting watching a chap come out of the pub the worse for wear. He staggered across the bomb site to then stumble flat on his face, but after a few minutes picked himself up to carry on stumbling until he got to the road. We knew from experience that it might profit us to go and inspect where he fell as he might have departed with some coins. To our delight a few coins had slipped from his pocket for us to retrieve, and we skipped merrily to the sweet shop.

It was the normal thing on sultry summer nights for neighbours to sit outside their houses and have a gossip. I loved nothing better than to sit and listen to the many tales being told. I would listen attentively as they chatted about the War and other matters which I now realise that was not appropriate for an eight year old to be eavesdropping on.

I loved to hear the stories being told by people that would have a holiday but would be hop picking as well. I loved watching them pack up and go as well, being green with envy because I knew they were off to the countryside. What a tale they would tell once they were back from the adventures and hard slog they had hop picking. But they enjoyed every minute of it and would return year after year.

I remember the family that lived next door to us had so many kids but I remember going to theirs one tea time and the mother having made a spotted dick pudding. It looked like thick wedges swimming in golden syrup, and this was served to the kids for tea. I looked on in awe, as it looked like heaven.

We shared our house with two other families and a couple occupied the attic room as well. I was often called to run errands and earning myself a treat or two. I recall buying a penny bag of crisps which was crumbs really, but the bag would be bursting and just as tasty and good as a whole potato crisp. It was excellent value at a penny a bag.

Another of my early memories of my childhood was when I was fostered out and I would be taken to visit an elderly lady. Her sitting room was lit by gas mantles and the room was very dark and eerie with shadowy corners and the lady looking like an old witch. I would just sit and watch in silence as she got out a little box and put a pinch of snuff up her nose which left a horrid brown stain, then to go on and predict one another's futures from the formation left by the tea leaves which had been swirled around the cup. One or the other could expect a little luck on the horses, no doubt.

I would sit, look and listen in awe. Those were the good old days.

Margaret Foster [Nee Warren]

I remember mum and her sister laughing over washing their legs in tea leafs to give them a tanned look and then getting a fine stick and wetting it to draw the fine line up the back of their legs so it looked like nylons they had on. The funniest was the pipe cleaners to make the hair curly or wavy, even years after the war until hair rollers came out mum would wind these white pipe cleaners around her hair.

The hair spray was sugar water, if they could get the sugar, and use that in a squirt plastic bottle and for lips and rouge it was anything red if they could wet and get the dye from it, but mum had lipsticks from before the War so used her lipstick to use as a blush.

When mum was up in Aldershot she said they found a parachute on the way to work and about ten women were fighting over getting a part of it because they were made of pure silk.

As I was getting older it amazed me just how many jobs my mum had, she flitted from one to another, and was spoilt by some of her sisters who would help her out with money and stick up for her because she was so comical and had a heart of gold.

Sister Nora, once married, even cooked for her and one of the other sisters on a daily basis thinking they were out to work, but of course they were sat in pubs chatting the work hours away having a laugh and joke while Nora [Jagger, see page 33] and Dawsie had been to work, come home and cooked meals for them.

I was fascinated to hear my aunt Nora talk about Alders the corset factory she worked in that was in Lake Road, she said it was a family run business and the owners were very stern but good people to work for and my aunt, because she had very small fingers, was asked to do the very fine stitching of the bows that were added to the front of the corset and later on to the brassier which was very boring, but because she could do such very small stitching they put her in charge of that job.

Mum worked in the slipper factory that was next door for one day and then on to Alders for a couple of days, then Twilfit's corset factory that was situated by Fratton Bridge but didn't really enjoy going to work, so after a couple of weeks gave that up too and would always get her sister Nora to go to the wage clerk and pick up what money owed to her. Then she worked as a clippy on the buses until she was made to work in the Munitions Factory which she kept for quite a while.

When her sister Nora went up to Essex to live with her husband Les mum missed her a lot but had the other sisters to help her out. Mum would tell us about her family house they lived in at Lake Road and how the roof was blown off in the bombing and how they would clean up the mess and still sleep in the beds looking up at the stars.

She didn't talk much in front of dad about her nights out in the dance hall at the bottom of Lake Road but as I got older I imagined all the girls would dance and drink with the American Firemen and the other nationals that used to go to the dance hall as it was in the one they had that was so near.

After the War when dad came out of the services they settled down together and had us six children, but I can remember how hard it was for food and other bits and pieces. My dad worked for the Water Company for many years and while we were young mum didn't work at all but dad also took a weekend job over at Hayling Island Fair to make ends meet. It was a struggle for mum trying to keep the family going with so little money and I remember having to go to the butchers when I was six and buying sixpenny worth of minced meat and that would feed eight of us. We always had lots of vegetables but never no luxuries, we would use soap for washing clothes and bathing in as well as washing our hair, but we were always clean apart from when we were out to play on all the bombed sites.

I remember the old black car that had been abandoned in St Georges Square, it was to me in them days a very large flash car, I would sit in with my friends for hours or we would get in the horse trough and play with the stagnant water then go look for old bits of treasure or shrapnel that would still be on the old sites for years after the War up until the council started the clearing up of the areas, and where Portsea and Landport was bombed so badly it took years to bring the community up to scratch.

With all the bombing that took place I still wonder how some people even today say the War years were the best days of their lives. I know they lived a simple life and worked the earth for fresh vegetables and fruit but when I hear about how they had ration books and went without so much I think how can they make such a statement?

But even though we went without such a lot after the War we had happy childhoods without a care in the world really, and that was all thanks to our fathers and grandfathers that fought in the War to make it a safer place for us to grow up in.

Listening to the stories people has given me for this book makes me so proud of the people that served and protected our country in the War and the stories from the evacuees has open our eyes to a lot of what really happened to them in the War.

Unsaid until now but never forgotten.

Mum always said it was a dream that came true for her when the Corporation offered her and Dad 18 Frazer House, St Georges Square as it was known then. It was a three bedroomed top floor flat and coming from the one room in her sister's house she shared with us kids it was heaven to have her own place.

Especially having an indoor toilet and bathroom, it was a luxury to have because her sister had a toilet in the back garden which was shared with rodents and any other garden creature. The bath was an old tin one that they would use in the parlour, but because mum and dad lived in that room it was the scullery which you had your bath in and from kettles of water that filled it and pots that would be boiled up on the stove.

Mum said in the summer months they would add a few rose petals to give the water a bit of scent and colour some times.

Mum also loved the fact that she had a coal cupboard to store the coal and coke so didn't have to go out in the bitter cold to bring a scuttle of coal in, and a pulley line to hang the washing out on that would dry in no time as we lived three floors up, the balcony was a god send because we could sit and play and she could keep her eye on us.

At the back of the flats was a big square so we could also play downstairs and she could pop her head out of the kitchen door to the balcony and watch what we were doing which wasn't too much only hopscotch or cricket or skipping or football. Summertime was lovely because the railway line was up on top of the embankment and we would climb over and sit and take train numbers down which was very dangerous but hey, we were kids and had no fear.

Mum said the War was bad but lots of good things had come after it, like being rehoused and ration books fizzling out and being able to buy eggs and sugar and other needy ingredients to make a meal out of, the radio was at last playing nice music, and having a boiler in the kitchen to heat the bath water, and able to wash clothes in was a luxury, scrubbing boards and pots and pans were back available in the shops - all life's little luxuries.

Television didn't come about for a while for big families like ours until the early sixties when we moved to a bigger flat which mum was over the moon about, four bedrooms and her mate Val, who also had six children, moved in the four bed roomed flat beneath ours in Privett House, Portsea.

Mum said yes, one will never forget the horrendous times but they will always remember the laughs they all had down the Anderson shelters and the nights dancing and making new friends. Fond memories she always said, a good laugh and a good cry and we will never forget those who lost their lives, civilians and those who served for King and Country.

We went without and made do with an awful lot, poverty as never seen before but we managed and because of the War people learned a little could go a long way, but of course coming out of the 1950s was the best times of all when things started to get back to normal, and jobs became available, and building work for new houses and flats started, and rows and rows of bombed out places were cleared and the Regeneration of Portsmouth got underway.

Butchers and other shops opened again mum would send us up Green's the butcher and cold meat shop for a shilling's worth of chitlins or half a pig's head that would be roasted, or pigs trotters. The offal you would not purchase today but was very well sold up until the old butcher shops closed and offal was then frowned upon.

The butcher would hang chickens and other items on show outside the shop - something we will never see again, coal scuttles carrying coal from the ships or to the ships and to our lorries waiting to deliver to depots, and most of our breweries now gone that bottled the beers and lemonades, our milkmen that had carts then vans has almost diminished because of supermarkets that sprang up in the late sixties and seventies.

Redevelopment and Regeneration was the new words people were learning and thankfully for all of us today we welcomed the changes that had come about because of the War, but like our parents and grandparents we to will never forget.